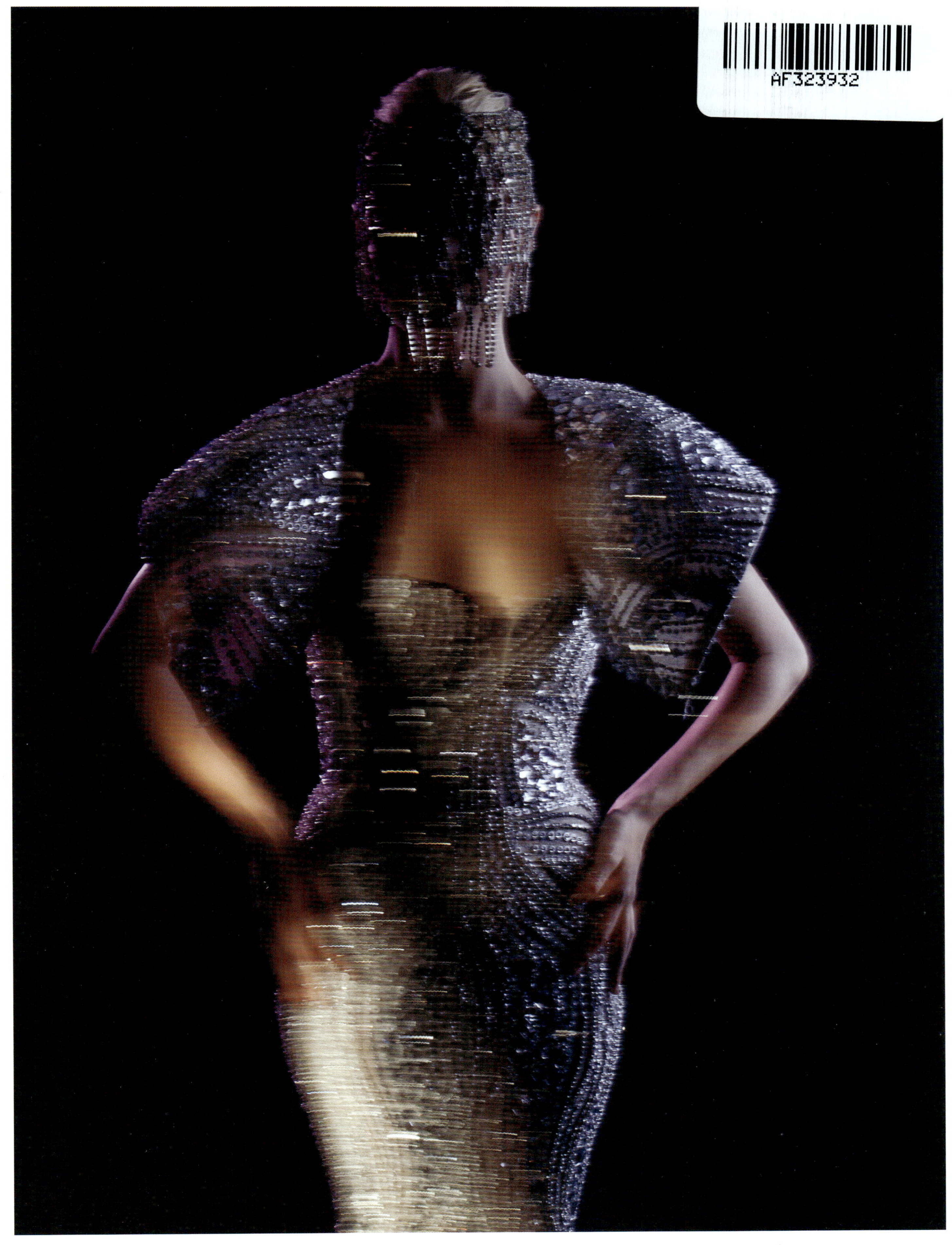

RAFAELCENNAMO
WHITE COUTURE
RAFAELCENNAMO.COM

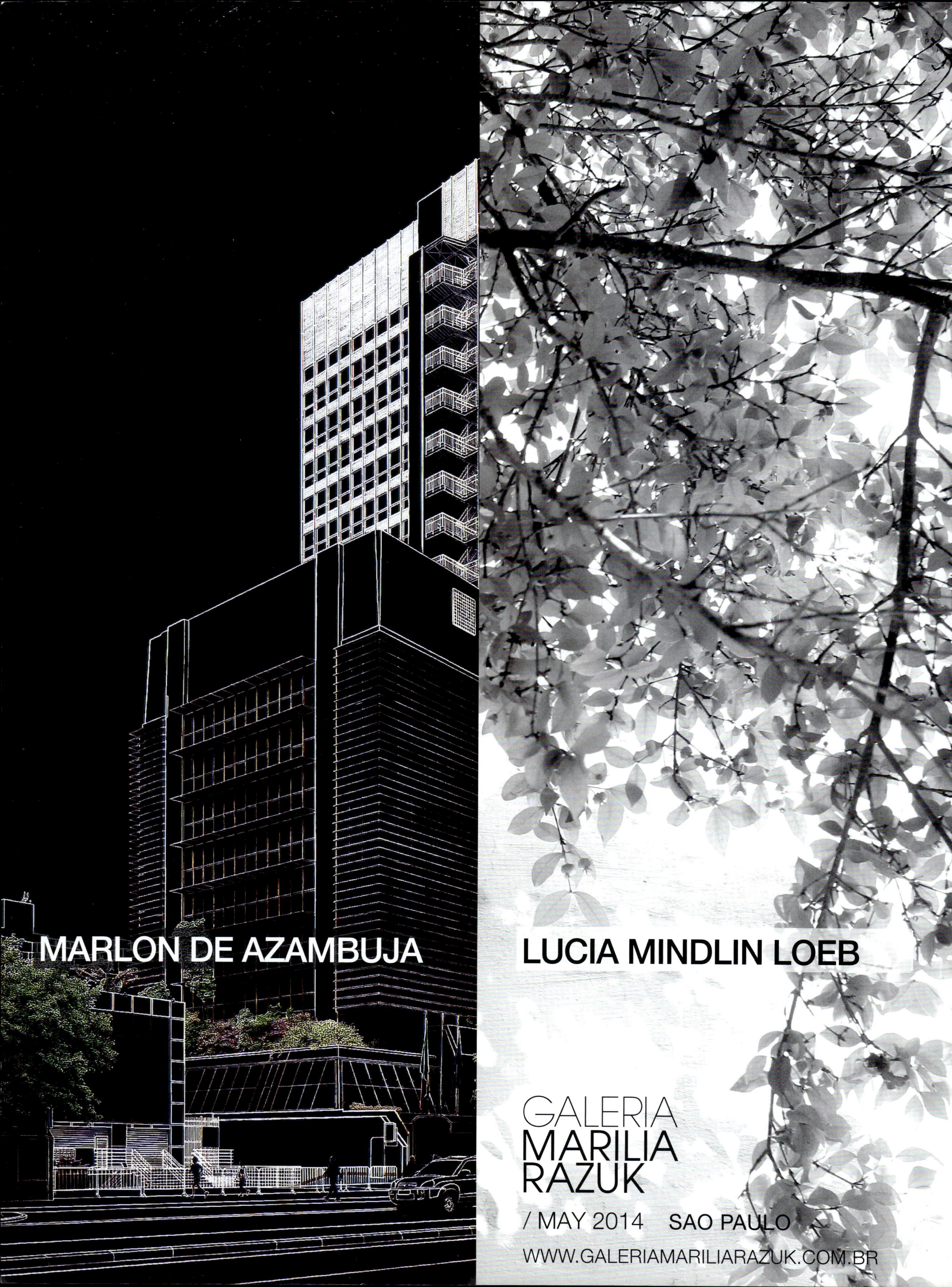

MARLON DE AZAMBUJA
LUCIA MINDLIN LOEB
GALERIA
MARILIA
RAZUK
/ MAY 2014   SAO PAULO
WWW.GALERIAMARILIARAZUK.COM.BR

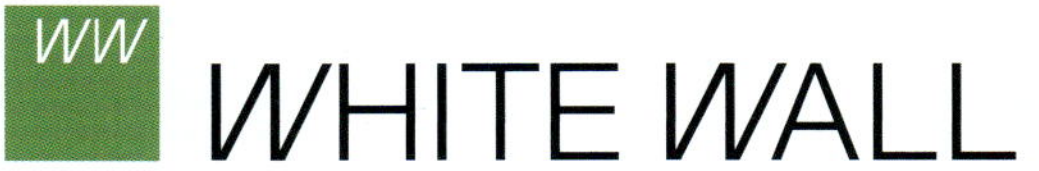

Proud winner of the TIPA award

"Best Photo Lab Worldwide"

awarded by the editors of 28 leading photography magazines

Lambda & LightJet prints on Fuji and Kodak paper, pigment & canvas prints

Mountings on aluminum and under acrylic

More than 3,000 framing options

Custom sizes

Over 220,000 satisfied customers

The lab of choice for 10,000 pros and 300 galleries

5-year guarantee

Winner of 45 awards from the photo press

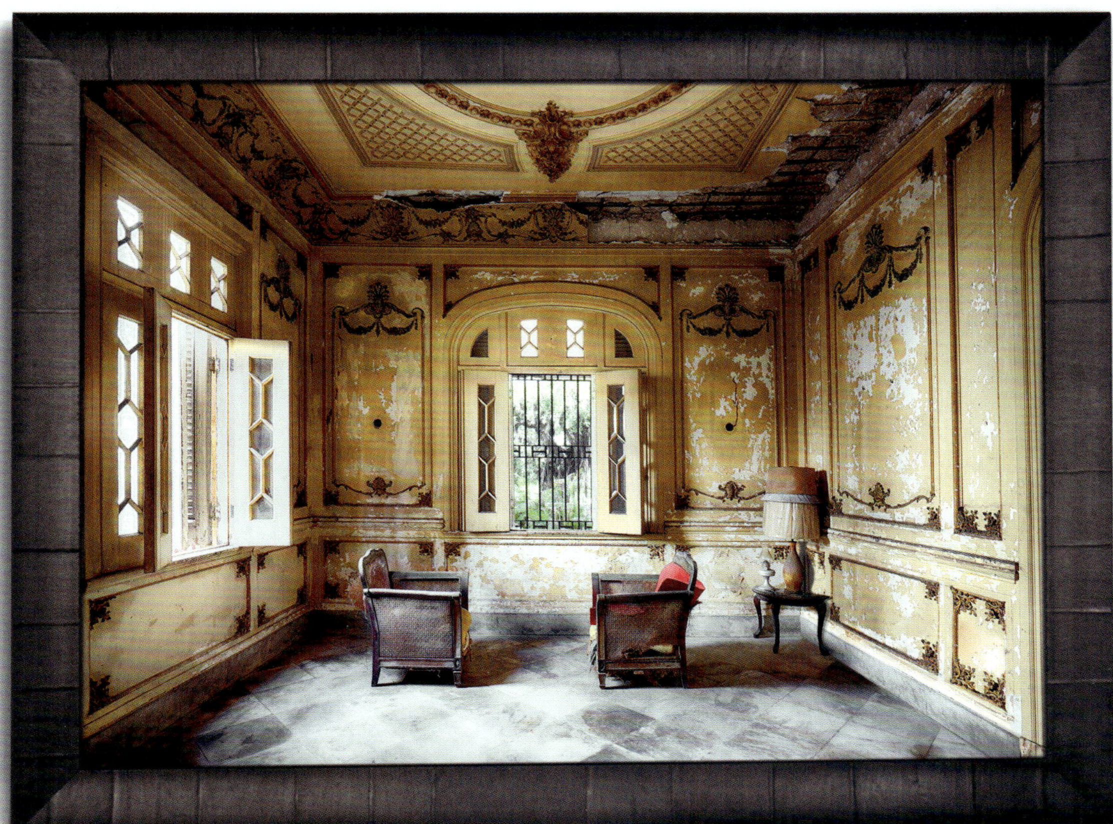

*Pictured: "House of Savreda" by Werner Pawlok, from LUMAS.COM

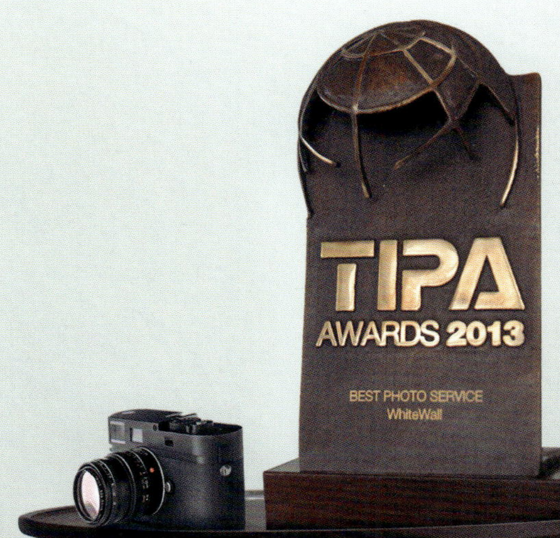

GALLERY QUALITY FOR YOUR PHOTOS

WhiteWall.com

America's Premier Book Prize in Photography

CDS/Honickman First Book Prize

- Publication of a book of photography with an introduction by **Sandra S. Phillips,** judge of the seventh biennial competition

- An award of $3,000

- A solo exhibition

- Inclusion in a website devoted to presenting and following the work of prizewinners

- Submissions accepted from June 15 to September 15, 2014

Visit our website at firstbookprizephoto.com for more information about the prize and full competition guidelines.

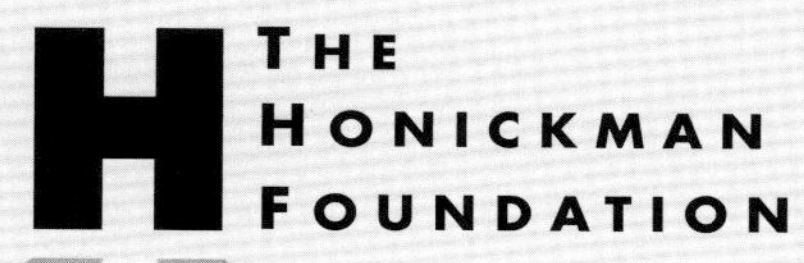

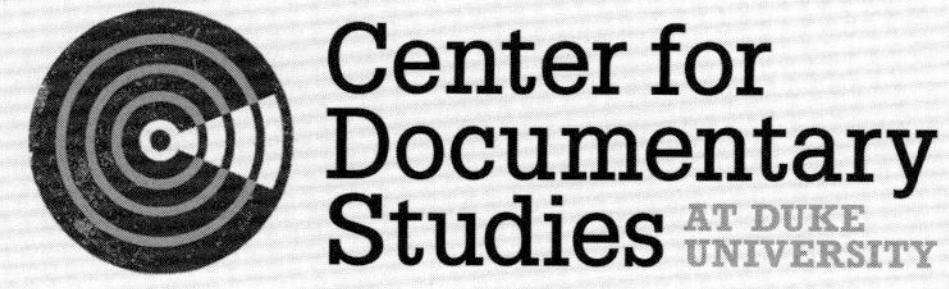

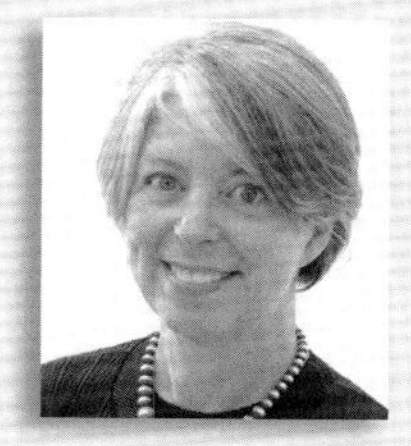

Sandra S. Phillips
Senior Curator of Photography, SFMOMA

PHOTOGRAPHY

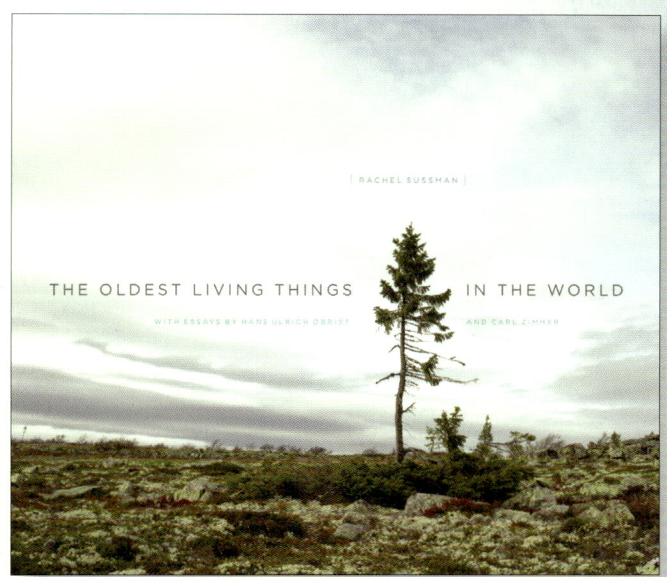

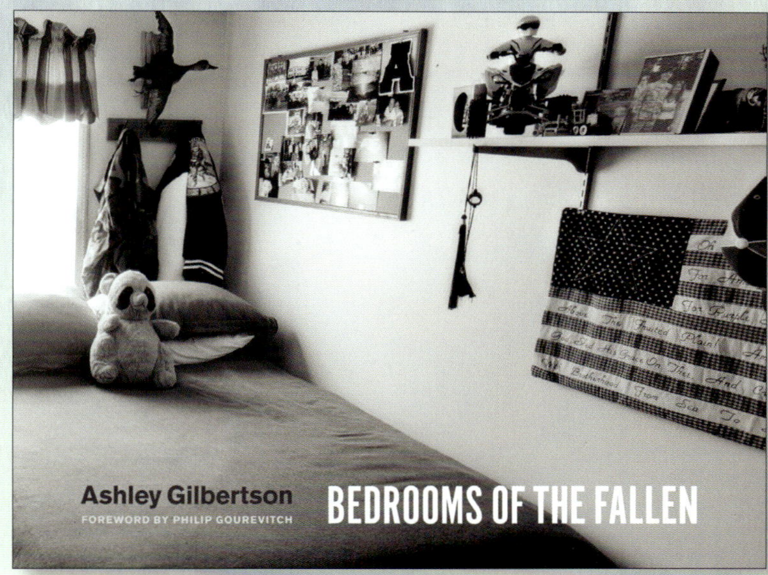

FROM CHICAGO

The Oldest Living Things in the World

Rachel Sussman

With Essays by Hans Ulrich Obrist and Carl Zimmer

170 p., 120 color plates, 5 halftones
Cloth $45.00

Bedrooms of the Fallen

Ashley Gilbertson

With a Foreword by Philip Gourevitch

120 p., 40 duotones
Cloth $35.00

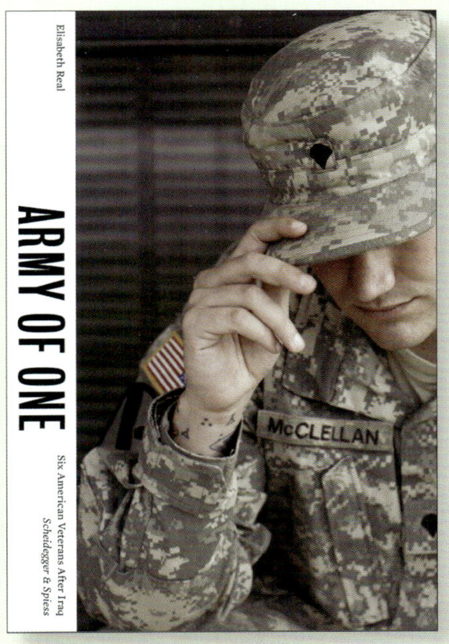

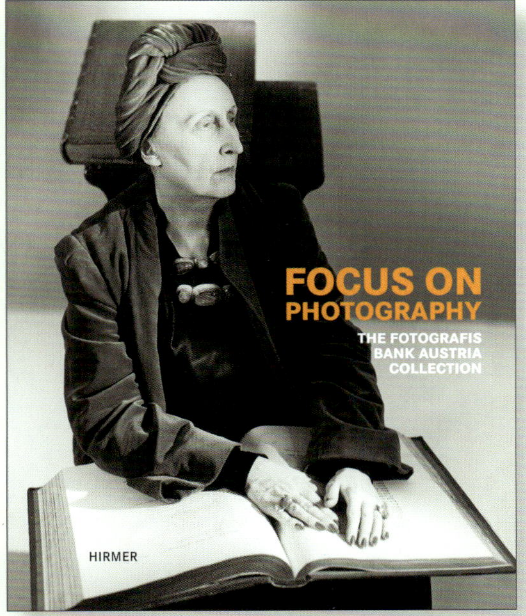

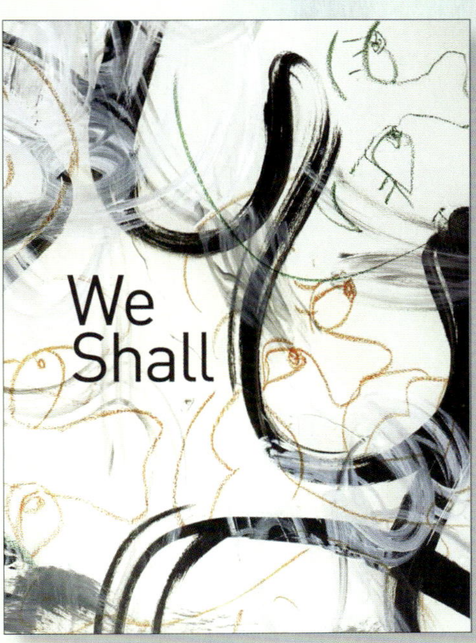

FROM SCHEIDEGGER AND SPIESS

FROM HIRMER PUBLISHERS

FROM THE DEPAUL ART MUSEUM

Army of One

Six American Veterans After Iraq

Elisabeth Real

376 p., 118 color plates
Paper $29.00

Focus on Photography

The Fotografis Bank Austria Collection

Edited by Toni Stooss

240 p., 131 duotones
Cloth $49.95

We Shall

Photographs by Paul D'Amato

Paul D'Amato

With Contributions by Gregory J. Harris and Cleophus J. Lee

102 p., 47 color plates
Cloth $45.00

THE UNIVERSITY OF CHICAGO PRESS   www.press.uchicago.edu 

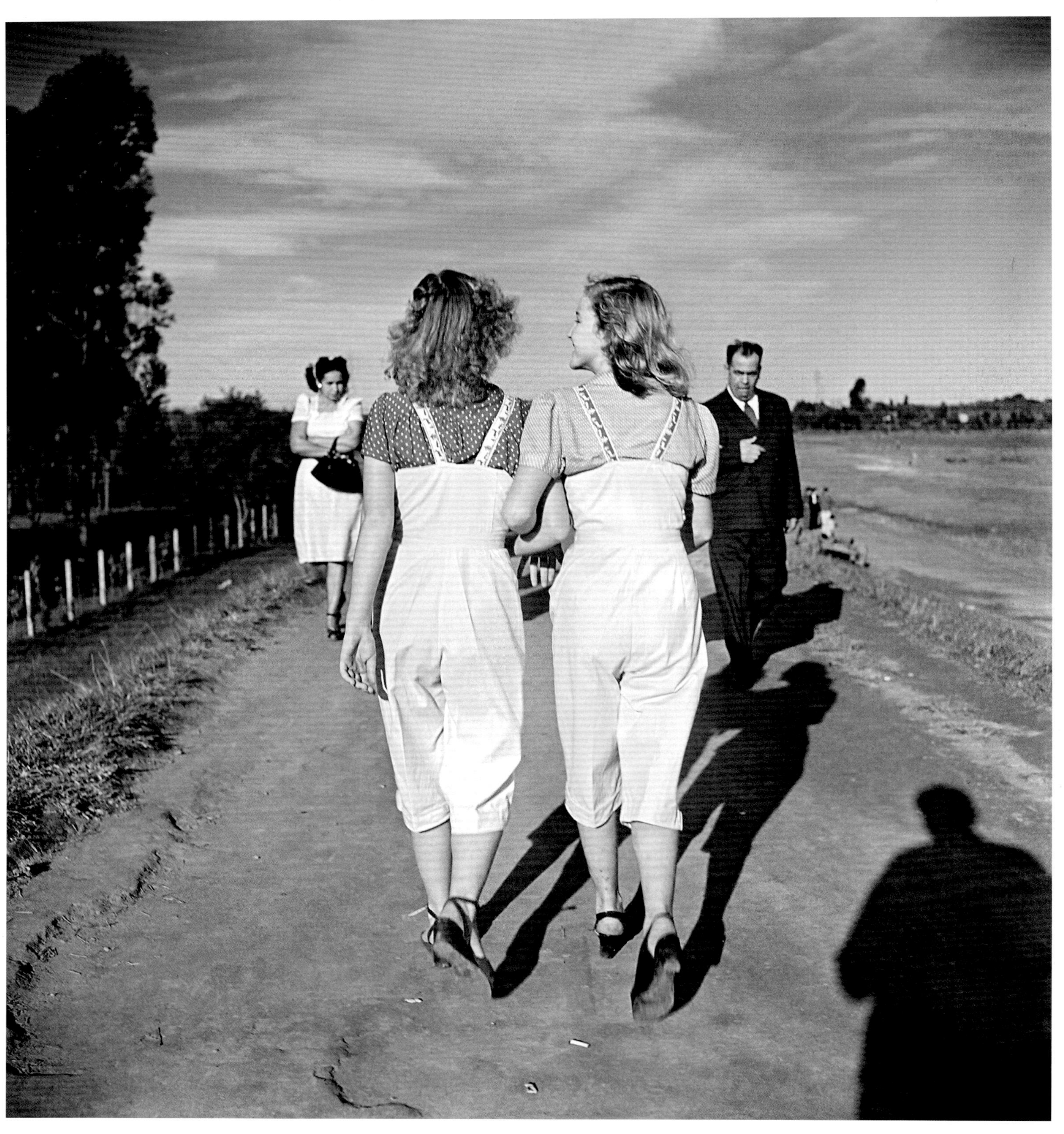

Opposite:
Peter Scheier,
Santo Amaro,
São Paulo, 1948
Courtesy Instituto Moreira Salles

Front cover:
Caio Reisewitz,
Casa Rua Santa Cruz (House on Santa Cruz Street), 2013 (detail)
© Caio Reisewitz and courtesy Luciana Brito Galeria, São Paulo

Editor
Michael Famighetti
Managing Editor
Paula Kupfer
Copy Editor
Claire Barliant
Production Manager
Matthew Harvey
Production Assistant
Luke Chase
Work Scholars
Jessica Lancaster, Hannah Max, Emily Myerscough

Art Direction, Design & Typefaces
A2/SW/HK, London

Translation from the Portuguese
David Auerbach, Jennifer Sarah Cooper,
Roberta Mahfuz, David Sharp

Editor-at-Large
Melissa Harris

Publisher
Dana Triwush
magazine@aperture.org

Advertising
Bill Besch
631-665-0467
bbesch1@verizon.net

Cultureshock Media
Sarah Haviland
+44 (0) 20 7735 9263
ads@cultureshockmedia.co.uk

Switzerland and Liechtenstein:
Affinity-PrimeMEDIA Ltd.
Eva Favre
+41 (0) 21 781 08 50
e.favre@affinity-primemedia.ch

**Executive Director,
Aperture Foundation**
Chris Boot

Minor White, Editor (1952–1974)

Michael E. Hoffman, Publisher and Executive Director
(1964–2001)

Aperture, a not-for-profit foundation, connects the photo community and its
audiences with the most inspiring work, the sharpest ideas, and with each other—
in print, in person, and online.

Help maintain Aperture's publishing, education, and community activities by joining our
new general member program. Membership starts at $75 annually and includes invitations
to special events, exclusive discounts on Aperture publications, and opportunities to meet
artists and engage with leaders in the photo community. Aperture Foundation welcomes
support at all levels of giving, and all gifts are tax-deductible to the fullest extent of the
law. For more information about supporting Aperture, please visit aperture.org/join or
contact the Development Department at membership@aperture.org.

Aperture (ISSN 0003-6420) is published quarterly, in spring, summer, fall, and winter,
at 547 West 27th Street, 4th Floor, New York, N.Y. 10001. In the United States,
a one-year subscription (four issues) is $75; a two-year subscription (eight issues)
is $124. In Canada, a one-year subscription is $95. All other international subscriptions
are $105 per year. Visit aperture.org to subscribe. Single copies may be purchased
at $24.95 for most issues. Periodicals postage paid at New York and additional offices.
Postmaster: Send address changes to *Aperture*, P.O. Box 3000, Denville, N.J. 07834.
Address queries regarding subscriptions, renewals, or gifts to: *Aperture* Subscription
Service, 866-457-4603 (U.S. and Canada), or e-mail custsvc_aperture@fulcoinc.com.

Newsstand distribution in the U.S. is handled by Curtis Circulation Company,
201-634-7400. For international distribution, contact Central Books, centralbooks.com.

Library of Congress Catalog Card No: 58-30845.

ISBN 978-1-59711-281-9

Printed in Turkey by Ofset Yapimevi

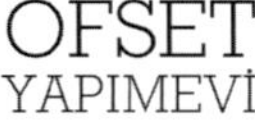

aperture.org

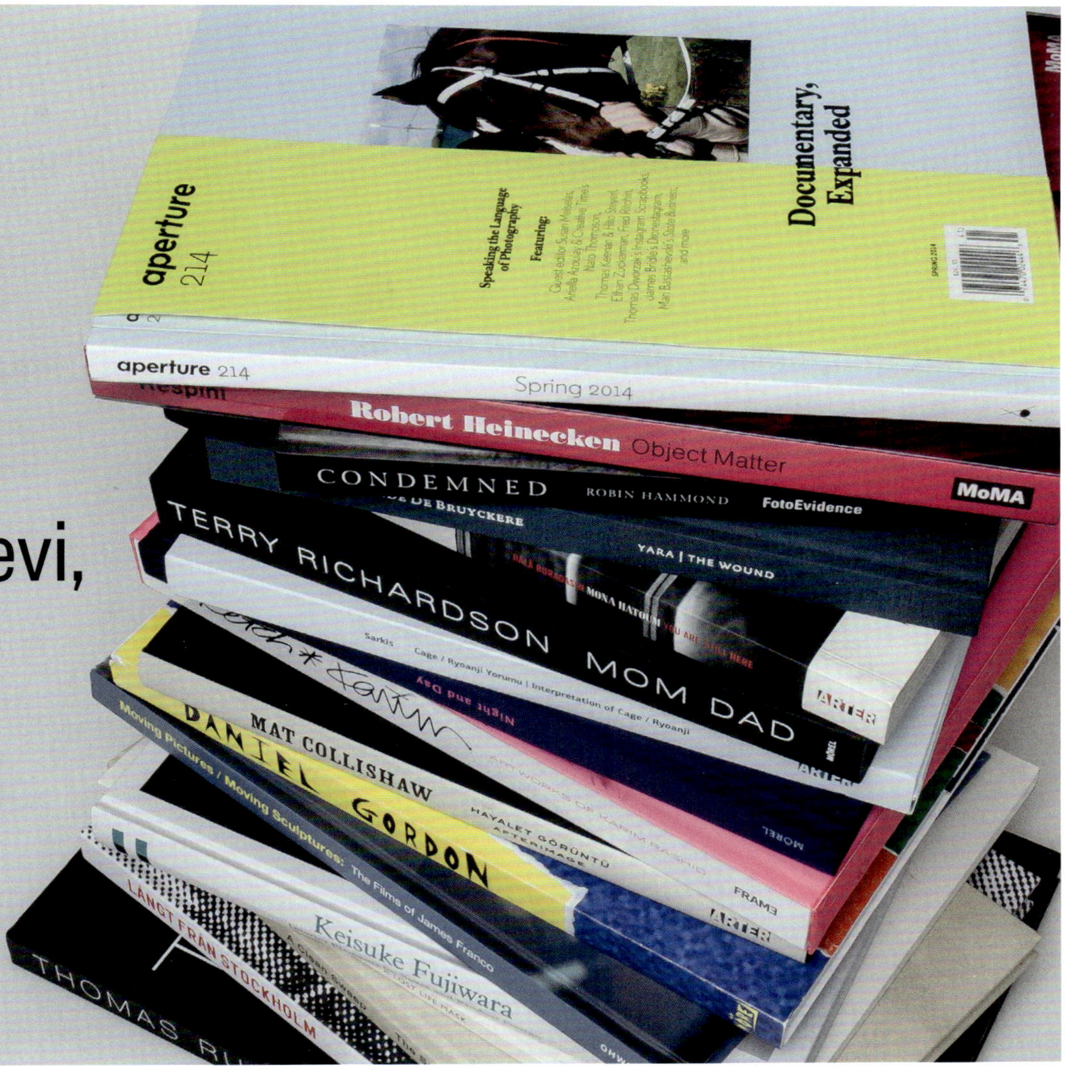

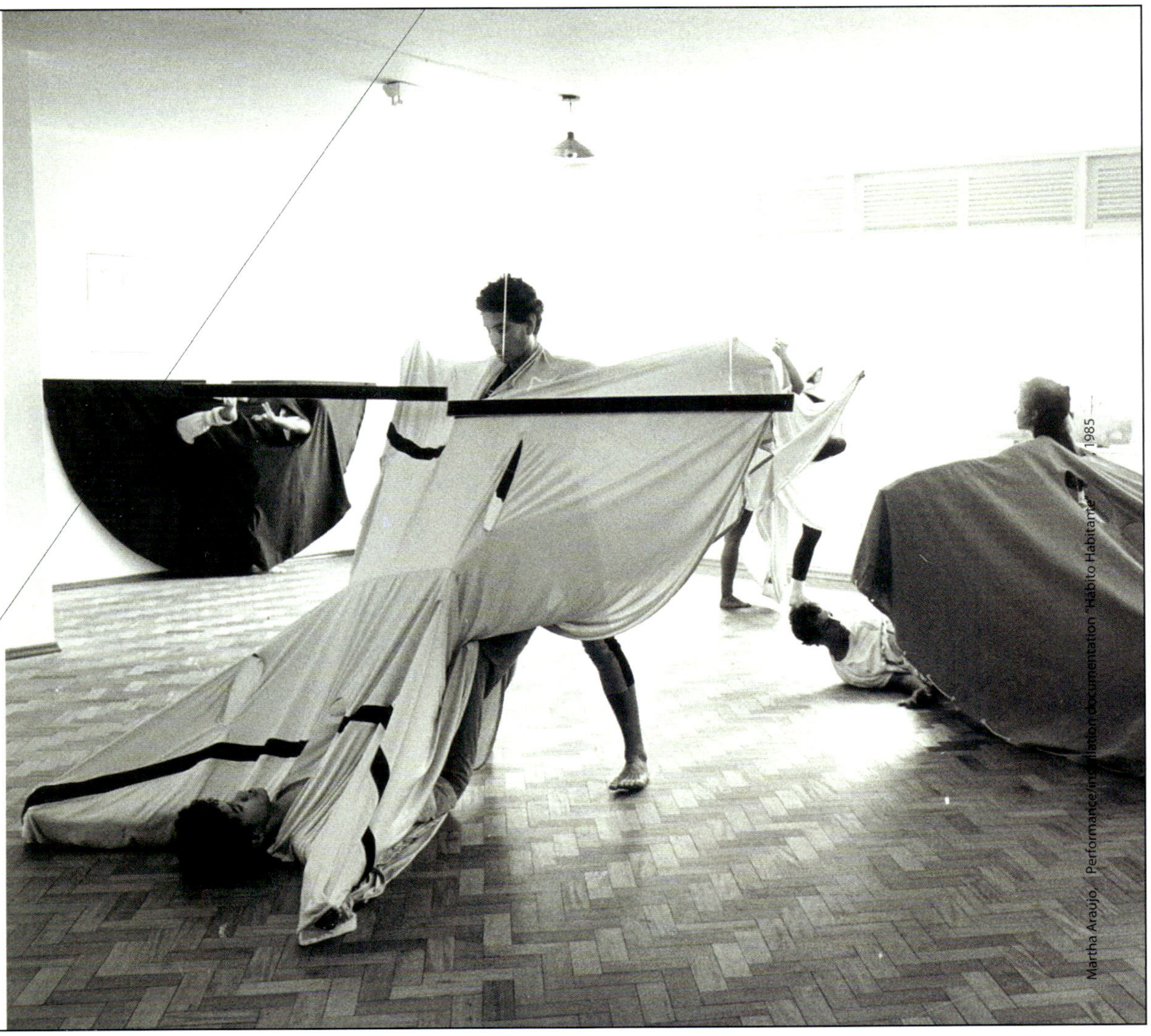

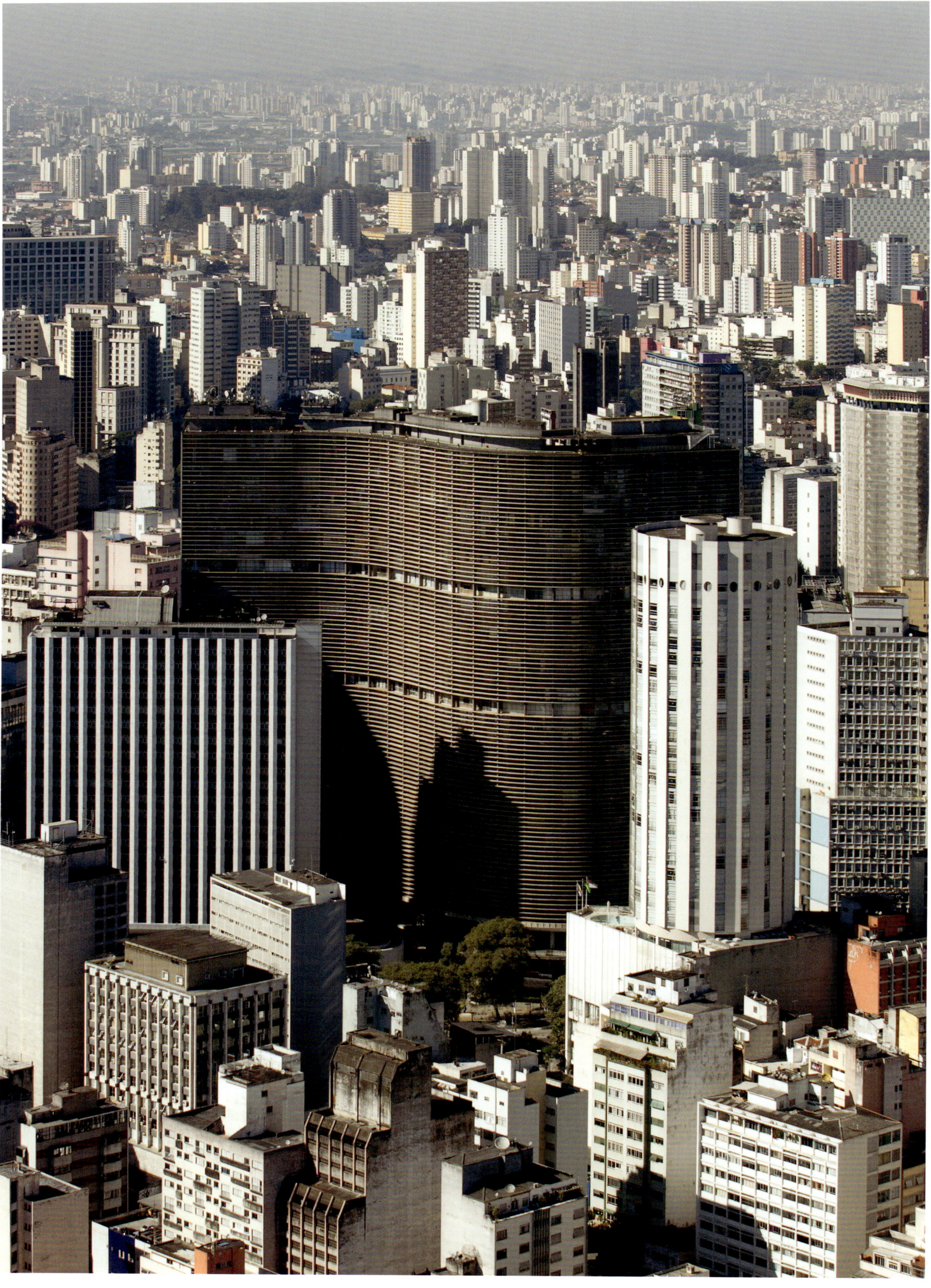

The São Paulo Issue

Was photography invented in Brazil? Possibly, according to the story of Hercule Florence, a tireless inventor and adventurer who pioneered an early form of photography in the 1830s. More likely, photography was invented simultaneously in many places, but Florence's Herzogian story of entrepreneurial tenacity and Amazonian exploration gone awry is largely absent from the more familiar narratives of European figures attempting to fix light and shadow.

This São Paulo Issue is based on two extended visits to Brazil last autumn and winter. We wanted to expand our purview to find stories like Florence's, told here by Natalia Brizuela. Working with guest editor Thyago Nogueira, editor of *Zum* magazine and curator of contemporary photography at the Instituto Moreira Salles, one of Brazil's leading photography institutions, we visited dozens of photographers, writers, and curators. We came to better understand a history of photography largely untold in the United States—one mostly new to us—and were introduced to a vibrant contemporary scene supported by a growing network of museums, galleries, and emerging alternative spaces.

"Within cities like São Paulo there exist countless worlds that can be peeled away, layer by layer, to reveal hidden lives," Cassiano Elek Machado writes in these pages. With a population pushing twenty million, São Paulo extends vertiginously in all directions. A single magazine issue can only hope to peel back a few layers of curatorial and research activity, but in these pages you'll find a cross section of ideas and projects, an almost even split between historical and contemporary.

Waves of immigration shaped São Paulo, and its transnational story is evident in Sérgio Burgi's panoramic overview of the city's artistic activity across the twentieth century, and in Claudia Andujar's extraordinary story of fleeing Eastern Europe during the Second World War. Russian émigré Gregori Warchavchik's Casa Modernista appears on our cover in Caio Reisewitz's lush image. Modernism's enduring legacy and a fluid intersection of photography and design thread the issue—from Geraldo de Barros's diverse practice (from photography to furniture design) to Mauro Restiffe's tribute to legendary architect Oscar Niemeyer. With the exception of Bárbara Wagner and Jonathas de Andrade, each artist featured in the issue has roots in São Paulo. These two figures (whose work we discovered on view in São Paulo) may be more associated with the northern city of Recife, but their work taps into important areas of Brazilian culture and history—performance groups embodying Afro-Brazilian traditions and the years of military dictatorship, respectively.

Last year's social unrest, born out of debates about inequality in Brazil's fast-growing economy, played out dramatically as large-scale street demonstrations across the country. Politically engaged photography collectives, such as Mídia Ninja, were active in documenting the protests predicted to resume this summer when Brazil assumes the global spotlight as World Cup host. These forward-thinking collectives are redrawing the media landscape. Ronaldo Entler, in his overview of this phenomenon, notes how these groups "prove that it is possible to reinvent photography in times of crisis." It seems as long as photography has been around, it has been invented and reinvented in Brazil. This is the first time *Aperture* has embedded in a city abroad to uncover narratives of photography from a different perspective; we hope it will be the first of many.　—The Editors

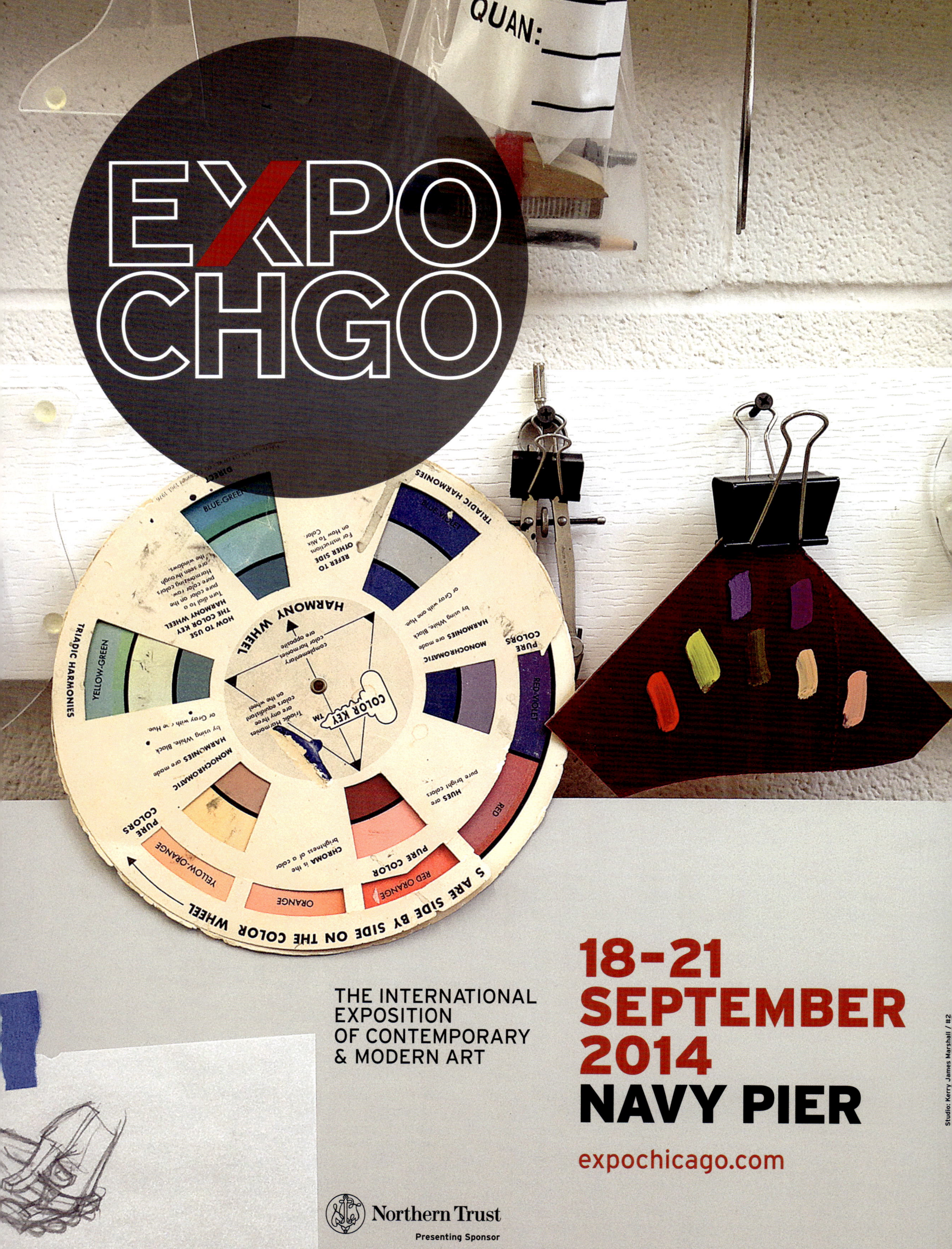

EXPO
CHGO
QUAN:
COLOR KEY
HARMONY WHEEL
THE INTERNATIONAL
EXPOSITION
OF CONTEMPORARY
& MODERN ART
18-21
SEPTEMBER
2014
NAVY PIER
expochicago.com
Northern Trust
Presenting Sponsor
Studio: Kerry James Marshall / #2

What Matters Now?
Photography, Technology, and the World

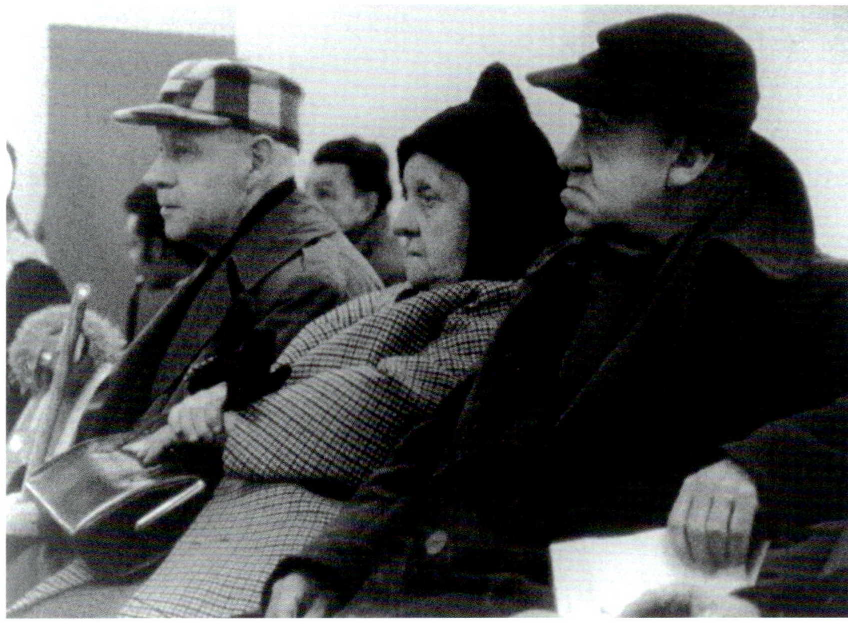

Above:
Three people waiting on a bench at a welfare center in New York, 1973 (film still)
Courtesy Zipporah Films, Cambridge, Mass.

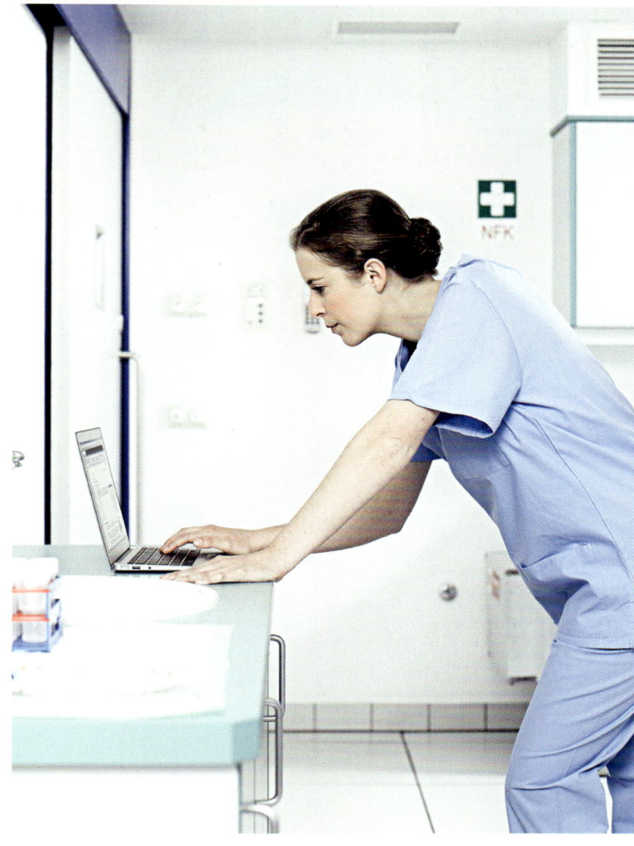

Above:
Doctor using laptop in hospital, from the Getty Images–*Lean In* collection
© Joos Mind/Getty Images

Welfare State

It is always a problem to know what an image "means." I like this still, taken from my film *Welfare*, of three people sitting on a bench at a welfare center in New York in 1973. I find it funny but I cannot explain why. Maybe because of the asymmetry of the three hats, balanced by the pointed one? Maybe it's the relationship of the jaws, and what they suggest—curiosity, patience, and anger. Maybe they just look like people who are used to waiting (though they might not be clients themselves but there to keep a son, aunt, nephew, or daughter-in-law company). Maybe the picture needs a caption: does "Three people waiting on a bench at a welfare center in New York" help? Perhaps it would be better to have a video so the reader could hear them think. Would that help us understand? Sometimes I think they may still be waiting and perhaps have not aged at all. Maybe they are eternally waiting, as Samuel Beckett understood so well, and that is what makes the photograph always feel contemporary. Finally, is all this blather a projection? If so, what does that say about me?

—**Frederick Wiseman, documentary filmmaker, most recently of *At Berkeley*, 2013**

Femme Total

Facebook Chief Operating Officer Sheryl Sandberg has curated a new Getty Images stock photo collection, branded *Lean In*, the same title as her recent advice tome for the working gal. The book speaks primarily to wealthy, white, straight working mothers, whom she encourages to embrace the patriarchal system of career advancement rather than advocating deeper systemic change. The *Lean In* gender safari set of images purports to offer portraits with which consumers can better identify, that is, more realistic or diverse figures, but still requires us to buy into the binary thinking espoused in Sandberg's book. On the menu are strong female characters, nontypical beauties (with slightly higher body mass index; glasses; hair that is gray, black, or curly), a few token brown faces, the happily coupled, unexpectedly tuned-in fathers, and the mother of all Western capitalist gender stereotypes: the Woman Who Has It All. The WWHIA is able to climb the corporate ladder, be an ideal mother, and have leisure time. Men are rarely praised for balancing work and fatherhood—perhaps they are not expected to do so, or we simply ignore those who do, or maybe it is more interesting to gaze at women capable of a full range of humanity, "in spite" of their assigned gender.

—**Marisa Olson, artist and media theorist based in New York**

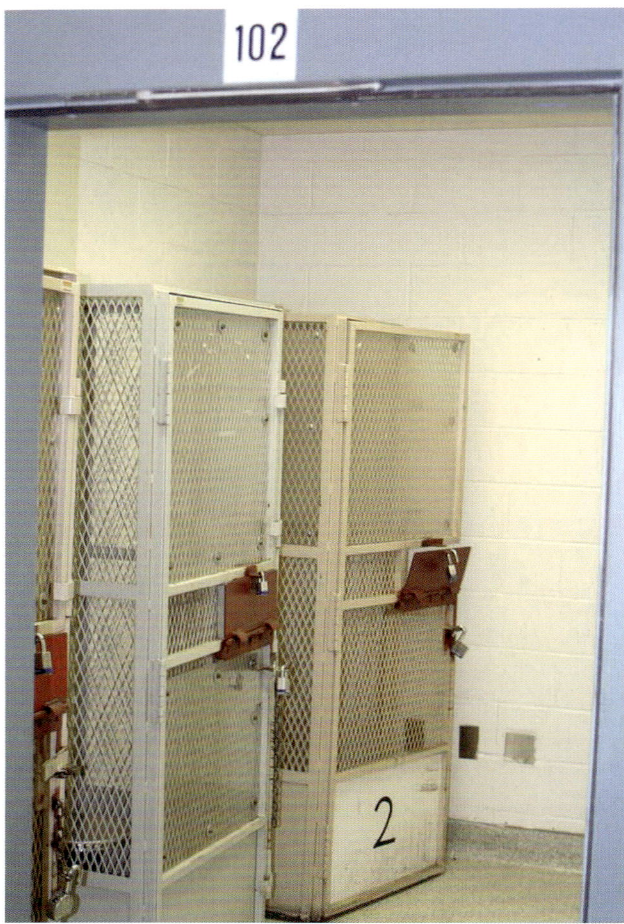

Above:
"Dry cages"
(holding cells) for
prisoners awaiting a
"mental health crisis"
bed, Correctional
Treatment Center,
Salinas Valley State
Prison, California,
July 29, 2008
Courtesy Rosen, Bien,
Galvan & Grunfeld LLP

Right:
*Law & Order:
Special Victims
Unit*, Episode 1,416
(pictured: Danny
Pino as detective
Nick Amaro and
Mariska Hargitay
as detective
Olivia Benson).
Photograph by
Michael Parmelee/NBC
Courtesy NBC Universal

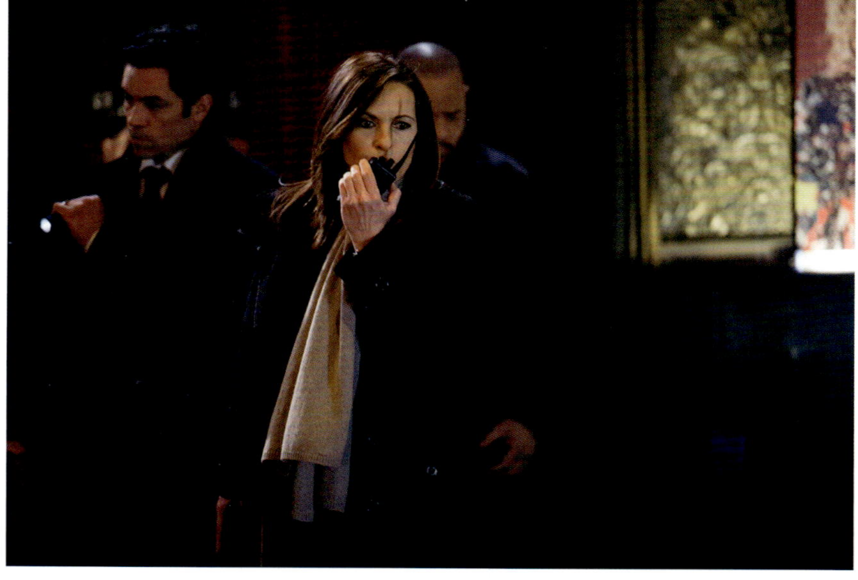

A Case for Photographs

In May 2011, the Supreme Court of the United States upheld an order to cut the prison population in California, on the grounds that overcrowding resulted in inadequate health care conditions and preventable deaths.

The majority ruling for the case, *Brown v. Plata*, was penned by Justice Anthony Kennedy, who took the unorthodox step of including in the appendix three photographs of prison conditions. Perhaps, in this case, the facts really needed to be seen in order to be believed?

The three images represented a cache of hundreds of low-resolution, anonymous, poorly lit photographs used in the initial filings and ongoing compliance stages of *Brown v. Plata*. Their inclusion spurred widespread consternation among some law boffins who believed that photographs are too emotive and too imprecise, and have no place in high-profile legal cases. I wonder, at what point did the legal community decide written and oral testimony is more legitimate than visual evidence?

For too long there has been arrogance among photography traditionalists that only professionally made documentary images can change the world. To find images that may change society, we'd be better off looking to legal briefs instead of newspaper front pages. The images made by prison officials and legal teams used in *Brown v. Plata* changed the daily living conditions of 165,000 men and women.

—**Pete Brook, editor of prisonphotography.org and columnist at** *Wired*

Veil of Clarity

In a Hamburg hotel room recently I was watching *Law & Order: Special Victims Unit*. The image quality was remarkably sharp. Watching it was like performing an act of forensic analysis. I had the impression of peering through an invisible space, one that was somehow sealed into the image itself. Beyond this peculiar veil of clarity was Mariska Hargitay talking on a cellphone with a kidnapped child who was stashed in a transport container, trying desperately to locate her before....

A non-analogue image has an extremely compressed life. It starts as *this* and, in increasingly short time spans, becomes *that*. Locked into an abstract context of technical progress, we climb an endless ladder of previously unexperienced clarities. Each fresh degree of definition offers a continuously new version of new. This succession permeates every level of consciousness both individual and collective, recalibrating awareness, altering identity itself.

—**Roni Horn, visual artist based in New York and Reykjavík, Iceland**

Art | Basel

Basel | June | 19–22 | 2014

artbasel.com | facebook.com/artbasel | twitter.com/artbasel

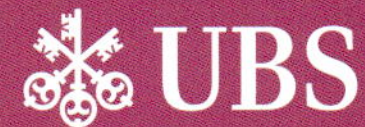

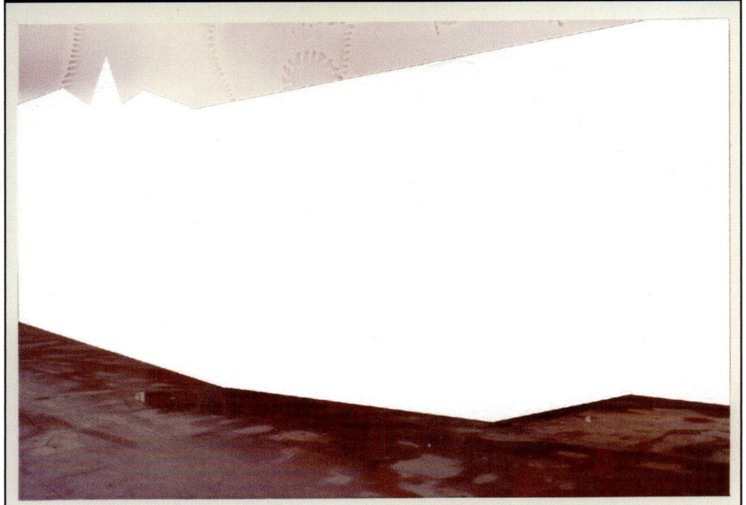

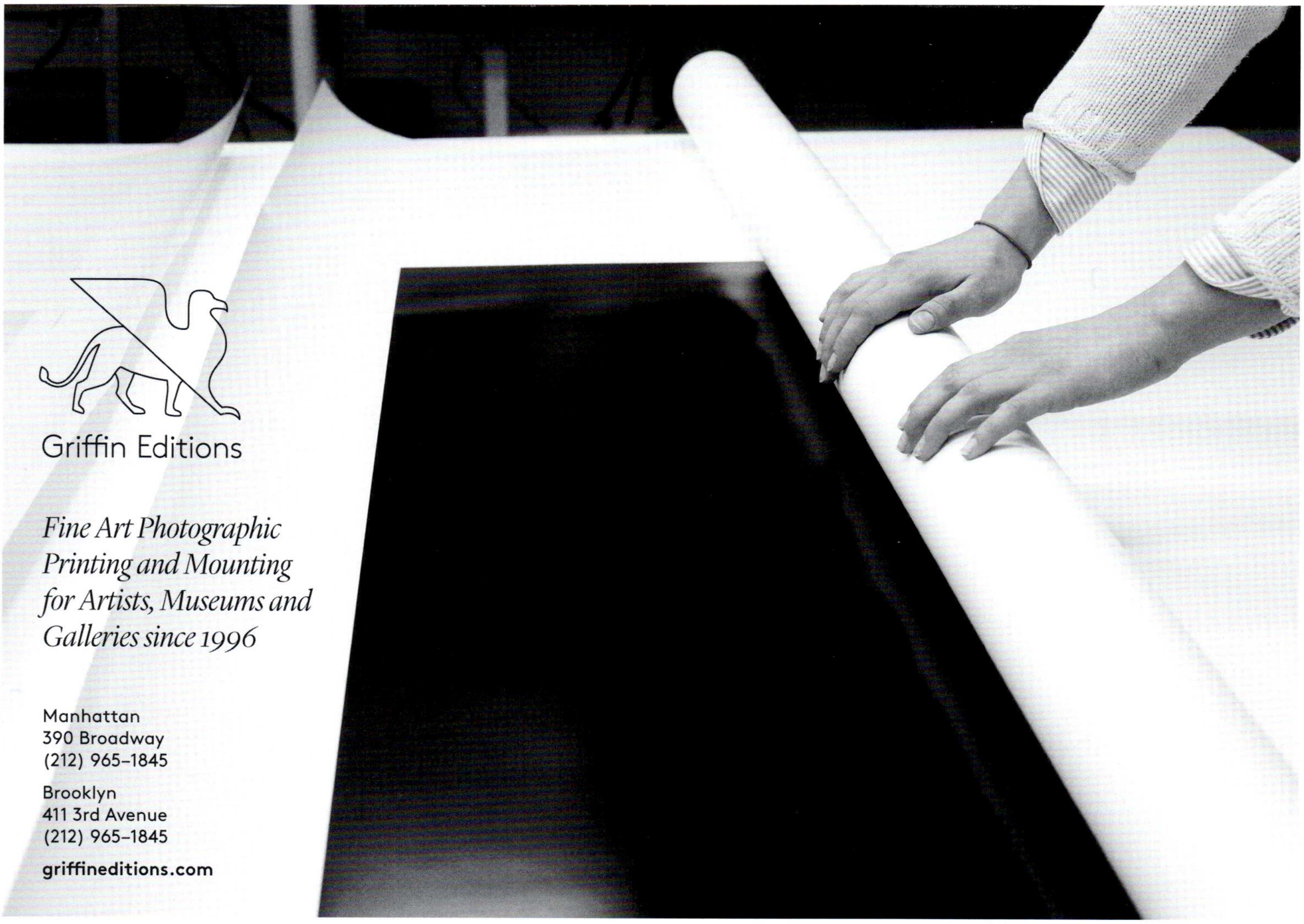

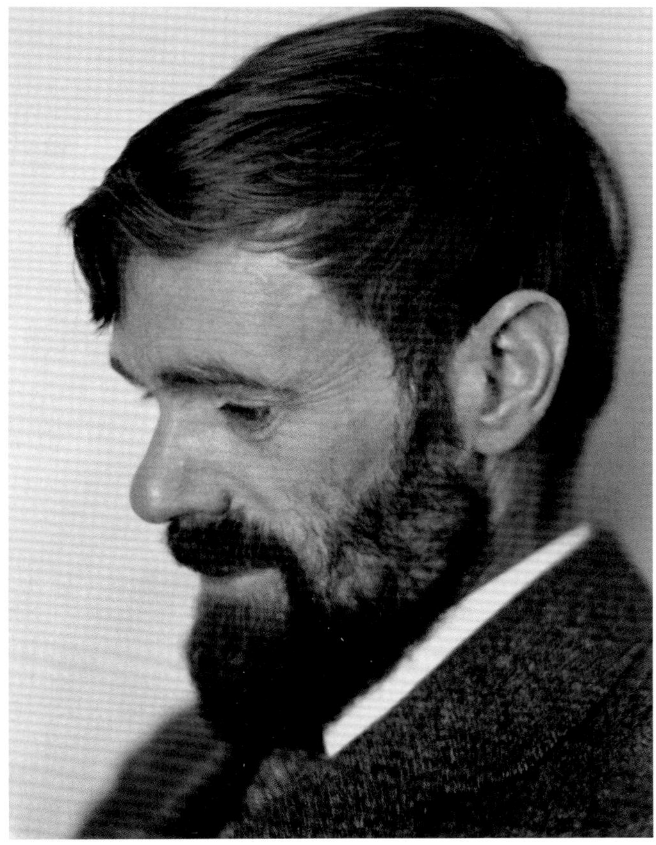

D.H. Lawrence's "Art and Morality"
Geoff Dyer

Edward Weston,
D.H. Lawrence, 1924
© 1981 Center for Creative
Photography, Arizona Board
of Regents

In November 1924 in Mexico City, a brief meeting took place between four remarkable—and remarkably different—people. Given the odd symmetry of their circumstances, it makes sense to introduce these two couples as if they were participants in a friendly set of mixed doubles. On one side of the net we have thirty-nine-year-old Englishman D.H. Lawrence (son of a miner, widely revered and derided both as a novelist and as a prophet of psychosexual revolution) and his wife, Frieda, an aristocratic German, five years his senior, who had abandoned her then-husband and children to elope with the writer back in 1912. On the other side we have Edward Weston, a photographer from Illinois, a year younger than Lawrence, who, having abandoned *his* family, was living in Mexico with the stunning Italian Tina Modotti. This last—and youngest—member of the quartet ended up having four claims to fame: as an actress, as Weston's model in some of his best-known Mexican photographs, as a major photographer in her own right, and, finally, as a revolutionary.

Apart from a few words in Lawrence's letters and in Weston's diaristic *Daybooks*, there is almost no record of what was said over the course of this encounter, but there was time for Weston to do two portraits of Lawrence. Weston took no pride in the results—it had all been too hurried, he said—but Lawrence liked the pictures well enough to write Weston and ask if there was any way he could help him in his career. Unable to go more than a couple of paragraphs without offering instruction on how to live, he advised Weston to "tackle the world, it's a rather stupid bull, to be taken by the horns, not dodged."

Lawrence was writing from Oaxaca, Mexico, where, even by his standards, he became terribly sick: with influenza, malaria, and typhoid fever to go along with (though he refused to admit this) the tuberculosis that would kill him less than five years later. By the time the Lawrences made it back to their little ranch in New Mexico in April 1925, Lorenzo was "a mere wreck." Being Lawrence, though, this was not sufficient impediment to stop him working on numerous writing projects, including a little essay called "Art and Morality," which ends up being a remarkable and slightly crazed consideration of photography.

He begins by asking why people are offended by Cézanne's still lifes of apples. It's because of "the slowly formed habit of seeing just as the photographic camera sees." Slowly formed the habit may have been, but with the advent of the Kodak camera it accelerated to the point where a man only "sees what the Kodak has taught him to see." And that's not all: "As vision developed toward the Kodak, man's idea of himself developed toward the snapshot. Primitive man simply didn't know *what* he was: He was always half in the dark. But we have learned to see, and each of us has a complete Kodak idea of himself." In his stride by now—and having left behind any readers who were

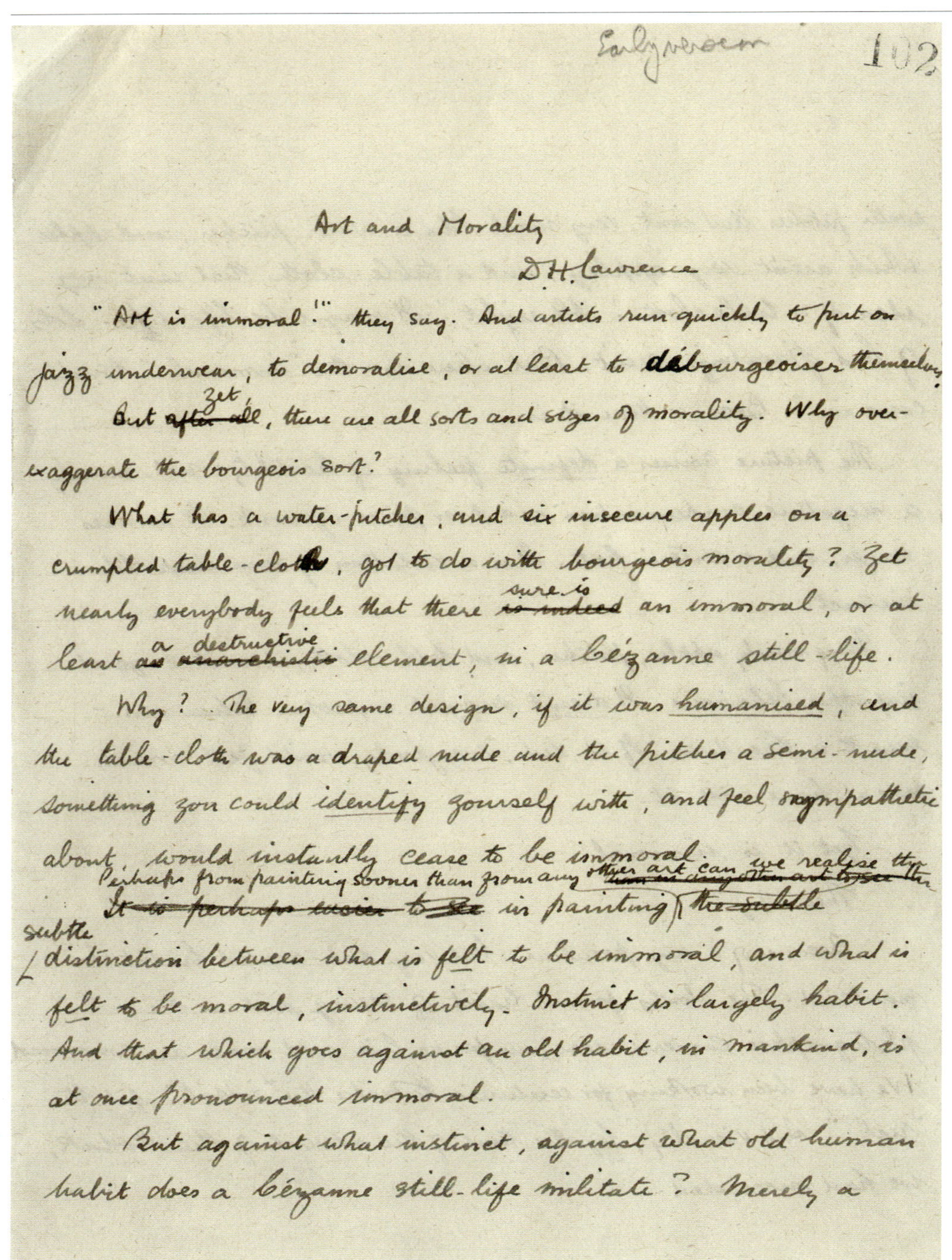

Early version   102

Art and Morality

D.H. Lawrence

"Art is immoral!" they say. And artists run quickly to put on jazz underwear, to demoralise, or at least to débourgeoiser themselves.

But [Yet] there are all sorts and sizes of morality. Why over-exaggerate the bourgeois sort?

What has a water-pitcher, and six insecure apples on a crumpled table-cloth, got to do with bourgeois morality? Yet nearly everybody feels that there sure is [is indeed] an immoral, or at least a destructive [anarchistic] element, in a Cézanne still-life.

Why? The very same design, if it was humanised, and the table-cloth was a draped nude and the pitcher a semi-nude, something you could identify yourself with, and feel sympathetic about, would instantly cease to be immoral. Perhaps from painting sooner than from any other art can we realise the subtle distinction between what is felt to be immoral, and what is felt to be moral, instinctively. Instinct is largely habit. And that which goes against an old habit, in mankind, is at once pronounced immoral.

But against what instinct, against what old human habit does a Cézanne still-life militate? Merely a

Weston found himself "convulsed with laughter" at Lawrence's attempts to probe the Mexican psyche via a "tiresome allegory of Quetzalcoatl" in the novel he was writing when they met, *The Plumed Serpent*.) But the essay's appeal to the deep Nile of the past or its diagnosis of the state of human failings in the mid-1920s is less striking now, almost ninety years after it was written, than its power as prognosis.

It was difficult to open a paper or magazine last year without coming across so-called "think pieces" about either the selfie or, relatedly, the way that people can't just *do* things anymore but have to photograph themselves doing them (having sex, swilling beer, doing their homework, even *taking photographs*). It might have seemed, to middle-aged eyes, as if this was how people—especially the young—spent their lives, but, as with so many apparently new phenomena, this one had a lengthy prehistory. As Lawrence's prophetic essay makes clear, in many ways it is just the latest technological manifestation—in his terms, a technological *consummation*—of a habit that was "already old" in 1925.

naively expecting a reasonable treatise on "art and morality"—Lawrence launches into one of his characteristic surges of intuitive analysis:

"Previously, even in Egypt, men had not learned to *see straight*. They fumbled in the dark, and didn't quite know where they were, or what they were. Like men in a dark room, they only *felt* their own existence surging in the darkness of other creatures.

"We, however, *are* what is seen…. A picture! A Kodak snap, in a universal film of snaps…. The identifying of ourselves with the visual image of ourselves has become an instinct; the habit is already old. The picture of me, the me that is seen, is me."

There's much to love in this, not least the way that he talks with such authority and confidence about the ancient Egyptian psyche. (Incidentally,

There's much to love in this, not least the way that he talks with such authority and confidence about the ancient Egyptian psyche.

Geoff Dyer's latest book, *Another Great Day at Sea*, about his time aboard an American aircraft carrier, the USS *George Bush*, will be published by Pantheon this spring.

Understanding a Photograph, a new compilation of John Berger's essays, edited and introduced by Geoff Dyer, was published by Aperture last fall.

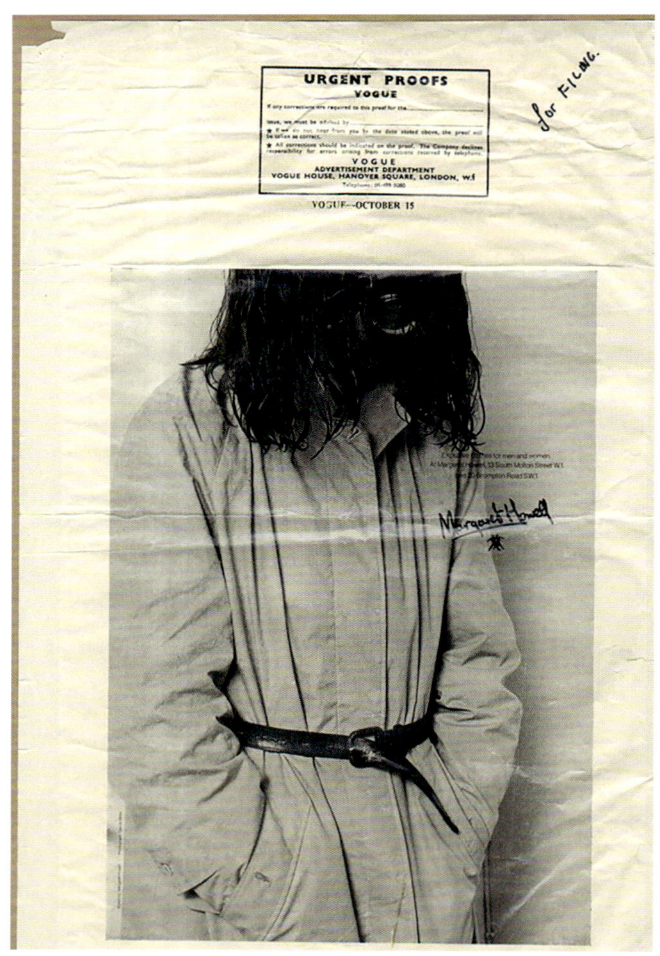
Proof of Margaret Howell's first women's ad campaign, 1975
Courtesy Margaret Howell

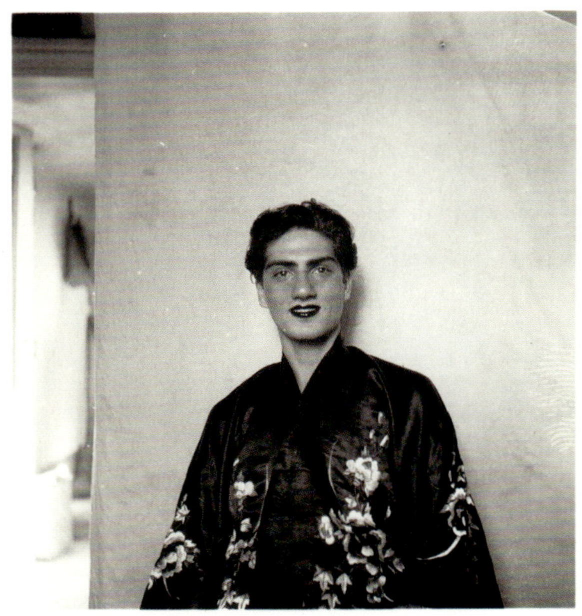
Van Leo (Leon Boyadjian), *Self-portrait*, Cairo, Egypt, June 26, 1940
© American University of Cairo and courtesy Arab Image Foundation

Negar Azimi

It's 1940. A young man dressed in a kimono stands against a white wall. His lips are smeared with lipstick and he may or may not be wearing rouge (the photo is black-and-white). On the back, in light pencil, is written "In the Chinese House." Why Chinese? Who took the picture? The photograph is part of a collection I've been working on since 2002 around the life and work of the late Armenian-Egyptian photographer Van Leo. A well-regarded studio photographer in Belle Époque Cairo, Van Leo took a thousand or more self-portraits throughout his life. Ambiguities, secrets, and dead ends abound, for while Van Leo, born Leon Boyadjian, was a fastidious hoarder—of everything from letters to electricity bills—much about him remains unknown. Today his collection is split between the American University in Cairo and the Arab Image Foundation in Beirut, where Karl Bassil and I are at work on a book and exhibition project about this enigmatic man and his idiosyncratic practice.

Negar Azimi is the senior editor at *Bidoun*.

Penny Martin

Last June I agreed to be "the other half" of the first public talk by designer Margaret Howell in the forty-or-so years she's been in business. Knowing that chronic nerves had kept Margaret silent all those years, I felt responsible for ensuring that her vocal debut would go smoothly. On the morning of the event at the Victoria & Albert Museum, I printed out this slide from her PowerPoint—an image from Margaret Howell's first women's ad campaign in 1975. It's hung on the noticeboard opposite my desk ever since, a reminder that one needn't be brimming with confidence to communicate stylishly.

Penny Martin is the editor of *The Gentlewoman*.

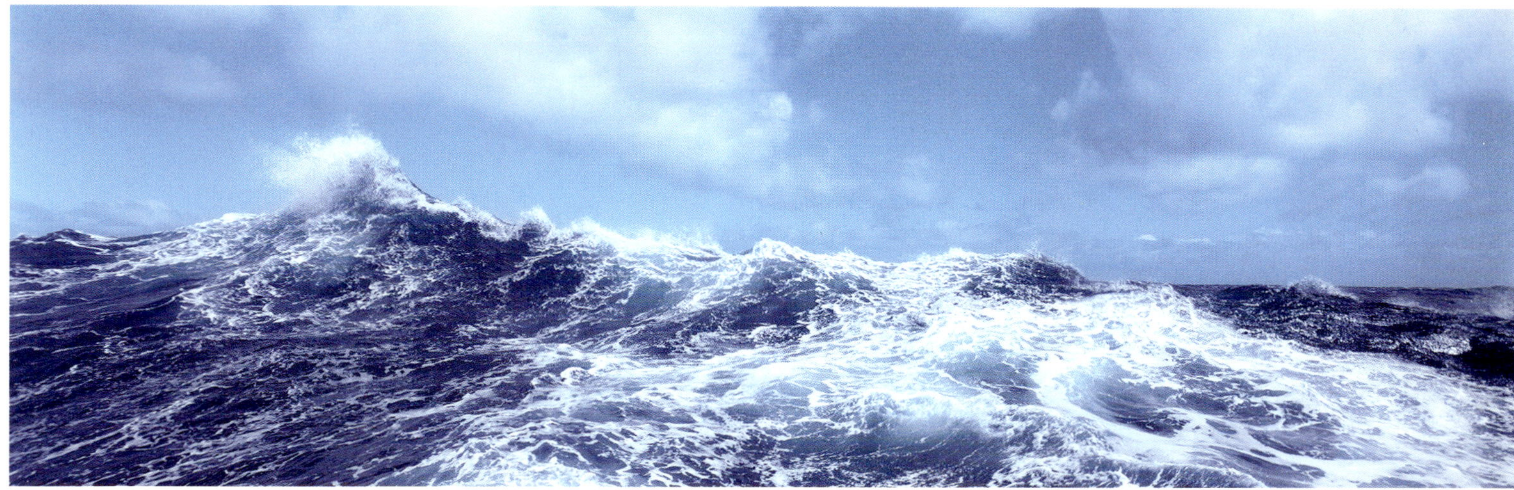

Stuart Klipper, *Swell, near 50° S, Southern Ocean, Antarctica*, 1992
Courtesy the artist

Josh Tyrangiel

I was wandering through the Museum of Modern Art several years ago, dodging tourists and suffering the usual museum-going misery, when I stumbled upon a massive print of Stuart Klipper's *Swell*. A smaller version hangs in my apartment now, and after hours of couch study I can say that it's "about" vastness and intimacy, stillness and motion. (It's also about as far away as you can get from the pictures of suited executives that fill so much of my professional viewing.) But I own it because it defies analysis or rationalization. It's a reminder that the world is enormous and forceful and inexplicable. I own it for the simplest reason: because it's beautiful.

Josh Tyrangiel is the editor of *Bloomberg Businessweek*.

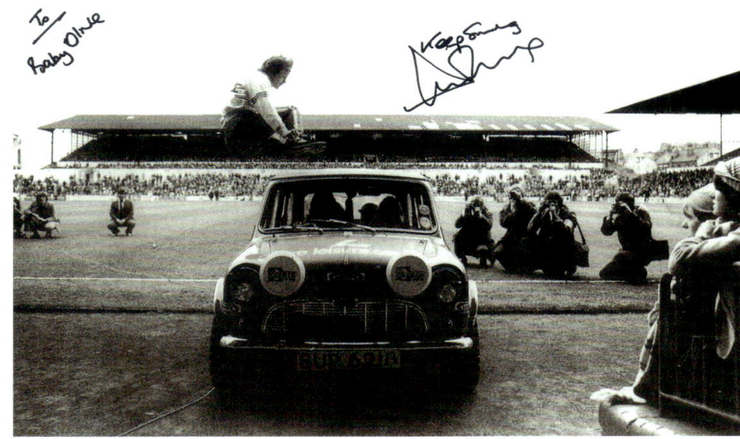

Duncan McKenzie jumps over a Mini, Leeds United, Elland Road, August 1975
Photographer unknown Courtesy Tony Chambers

Tony Chambers

The jumping man is Duncan McKenzie, an English football star in the 1970s and also one of my all-time favorite players. Duncan was famed for some unorthodox party tricks, including throwing a golf ball the length of a football pitch (approximately 110 yards) and hurdling a Mini (seen here). It is unimaginable that a football club, or agent, would allow one of their prized assets to risk injury performing such a prank today. The fact that this was just before a match kickoff makes it even more incredible.

I bought the photograph from Duncan himself. He carries a small portfolio of them whenever he attends a game; a signed print costs £5. Witnessing such a talented and successful ex-footballer touting memorabilia just doesn't seem right. Only twenty-five years separate Duncan McKenzie's generation from David Beckham's. The story behind this photograph illustrates the gulf in financial rewards available from the profession they both excelled in. However, this inequality does not seem to bother Duncan. He's always smiling, looks fit, and could probably still jump that Mini.

Tony Chambers is the editor-in-chief of *Wallpaper.**

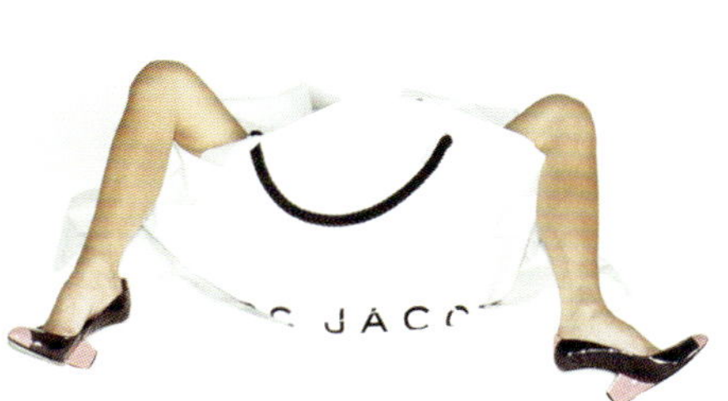

Juergen Teller, *Victoria Beckham, Marc Jacobs Campaign SS08, Legs, Bag, and Shoes, LA*, 2007 © Juergen Teller and courtesy Lehmann Maupin, New York

Stefano Tonchi

I love it when a single image can very simply articulate the otherwise abstract. This photograph of Victoria Beckham by one of *W*'s most iconic photographers, Juergen Teller, represents the perfect blend of art, commerce, and celebrity. For me, that is so much of what photography is about. It's featured in the Steidl book *Marc Jacobs Advertising 1998–2009*, but I also have a copy of the print at home. Teller's playfulness and flair for originality elevate this from a fashion image to cultural commentary.

Stefano Tonchi is the editor-in-chief of *W*.

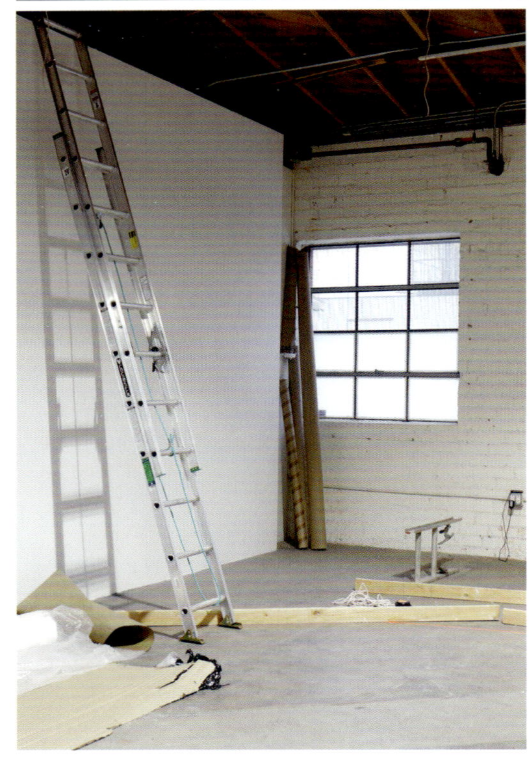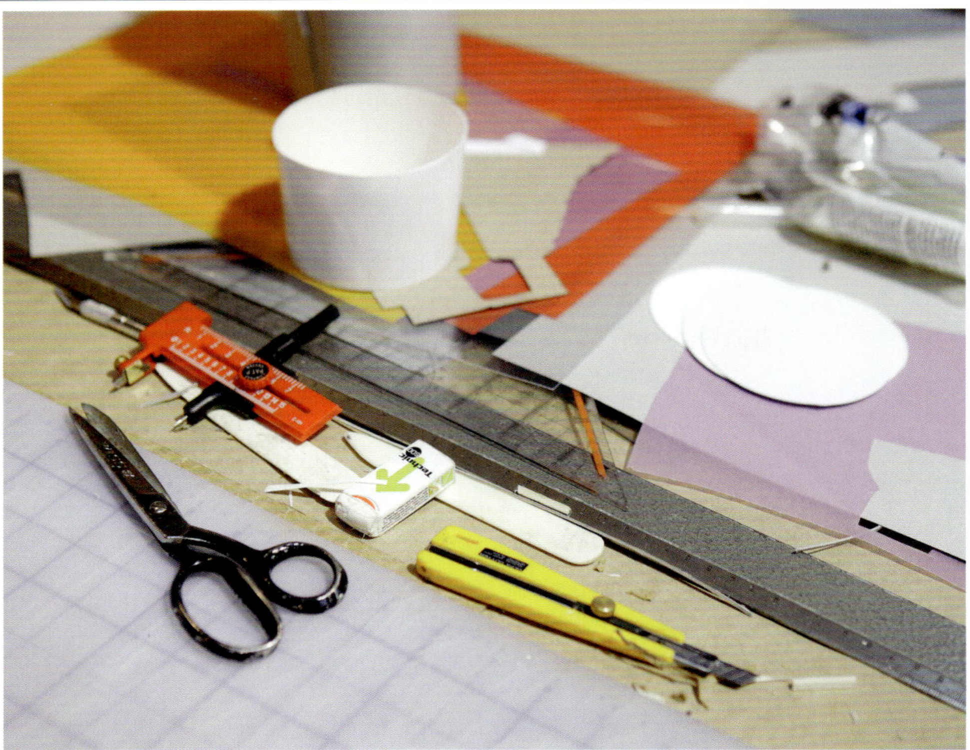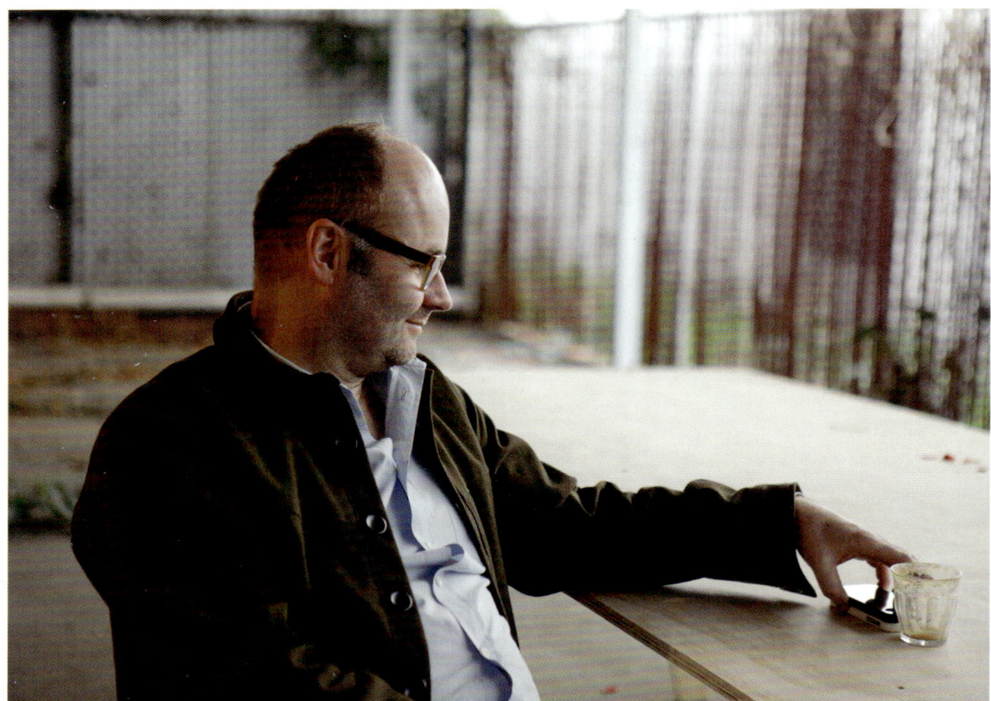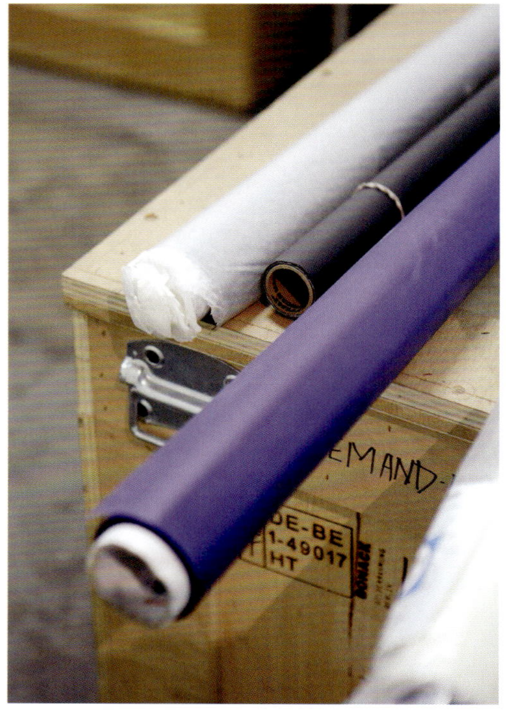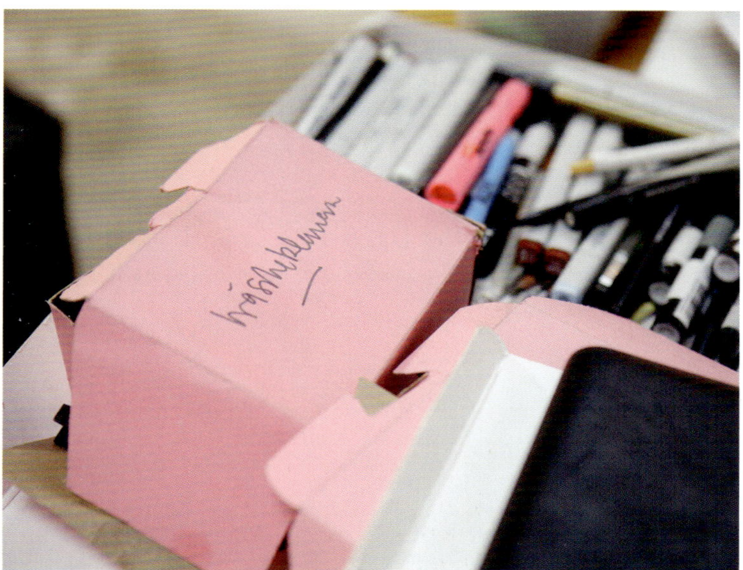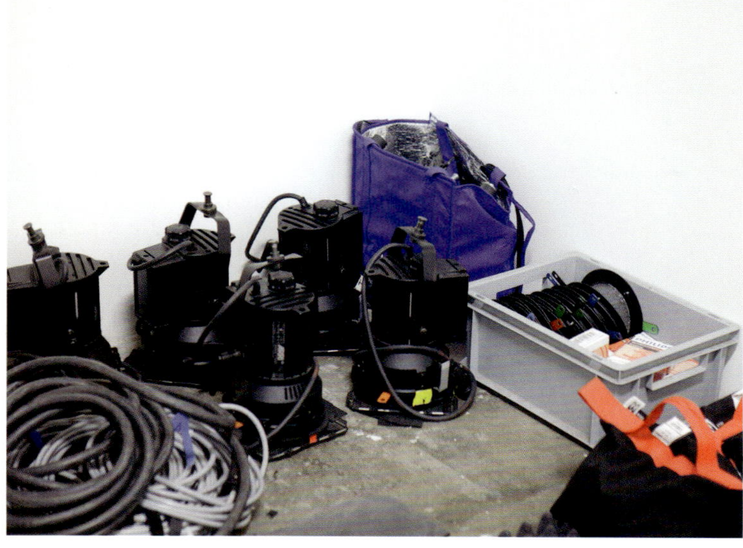

Studio Visit
Photographers at Work

With Thomas Demand in Los Angeles
Jonathan Griffin

Early last December, Thomas Demand's studio of twelve years, next to the Hamburger Bahnhof in Berlin, was bulldozed. Demand had known that sooner or later this day would come—the building's prime location made it vulnerable to developers—but it marked the end of an era for the German artist. He had lived in the city since 1995, around the time that he first became known for his photographs of life-size card-and-paper models of vacant interiors re-created from found photographs, often associated with poignant human narratives.

Demand first began spending time in Los Angeles in 2010 as a scholar at the Getty Research Institute. After three and a half years in planes over the Atlantic, he has resolved to settle, at least for the time being, in California. He had long nurtured an ambition to live in Los Angeles, and in 2012 his gallery, Matthew Marks, opened a space there. When we met at his Culver City studio a week after the demolition, Demand admitted that his relationship with the city is still in its honeymoon phase: "I come here, I see the sun, I'm happy: I have an empty space, I'm still the master of my own schedule. I'm enjoying this freedom quite a lot." Following a hectic 2013, Demand had almost entirely cleared his calendar of commitments for the coming year.

The space in which we were sitting was, indeed, quite empty. I had expected a bustling operation involving a platoon of assistants, card-and-paper models mid-construction, administrative staff, and storage areas for prints and materials. Demand had warned me that there was "not much to see"; I should have taken him at his word. He had moved into the building only two months before. "I'm like a hermit crab. I basically have a pop-up studio," he explained. A couple of robust plastic trunks carry almost everything he needs: cutting tools, adhesives, and some power cables. Two plywood chests contain his archive of colored papers, and another crate contains his photographic equipment. Everything else he orders specifically for each project. My expectations were calibrated, perhaps, by a lecture I'd heard Demand give about the complexity of his recent project *Pacific Sun* (2012), a one-hundred-second animated film that reenacted the cataclysmic effect of two gigantic waves on a cruise ship restaurant, as captured by a security video. Fifteen months in the making and requiring dozens of specialist assistants, it was his most logistically ambitious work since *Grotto* (2006), a photograph of a fifty-two-metric-ton life-size cardboard model of a cave. *Pacific Sun* was made in Los Angeles—in a previous studio, bigger than Demand's current premises but lacking air conditioning. The fluctuating humidity (along with occasional seismic tremors) caused Demand's card-and-paper models to move, incrementally, overnight, which is disastrous for the stop-motion process. While making *Pacific Sun*, Demand realized that it might not always be the most efficient use of his time to be present in the studio while assistants painstakingly adjusted models and equipment.

His series *Model Studies* (2011), in which he photographed the maquettes of unrealized structures by architect John Lautner, was made during this time in the archives of the Getty Research Institute. It was the first time that Demand had taken photographs of models not made by him, and it permitted a quicker and more liberated mode of making images. These changes of pace, he says, are crucial. "The good thing about paper is that it is actually really fast," he told me. Since the acquisition of a digital paper cutter during the making of *Grotto*, not everything in Demand's photographs is necessarily a feat of astonishing handcraft. In *Control Room* (2011), which shows the Fukushima Daiichi power plant after the Tohoku earthquake, gridded panels dangle from the ceiling. "If you made them by hand," Demand said, "the picture would be about those things taking forever to make. That's not what it is about. They need the appearance of industrially made objects. This is a corporate headquarters. I needed that kind of coldness of material, and that's why I used a mechanical process."

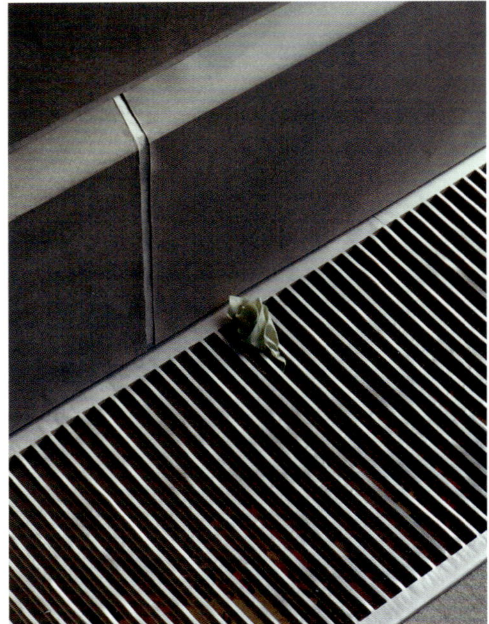

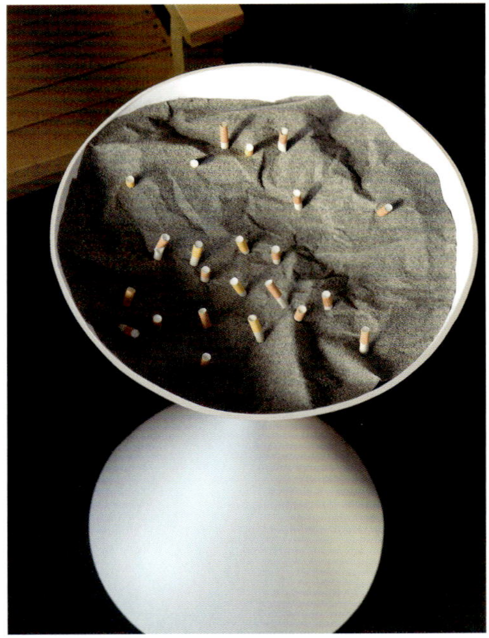

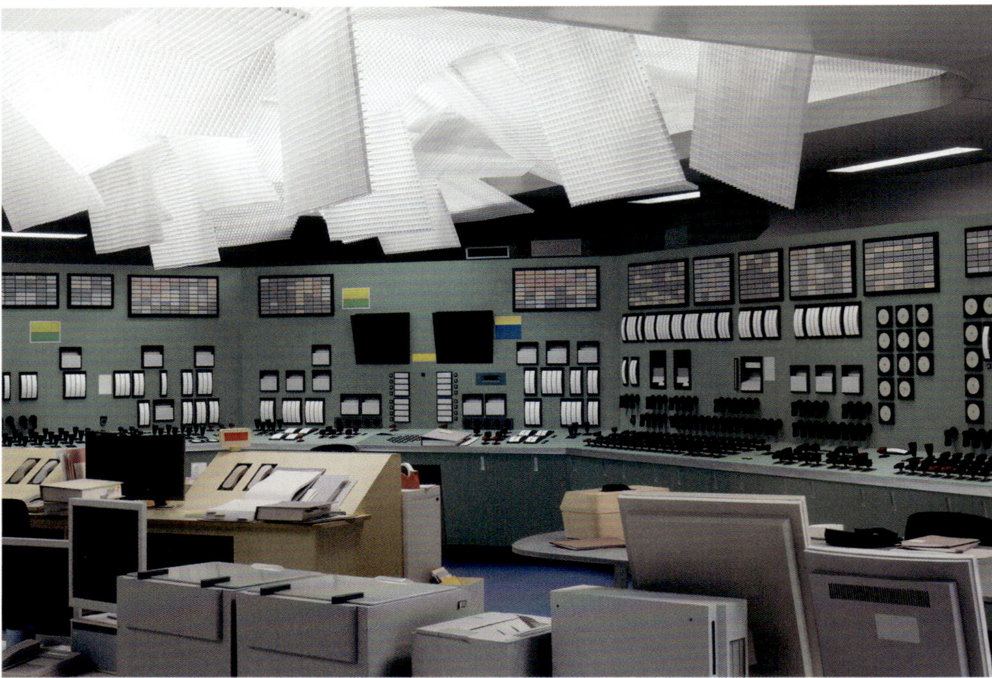

He was thinking a great deal about time when he decided to print his series *Dailies* (2008–ongoing) using the dye transfer process. In 1992, Kodak ceased production of the paper and chemicals necessary for this technique; only a few people in the world still have the stockpiles of materials necessary to create these superbly rich archival prints. Each print, Demand said, takes days. The time invested, and the resultant longevity of the prints, contrasts with the casualness of the original images: snapshots taken by the artist on his iPhone.

The fleeting nature of the photographic moment is a central preoccupation in Demand's work. Pinned to his studio wall is a photograph torn from a newspaper of a woman standing between two buildings; behind her, over a wall, is a magnificent cherry blossom tree in full bloom. When I next visited Demand, a month later, two tables were laid out with stalks, painted stamens, and pale pink petals in bags, cut by the digital plotter in Berlin. Three assistants sat at a table and assembled the flowers, curling petals and binding them to stalks with strips of crepe. At this stage, Demand did not know how much of the photograph he would re-create or how long the work would take. He had been commissioned to produce wallpaper featuring a detail of the blossoms for the café of the Neue Nationalgalerie, Berlin; he planned to coincide his project with the cherry blossom festival in Tokyo, which usually takes place in April. As always, time was of the essence.

Top left: *Daily #7*, 2008;
top right: *Daily #2*, 2008;
bottom: *Kontrollraum /
Control Room*, 2011
All photographs by
Thomas Demand
© Thomas Demand/Artists
Rights Society (ARS),
New York and courtesy
Matthew Marks Gallery,
New York

Demand contrasts the grids with an earlier work, *Lawn* (1998), in which every blade in a patch of grass was cut and bent by hand. "People ask me, 'What happened on that lawn?' Well, the picture is about not having anything happening; it's about the complexity of the banal, the everyday. How much is on that lawn is just unbelievable." In that instance, it was vital that Demand made the work entirely himself. But even when working with mechanized processes or groups of assistants, he retains control over every part of the picture. "While I'm doing it I'm thinking about it. And I don't want to get rid of that thinking process by industrializing my approach. I think the world can only take so many Thomas Demands anyway. I'd rather be the master of my own work than master of my own career."

Jonathan Griffin is a
writer living in Los Angeles
and a contributing editor
for *Frieze*.

Words

Hans Günter Flieg,
*Centro de São Paulo,
visto do terraço do edifício
Altino Arantes* (Center
of São Paulo, seen from
the terrace of the Altino
Arantes building), 1950
Courtesy Instituto Moreira
Salles

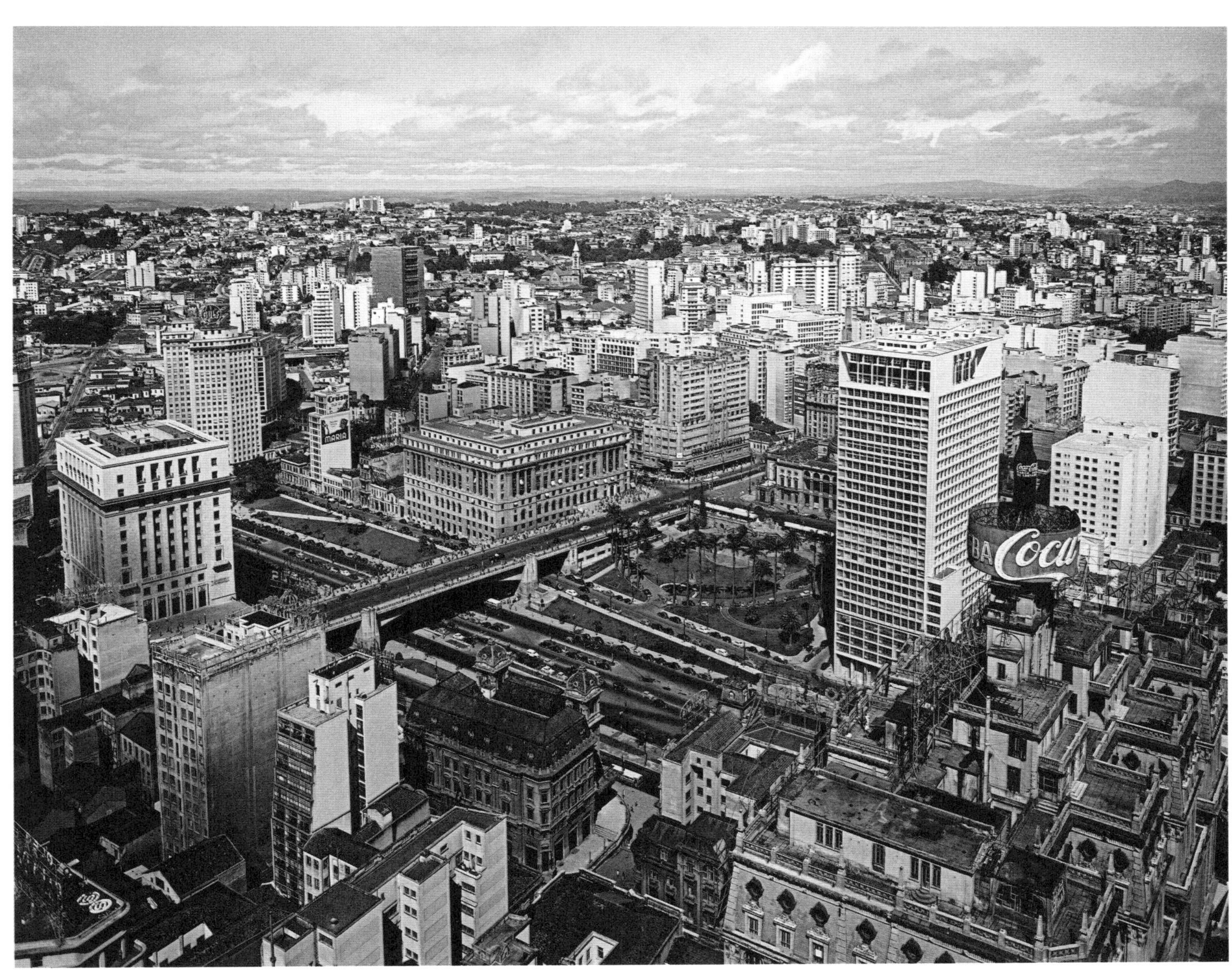

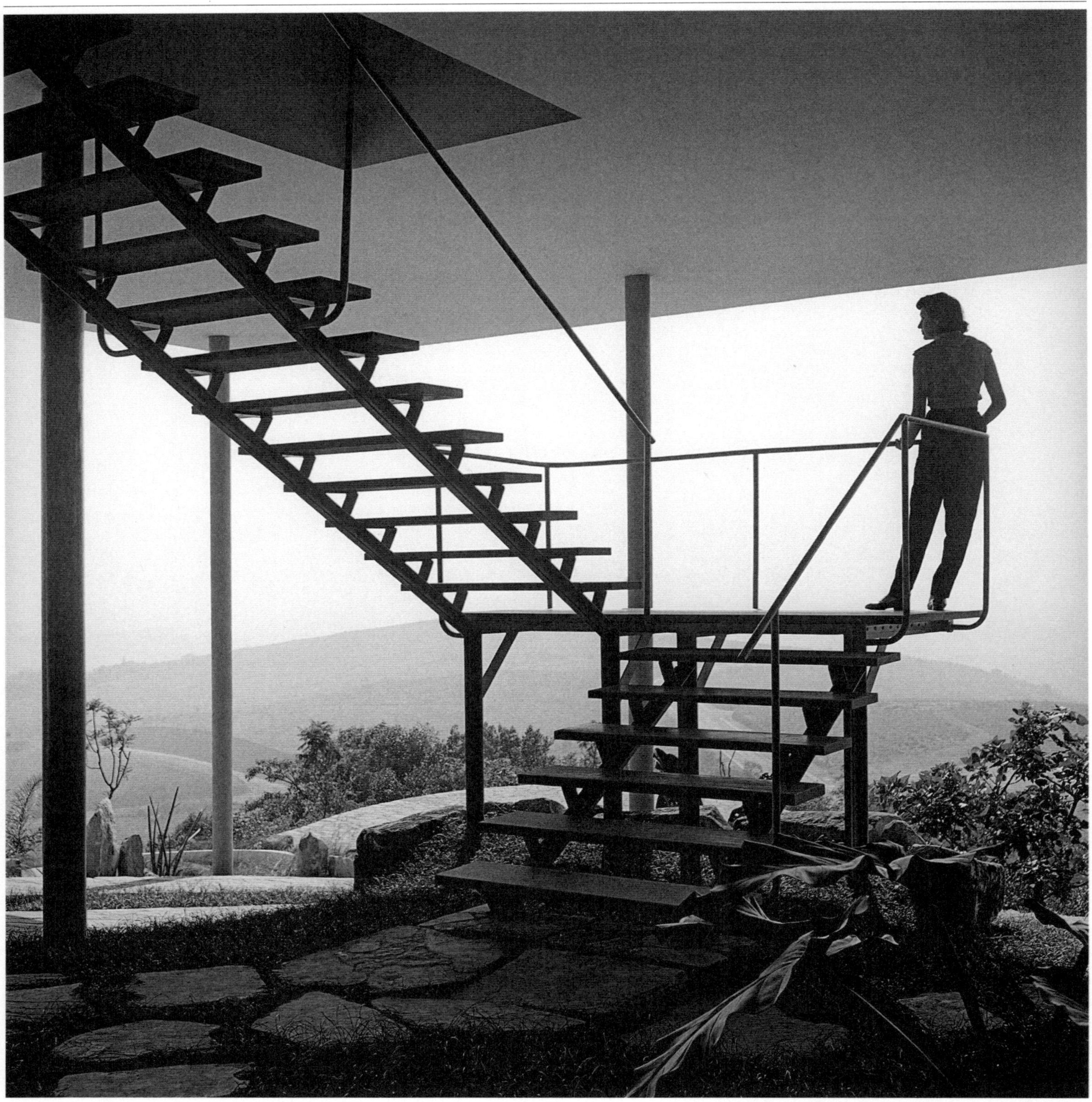

Chico Albuquerque,
Lina Bo Bardi na Casa
de Vidro **(Lina Bo Bardi**
in the Glass House),
São Paulo, 1952
Courtesy Museu da Imagem
e do Som, São Paulo/
Instituto Moreira Salles

From the pictorial magazines that shaped a legacy of photojournalism to the avant-garde postwar photo clubs that transformed the medium, the layered narratives of photography in São Paulo reflect the city's cosmopolitan spirit.

An Itinerant Photography
Sérgio Burgi

It is difficult to conceive of photography in São Paulo without Militão Augusto de Azevedo. Militão moved to São Paulo in 1862 after attempting a career as a theater actor in Rio de Janeiro, and produced the first comprehensive photographic documentary of the city. His *Álbum comparativo da cidade de São Paulo 1862/1887* (Comparative album of the city of São Paulo 1862/1887) comprises images taken from the same viewpoints over twenty-five years. Of his ambitious project, Militão remarked: "It seemed to me a very significant work, and perhaps the first one to be executed in photography, possibly because very few at that time would have preserved negatives for twenty-five years." Militão seems to have been presciently aware of photography's ability to create a lasting record of the exponential expansion of the city. Over the next century and a half, São Paulo would grow from approximately twenty-five thousand inhabitants in 1862 to close to fifty thousand by 1887, before surging to today's twenty million.

The growth of photography in São Paulo throughout the twentieth century parallels the urban growth witnessed by Militão—it's a story shaped by the movement of people from abroad and across Brazil, arriving with ideas and creative energy. As Europe slid into crisis in the 1930s, intellectuals and artists emigrated to Brazil from across Western and Eastern Europe and Turkey, establishing themselves in industry, communications, and visual arts, and in turn reshaping those fields. With the rise of mass media, visual communication was transformed radically between the mid-1940s and '50s, and fine arts, photography included, intersected with this new media environment. In the early 1940s, *O Cruzeiro* (1928–1975) was reconceived to become the first magazine in Brazil dedicated to photo-reportage, taking inspiration from French and German pictorial magazines, such as *Vu* (1928–1940), *Voilà* (1931–1950), and *Illustrierte Zeitung* (1892–1945). *O Cruzeiro* covered myriad topics, from politics and culture to sports. José Medeiros, for example, documented indigenous tribes recently contacted by outsiders for the first time, including the Xavante and Caiapó peoples, who lived in unsettled areas near where the modernist capital Brasília would rise a decade later. Peter Scheier, a Jewish photographer who fled Germany in 1937, became a regular contributor to *O Cruzeiro* in the late 1940s, publishing on a variety of subjects— São Paulo's new art museums, the working-class neighborhood of Brás, a small business run by poor Jewish residents, and the leisure activity around the city's reservoirs. Throughout the postwar years, the magazine adopted a humanistic and engaged visual journalism. Enrico Bianco, the magazine's art director in the mid-1950s, summed up his mission: "My intention from the very beginning was to intensify the transformation of *O Cruzeiro* from a variety-oriented magazine with strong commercial interests and… subjects with no journalistic content, into a magazine committed to objective information and relevant subjects.…" Indeed, Bianco's bold graphic style helped achieve this goal; he created a dynamic visual texture, giving photographs cinematic punch on the printed page, earning the publication a loyal audience: By 1954, more than half a million copies were published weekly and distributed nationally.

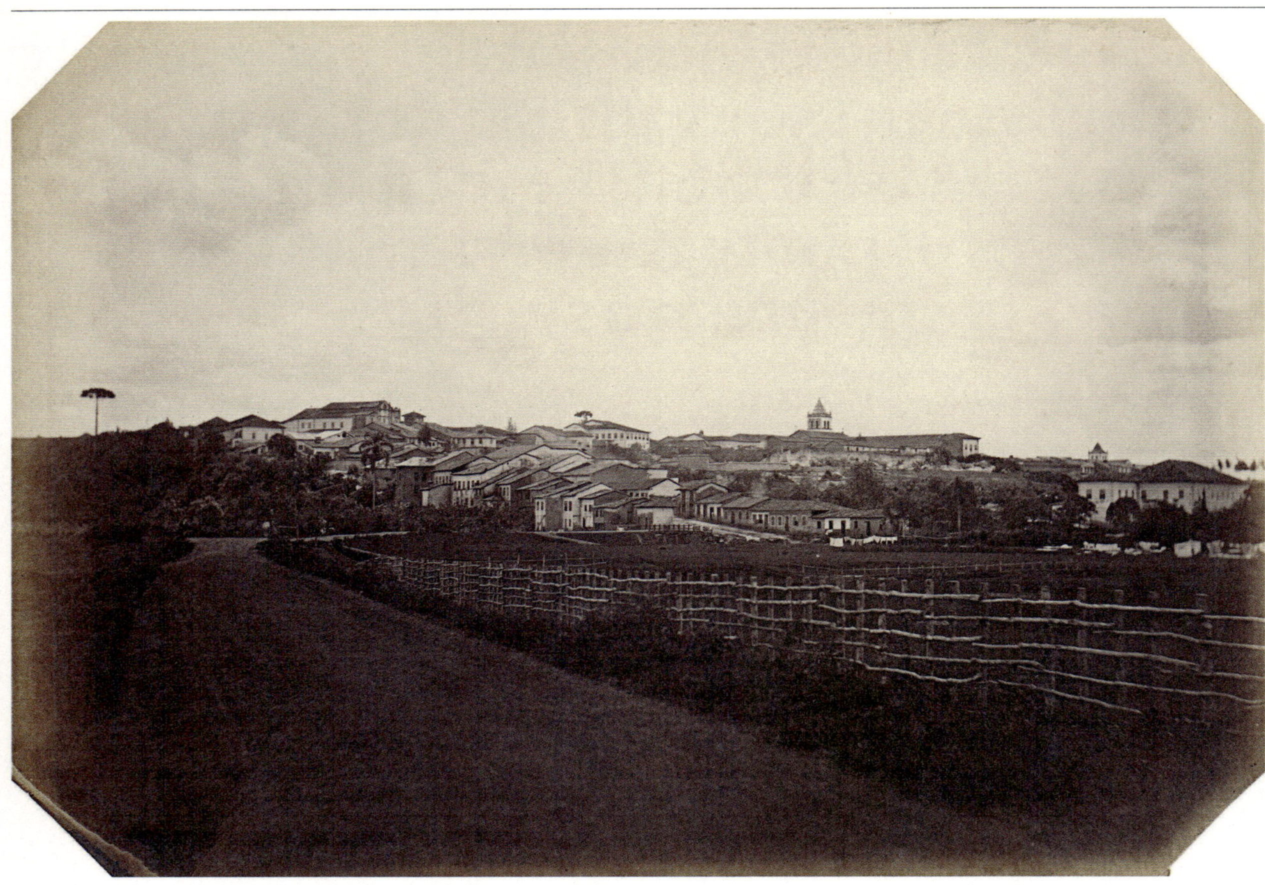

Photography in São Paulo throughout the twentieth century is a story shaped by the movement of people from abroad and across Brazil.

As photography's capacity for storytelling captured readers' imaginations through magazines, art circles, in parallel, advocated a radically different, less descriptive approach to the medium. The Foto Cine Clube Bandeirantes (Bandeirantes Photography and Film Club, or FCCB), an association of photography aficionados and professionals, created a space for debate about the aesthetic renewal of photography. Now-seminal figures like Thomaz Farkas, Geraldo de Barros, German Lorca, and Chico Albuquerque joined the FCCB during the 1940s. The society published an influential bulletin (first appearing in 1946), and their São Paulo International Photography Salons, held annually at Galeria Prestes Maia, a space devoted to the arts in downtown São Paulo, proved popular with the public.

Breaking away from pictorialism, the dominant style of photography societies of the day, the FCCB would form the foundation of modern photography in Brazil, reflecting the country's dramatic transformation after World War II. Like comparable movements in Europe, such as Fotoform in the 1950s, or those of the interwar period, including Neues Sehen (New Vision) and Neue Sachlichkeit (New Objectivity), the FCCB advanced a radical style defined by abstraction, formalism, and inventive composition articulated with light and shadow, as in Farkas's disorienting image of movie theater lights reduced to an elegant geometric abstraction, or in de Barros's *Fotoformas* (see portfolio on page 66). "[The photographs] cause a sense of strangeness that induces critical thinking," Farkas wrote in 1948. "[The observer] becomes more knowledgeable, opens new paths for himself, starts to see more …" The art going public would indeed have the chance to test Farkas's claims: Between 1949 and 1952, Farkas, de Barros, Lorca, and Albuquerque would each be the subject of one-person shows at the city's newly minted museums that had the foresight to immediately include photography in their programming—the São Paulo Art Museum (MASP) and the São Paulo Museum of Modern Art (MAM). Italian-born architect Lina Bo Bardi, whom Albuquerque photographed in silhouette on the steps of her Glass House, designed both museums and later oversaw their installation design.

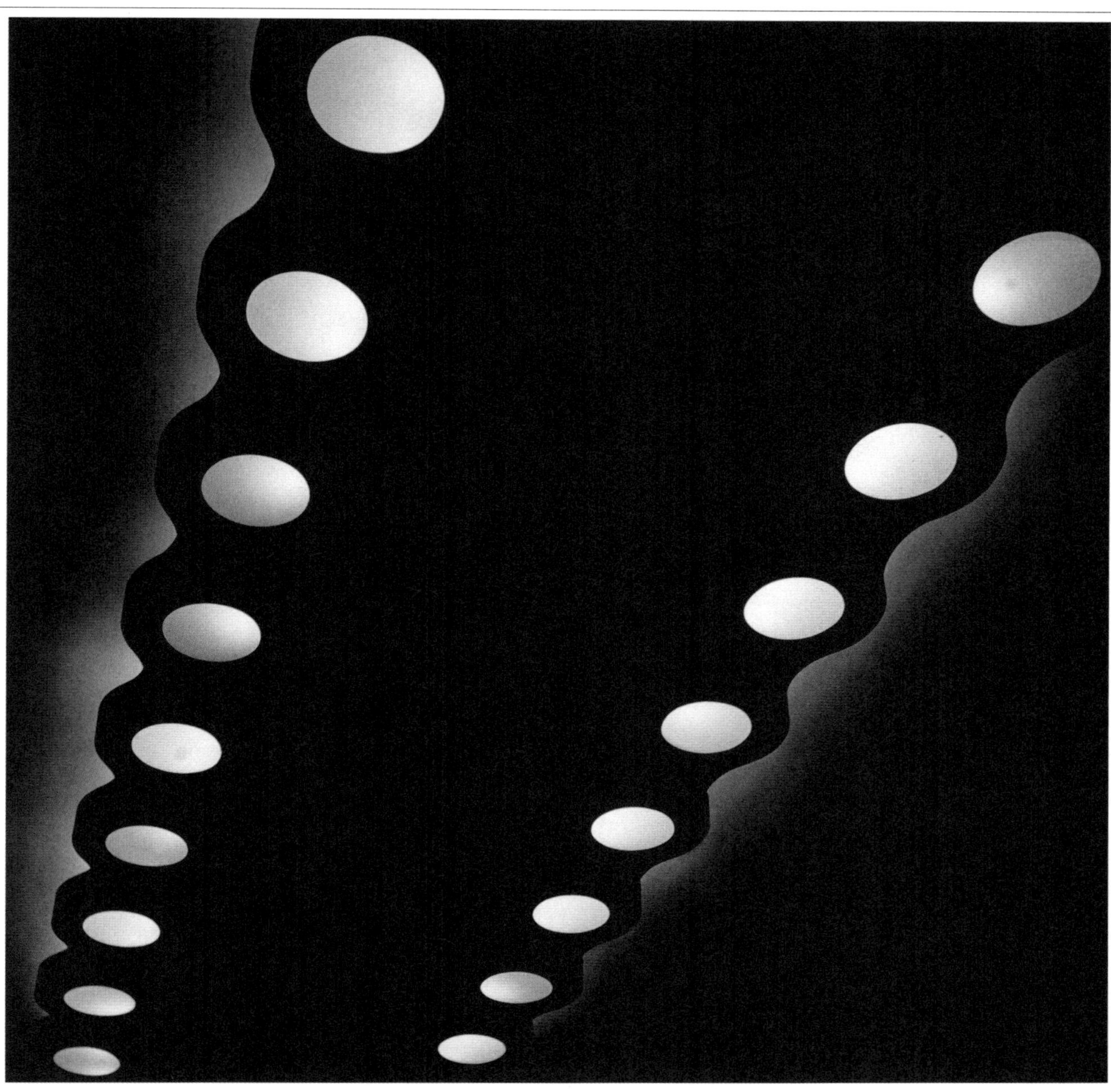

The culminating moment, though, for this group of avant-gardists would be their inclusion in the 1953 São Paulo International Art Biennial (the second edition), which involved a stroke of luck but was in actuality the culmination of a long process of shifting cultural conditions that allowed for a rethinking of the medium. The Biennial quickly established itself as the first large-scale modern art exhibition outside Europe and the United States. The first edition in 1951 included artists Max Bill and Ivan Serpa; Picasso's *Guernica* was exhibited at the second. Naturally, the FCCB wanted to be included in this context, and the opportunity arrived when two Mexican mural painters— José Clemente Orozco and David Alfaro Siqueiros—along with the Haitian team of artists, withdrew at the last minute, leaving a gap in the exhibition program, an inconvenient snag for MAM's director, Wolfgang Pfeiffer. De Barros later described the circumstances leading to the FCCB's inclusion in their bulletin: "Several problems arose with the news about Siqueiros's and Orozco's inability to take part in the Biennial and with Haiti's withdrawal. (…) It was during one of these conversations, when attempting to find a solution, that suddenly Aldemir [Aldemir Martins, a Brazilian painter] and I said almost at the exact same time: PHOTOGRAPHS, Dr. Pfeiffer! In fact, during a conversation [we] had already discussed the need to expand photography and had dreamed of exhibiting photography at the Biennial…." This dream became more than a reality: the FCCB's inclusion in the show would cement photography's position in the art world.

Meanwhile, the quickly professionalizing advertising industry—expanding in part due to advances in offset printing— was well aware of the talents of the city's most inventive photographers. Chico Albuquerque established a solid relationship with major advertising agencies such as McCann and Standard, shooting campaigns for clients from the automobile, food, and architectural industries. Mercedes-Benz, among other companies, hired Hans Günter Flieg to document the construction and design of their products. Flieg produced an in-depth study of São Paulo's industrialization, through crisp black-and-white images of machinery, production lines, and products, and sharp views of the bustling city itself. Albuquerque, who once referred to his time with the FCCB as "my diploma in photography," would go on to direct the Estúdio Abril (Abril Studio), which in turn served as an unofficial photography school, instructing a new generation of commercial photographers, including now-renowned fashion photographer Bob Wolfenson.

Editora Abril (the studio's publishing arm) launched *Realidade* in 1966, a magazine devoted to portraying Brazil through literary journalism and photography, giving writers and documentarians freedom, time, and resources to produce stories aimed to inform the public and, within the acceptable limits, question the broader policies of the military regime that assumed power in 1964 (and remained until 1985). *Realidade* lasted for a decade and in that time brought together a mix of foreign and Brazilian photographers: Lew Parrella, David Drew Zingg, and George Love (all Americans);

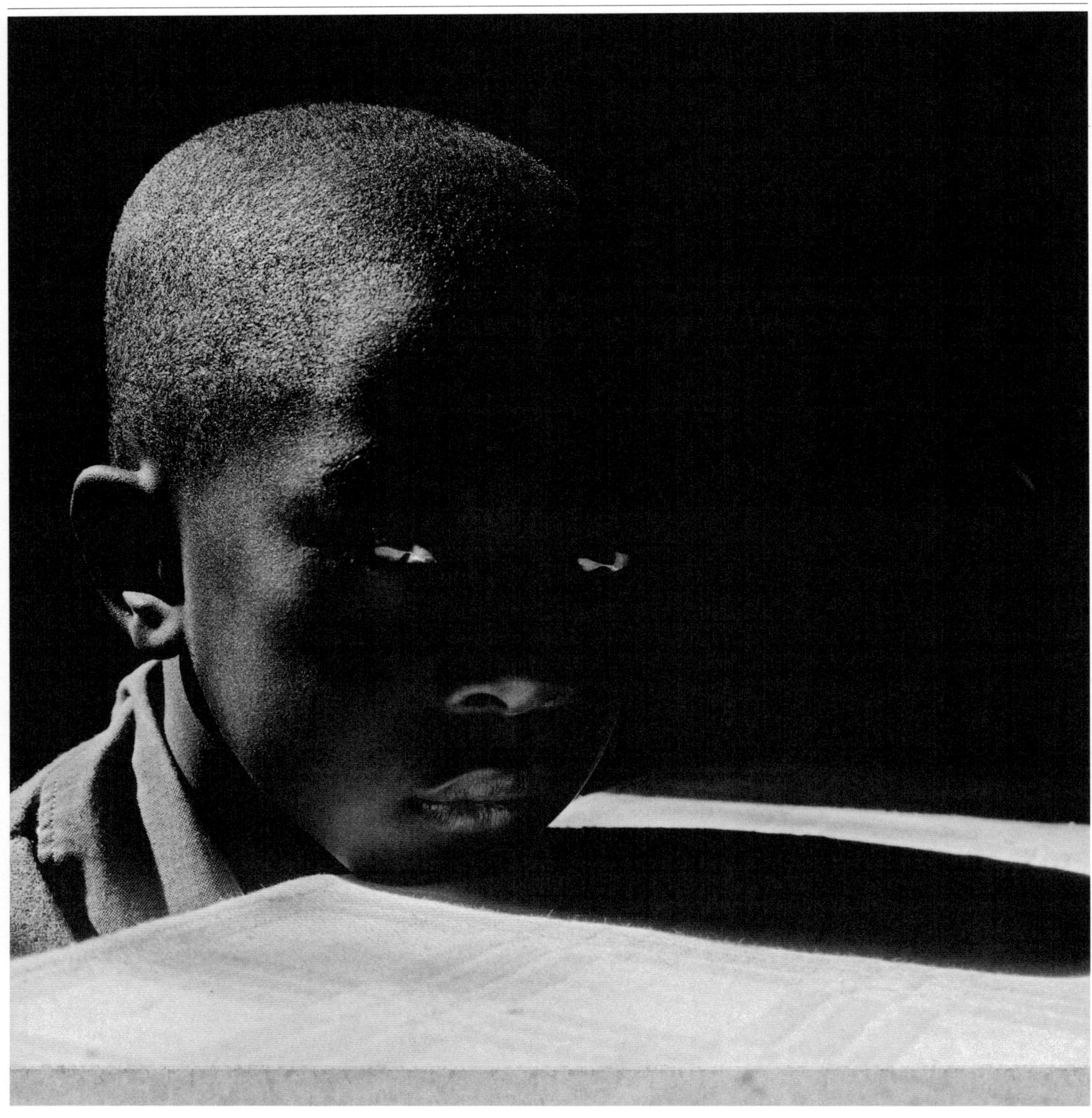

Claudia Andujar (Hungarian/Swiss-born); Luigi Mamprin (Italian); Maureen Bisilliat and Roger Bester (both English); Jean Solari (French); and Walter Firmo (Brazilian). From 1969 onward, censorship increased and civil rights were eliminated by a military regime tightening control through the draconian AI-5 (Institutional Act 5). Photographers used ambiguity and irony to work around censorship. One example is Bisilliat's 1970s piece on crabbers on the coast of the northeastern state of Paraíba, struggling to survive in the middle of what the military regime called an economic miracle. Bisilliat's subjects, mostly women, are portrayed smiling, seemingly joyful; the pictures obliquely point to exploitation and inequality, without an overtly ideological critique of the economic system. Other prominent stories in the magazine included Andujar and Love's regular coverage of the Amazon and the fraught politics surrounding the region's indigenous peoples (see interview with Andujar on page 116).

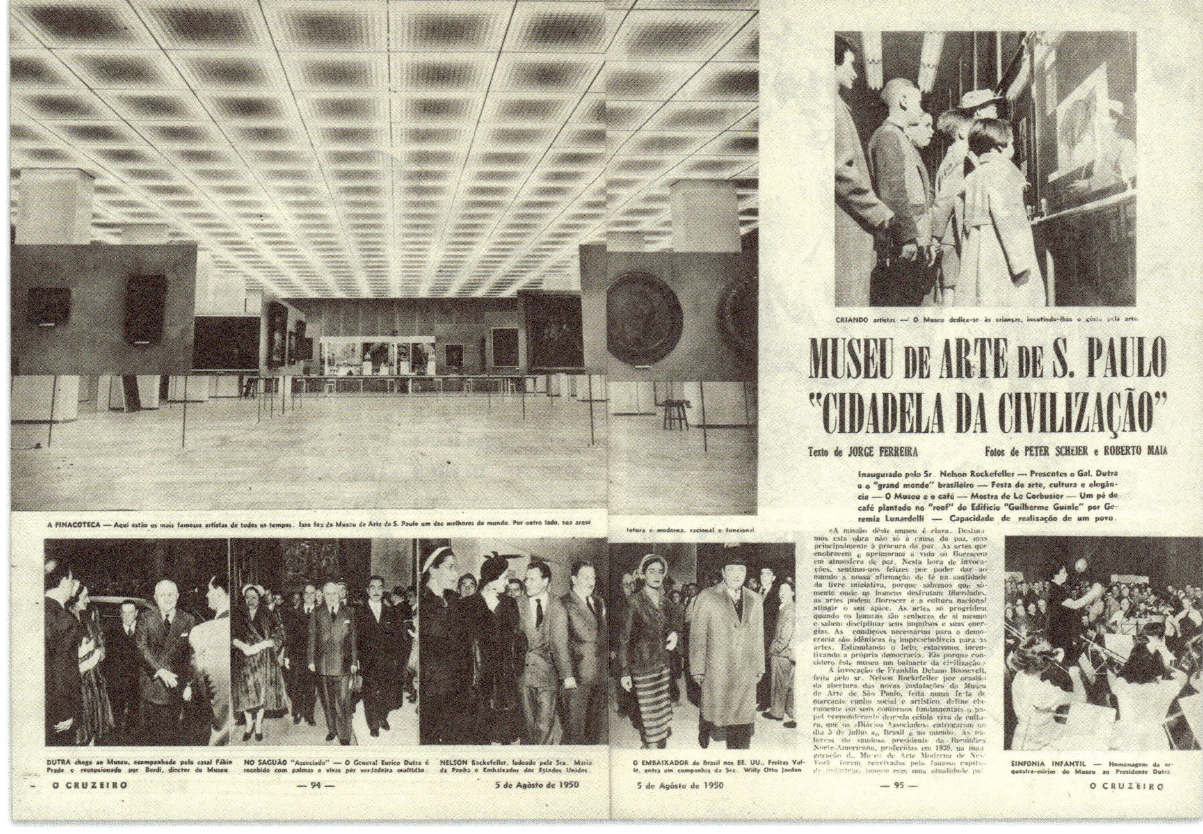

Spread from *O Cruzeiro* (August 5, 1950), featuring "Museu de Arte de S.Paulo — Cidadela da civilização" (São Paulo Museum of Art — Citadel of civilization), with photographs by Peter Scheier and Roberto Maia
Courtesy Instituto Moreira Salles

Andujar and Love would also contribute to a new wave of formalized photography education when they created classes at MASP. Elsewhere, photographer and writer Cláudio Kubrusly founded a school of photography called ENFOCO (1968–1976), and the influential Czech-born philosopher Vilém Flusser, seeking a new beginning after most of his family was killed in Nazi-occupied Europe, began teaching at the Polytechnic School of the University of São Paulo and at the School of Film and the School of Dramatic Arts. Now famous for his canonical 1983 book *Towards a Philosophy of Photography*, Flusser established himself as an active participant in the artistic life of the city, regularly contributing to the literary supplement for the São Paulo newspaper *O Estado*, on topics of language and reality. Throughout the 1970s and '80s, the University of São Paulo fostered critical thinking about the medium and established new programs, where Cristiano Mascaro, João Luiz Musa, and Raul Garcez taught. Still, it took some time for academia to officially catch up with the dialogue initiated by avant-garde clubs and magazines: Brazil's first bachelor's degree program in photography was not established until 1999.

Although the growth of photography paralleled the growth of São Paulo, their rapid transformations didn't always occur in perfect tandem. As the populace expanded and diversified, photography evolved by necessity as an itinerant visual language. The dramatic urban changes observed by Militão in his day were already so significant that he recognized the importance of capturing them in a body of work at the end of his career. "Like Verdi," he wrote, "who created his *Otello* as his farewell to the world of Music, so did I with my [*Comparative Album*]." The nature of Militão's finale meant that the project could never be "finished"; it exists as an enduring reminder of the pace of change that the city was then only beginning to experience. São Paulo continues to be a story of images and individuals, local and international, in permanent motion and exchange; the result is the vibrant artistic activity taking place today that is truly transnational, much like the spirit of the city.

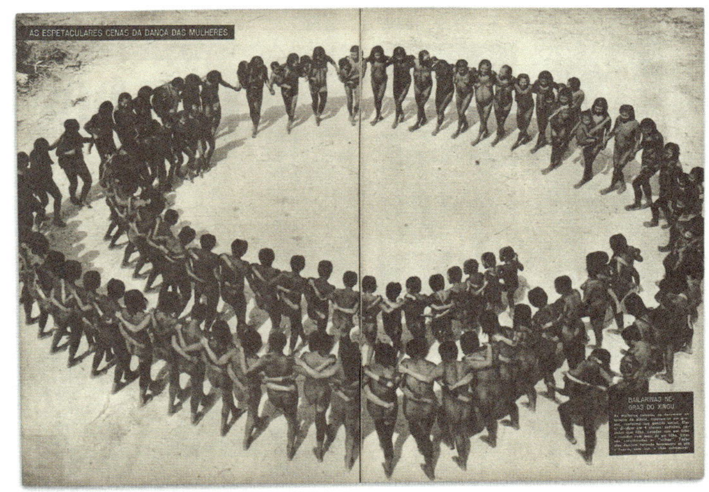

Spread from *O Cruzeiro* (June 7, 1952), featuring "Homens brancos na aldeia dos Caiapós" (White men in the village of the Caiapó), with a photograph by José Medeiros
Courtesy Instituto Moreira Salles

Sérgio Burgi is the photography coordinator at the Instituto Moreira Salles, Rio de Janeiro.

In the 1830s, an adventurer and inventor named Hercule Florence sought to score the Amazon's abundant birdsong. When attempting to print his peculiar manuscript about nature's sound archive, he also invented an early form of photography.

Light Writing in the Tropics
Natalia Brizuela

In a letter dated June 1839, William Henry Fox Talbot wrote to a botanist living in Italy that his "photogenic" drawings, as he named his first proto-photographs made with the aid of a solar microscope, would be "a big help to botanists." In a later letter Talbot insisted that his invention would be "useful especially to the naturalists, since one can copy the most difficult things with much ease, for example crystallizations, tiny parts of plants, etc. etc." Little did Talbot, largely credited as one of photography's inventors, know that six years earlier a twenty-nine-year-old man in Brazil, far removed from the conversations happening in Europe about how to fix light and shadow (including French scientist and politician François Arago's presentation of the daguerreotype at the Academy of Sciences in Paris in 1839, and British scientist Sir John Herschel's supposed coining of the word *photography* the same year with his now-famous phrase "picture obtained by photography" at the Royal Society in London), had invented his own form of "photogenic" writing aimed to aid naturalists.

In 1833, Hercule Florence, a Frenchman who settled on the outskirts of São Paulo after surviving a four-year stint as a draftsman for a Russian Naturalist expedition up the Amazon River basin in the 1820s, invented a mode of reproduction that he called *photographie* (light writing)—the same words Fox Talbot used years later to describe his invention. Florence arrived at his form of light writing somewhat accidentally. In contrast to the narrative typically used to describe photography's invention in Europe, it was not the joint achievement of nineteenth-century chemists and artists experimenting with light and silver compounds, nor that of Romantic poets desiring to apprehend that unruly living organism called nature. Instead it was the end result of a long search for a mode of printing. Specifically, Florence wanted to print and distribute a transcription method he had developed to organize and systematize the sounds of nature found in the Amazon region.

Portrait of Hercule Florence, ca. 1875
Courtesy Instituto Hercule Florence (Arnaldo Machado Archive), São Paulo

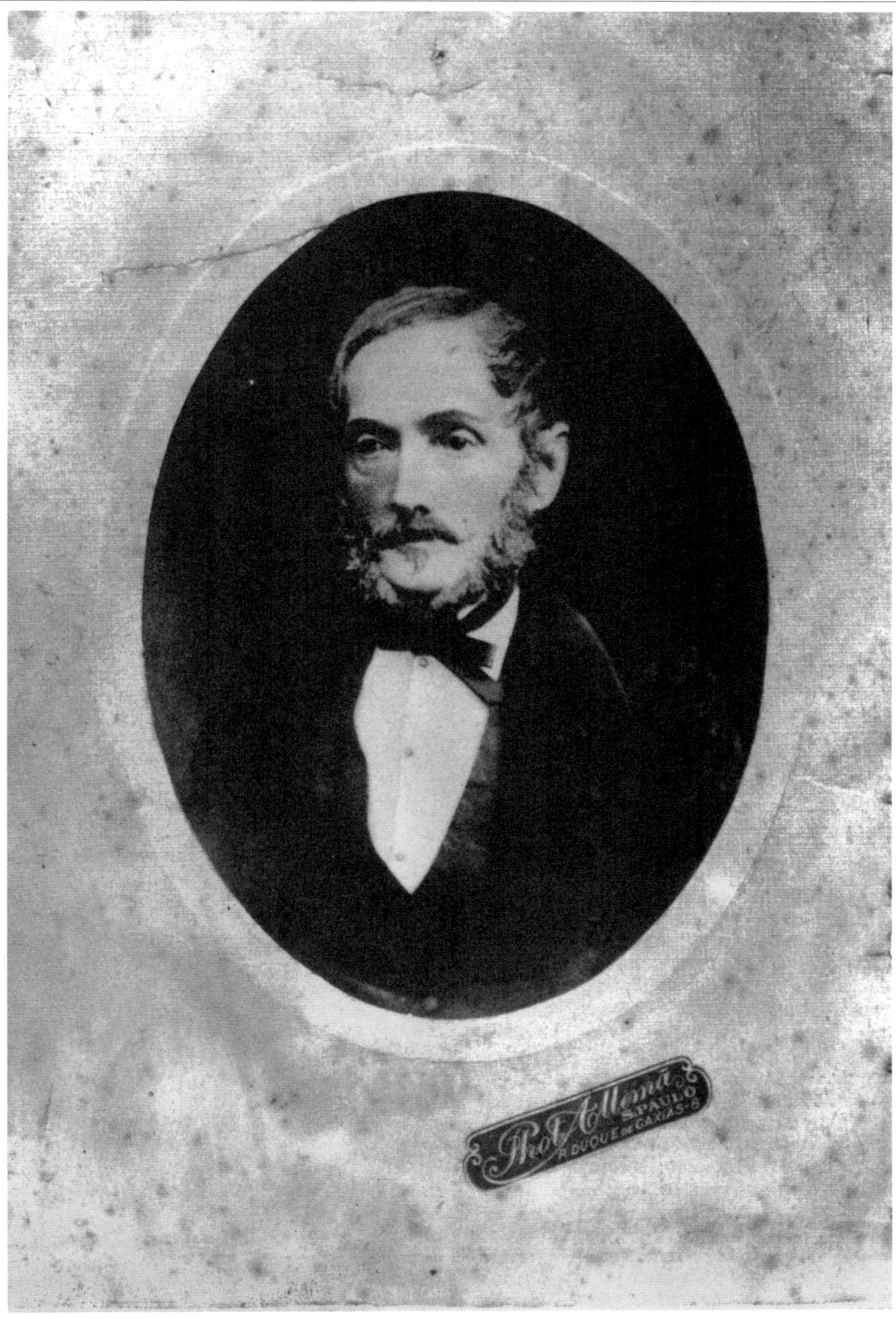

Florence was twenty when he arrived in the newly proclaimed Brazilian Empire in the early 1820s, living first in Rio de Janeiro, where he worked at a bookstore and printing press, before settling down some years later in the small village of São Carlos (Campinas), outside of São Paulo, for the remainder of his life. He hadn't been living in his adopted country for long before he responded to an advertisement for an expedition led by Georg Heinrich von Langsdorff and was hired to be the group's second draftsman (along with the well-known German painter Johann Moritz Rugendas and a younger artist named Aimé Adrien Taunay, although Rugendas would be dismissed before the journey began, after falling out with Langsdorff). The expedition's aim was to reach Pará, in the Amazon basin, through a fluvial route, while engaging in botanical, astronomical, and cartographic observations typical of such ventures. Close reading of Florence's sporadic diary entries from these years reveals that despite his penchant for travel and adventure—a trait that brought him to Brazil—he found the expedition tiresome, describing the journey as a "grueling, anguished, and unfortunate peregrination" and noting time and again that "to see one Brazilian village is to see almost all of them." These observations are not surprising for a man who often commented on the lack of culture and excess of nature in his adopted homeland. The watercolor views and landscapes that Florence produced as a hired painter bored him. What was the purpose, he asked in his diary, of visually reproducing the natural world, of composing collections that could only imitate existing collections and inventories gathered and archived throughout Europe? Was there nothing uncharted and original left to continue expanding the inventory of the world? Had nature been turned, in this way, into nothing more than a dead still life—obvious and trivial, predictable, lifeless?

Craving a recording of the natural world that offered infinite uniqueness, singularity, and power, Florence fixated on the idea that while the naturalist expeditions of the first decades of the nineteenth century had created encyclopedic and cartographic knowledge, they never contemplated the possibility of a sonic

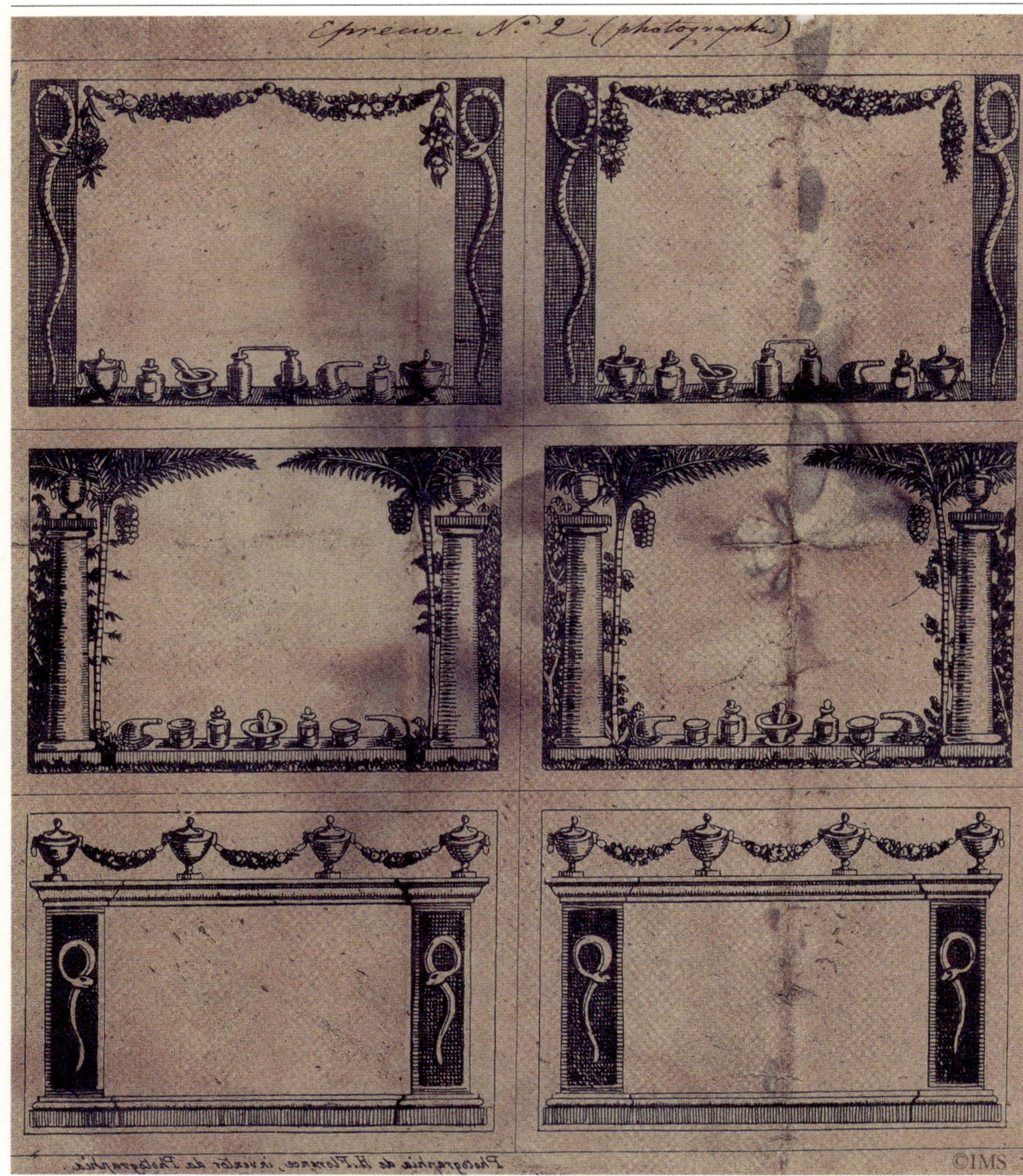

Hercule Florence, Photographic copy of pharmacy labels obtained through direct contact with photosensitive paper under the action of sunlight, ca. 1833. The lower left margin reads (in reverse): "Photography by H. Florence, inventor of Photography."
© Instituto Moreira Salles

These observations are not surprising for a man who often commented on the lack of culture and excess of nature in his adopted homeland.

inventory. "With great zeal we have tried to, and continue to try to, learn everything that is known about animals," Florence wrote. "Even the most minimal details have not been ignored; for this reason expensive and arduous voyages have been made to almost every point on the globe; collections of animals were thus made at an enormous cost to the museums of the great cities; the descriptions and drawings allow them to become known throughout the world." Ironically, Florence would have more opportunities to indulge his theories about sound as the expedition ran into grave problems, derailing hopes of becoming the most scientifically important journey of its kind in the region: Taunay would drown crossing a river; the group's astronomer came down with beriberi, a tropical disease that afflicted many slaves in colonial Brazil; Langsdorff, as well as half of the team, was stricken with malaria and suffered high, debilitating fevers, resulting in his complete insanity and loss of memory. Amid this chaos, Florence sidelined his official work and turned his attentions to the universe of sounds enveloping him. He began a series of notations recording the calls of birds, the croaks of frogs, and noises made by other animals. Of a bird called *araponga*, Florence writes that "it is beautiful…it makes a sound that imitates well the banging of a hammer on an anvil," and of the singing of the *anhu-póca*: "it is big, its voice strong and euphonious; repeats this sound every fourth of a minute." Florence approximated the corresponding notations to the

sounds he heard and then produced musical scores, a method
he dubbed *zoophonie*. The outsized ambition of his desire
to catalogue all the jungle's birdsong was not lost on Florence:
"when one considers how much animals' voices vary to infinity,
one tends to think that it is almost impossible to transcribe them
without using an infinite number of signs … the method that
I am here giving is only a first attempt …."

In 1831, after returning home from his journeys, Florence
attempted to print and circulate his notes and manuscript
outlining his *zoophonie*. The cumbersomely titled text, *Research
on the Voice of Animals or Essay on a New Subject of Study Offered
to the Friends of Nature*, detailed his discovery of nature's
potential sound archive and proposed his novel method of
capturing and recording the immaterial, enchanted animal sounds
of the Brazilian tropical forests. Florence, however, ran into
difficulties finding a printer for his manuscript—a struggle that
reveals how his experimentation with photography belongs to
the story of a fragile, emerging early-nineteenth-century print
culture. Few printing presses then existed in Brazil because the
Portuguese Crown sought to control the spread of anti-colonial
propaganda. But Florence would not be deterred. This obstacle
motivated him to find a more accessible and democratic mode
of reproduction, one that utilized a resource available to all,
sunlight. Unlike the European figures credited with the invention
of the medium, Florence used photography to reproduce symbols
and written artifacts, not the visible world. His first attempts with
the process resulted in a print made around 1833 of pharmacy
labels, likely produced for his friend and collaborator Joaquim
Corrêa de Mello, a chemist who at the time lived in Campinas,
the same village as Florence, and helped him learn the properties
of silver nitrate. These six pharmacy labels on a single sheet of
paper demonstrate how, for Florence, photography functioned
as a mode of reproduction analogous to printing. His method
worked much like a modern-day photocopy—and, significantly,
these labels reveal how seriality was ingrained in his work,
something that standard accounts of photography's history
attribute to the invention of the *carte-de-visite* decades later.
His notebooks and diaries also reveal that he worked on other
photographs: a photographic copy of a Masonic Diploma and
one of his own hand-drawn designs for a *camera obscura* and other
items needed for the photographic process. Ultimately, Florence
did not use this method to print his manuscript, as he finally
convinced a printing press in Rio de Janeiro to publish his findings,
though there is no record of how his *zoophonie* was received.

On May 1, 1839, the Rio de Janeiro–based newspaper *Jornal
do Commercio* announced the invention of what would become
known as the daguerreotype, calling the invention a "revolution
in the arts of design," in which "nature appears portraying itself,
copying its works as well as works of art…. Light, light itself was
the painter." Six months later, in response to the announcement
of Louis Daguerre's method, Florence published a press release
in the São Paulo–based newspaper *A Phenix* in which he stated
that he had already been working on photographic printing
methods for nine years and that these experiments led him first
to the invention of polygraphy (a form of printing that used
sunlight, stencils, and chemistry to reproduce texts or graphics)
and then to the "discovery" of "fixing of images in the *camera
obscura* through the action of light." He continued, "I will not
dispute anyone's discoveries, because one same idea can come
to two persons, and because I always considered my findings
precarious." When Florence's press release was reprinted in Rio
two months later, it was prefaced by a journalist's note stating,
"Let the readers compare the dates and decide if the world owes
the discovery of Photography, or at the very least of Polygraphy,
to Europe or to Brazil."

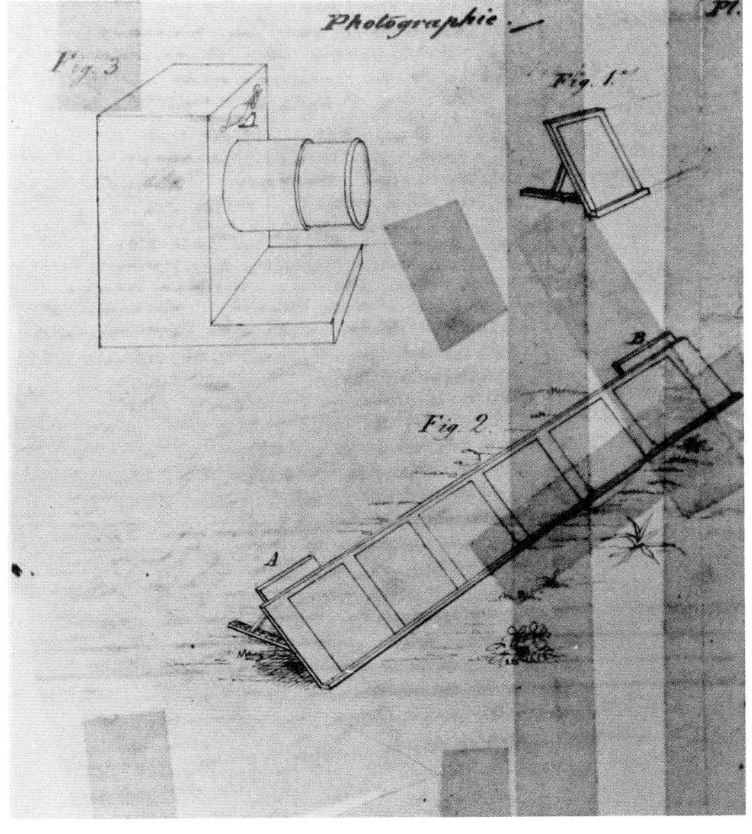

"Equipment used
for photography,"
originally appeared
in Florence's manuscript,
L'Ami des Arts…, 1837
Courtesy Instituto Hercule
Florence (Arnaldo Machado
Florence Archive)

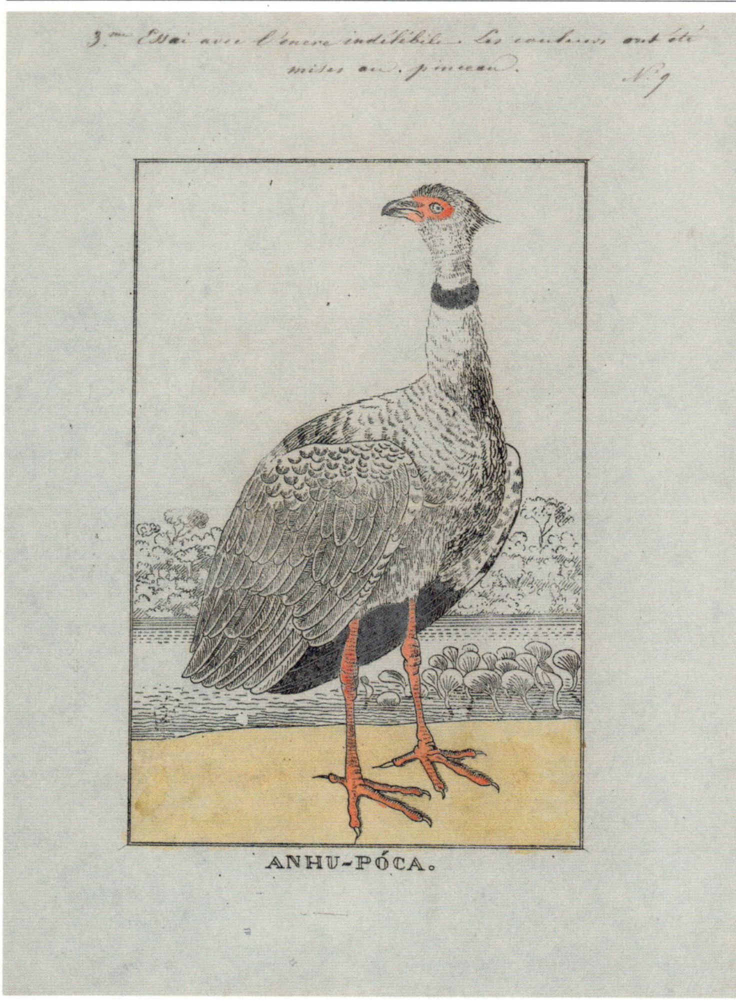
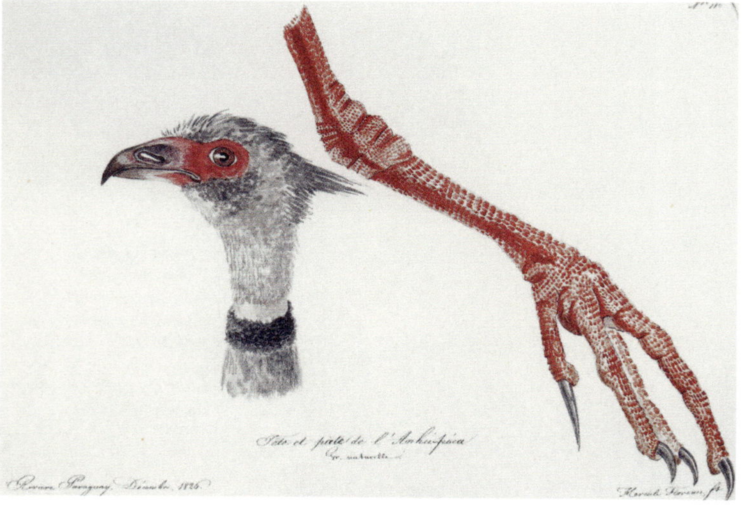

Top: Hercule Florence,
Anhu-póca, n.d.
(polygraphic drawing)
© Instituto Moreira Salles

Bottom: Hercule Florence,
Tête et pate de l'anhu-póca
(Head and feet of *anhu-póca* bird, or Southern screamer), Paraguay River, 1826, from *Expedição Langsdorff ao Brasil 1821–1829. Volume 3: Aquarelas e desenhos de Florence (Langsdorff Expedition to Brazil 1821–1829. Volume 3: Watercolors and drawings)*
Courtesy Instituto Hercule Florence, São Paulo, and Archive of the Russian Academy of Sciences, St. Petersburg

Daguerre had received a life pension from the French government, and Florence hoped to obtain the same. He wrote letters and made his case to the French Academy of Sciences but never received any serious response, and his diary entries from this time convey his resentment at being overlooked. "Photography is the wonder of the century. I had also already established the grounds, foreseen this art in all its majesty. I did it [photography] before Daguerre's process, but I worked in exile. I printed by means of sunlight seven years before photography was first talked about. I had already given it that name; however, all honors to Daguerre." The French invention caught on and became popular in Brazil; in 1840, fourteen-year-old Pedro II, about to be crowned Second Emperor of Brazil, had the daguerreotype technique demonstrated to him. The young emperor became enamored with the invention, turning into the first promoter of official photography within a monarchy, introducing the title of "Crown Photographer" before Queen Victoria in England.

A tireless inventor despite lack of fame, fortune, or even credit, Florence continued to experiment with reproduction. In the late 1830s, he purchased a typography machine, obtained the necessary license to operate it, and printed advertisements and the short-lived revolutionary newspaper *O Paulista* that became the "fuel of the liberal movement" until the anti-monarchical revolt had been squashed, forcing Florence to disappear his machine after printing only four editions. In the early 1840s, about a decade after his first experiments with photography, Florence invented unique and inimitable paper money. The move from photography to money might seem a stretch, but both share an inherent seriality. A banking crisis of 1864 that resulted in a reconfiguration of the banking and commerce system made it evident that money, both paper and coin, were difficult to authenticate. Florence seized on the economic tumult by introducing paper that, because of the "sharpness" it allowed in printing, the "microscopic traces," and the "indelible" quality of the printed colors and patterns could, as his 1842 advertisement claimed, "guarantee … against forgeries." But this, too, failed to catch on. Yet Florence never gave up: In 1859 he patented a reproduction technique he called "stereopainting" and, soon thereafter "solar painting," though we don't know much about what these intriguing projects entailed. His last known "invention" was what he called "The Sixth Order of Architecture, or Brazilian Order." This order consisted of columns, pediments, and other architectural details inspired by Brazilian palm trees, already an icon of the country. Greece produced the three known orders of architectural style—the Doric, Ionic, and Corinthian—that symbolized the roots of Western architecture. Florence seems to have wanted to put Brazil on the cultural map by inventing a style or order that reflected the country's tropical environs.

Why didn't any of Florence's ideas and inventions flourish? Most likely his status as an outsider within the highly structured political and class system in nineteenth-century Brazil, with its strong monarchy and organized cultural centers clustered in Rio de Janeiro and the northern city of Recife, is to blame for his lack of recognition. Though his name would fall into obscurity rather than becoming canonized in photography histories, he seems to have passed his later years rather contentedly in the small town of Campinas, where he fathered twenty children and lived on a beautiful *fazenda* (ranch).

A century passed before Florence's remarkable achievements were discovered. In the early 1970s, Boris Kossoy, a Brazilian photographer and photography historian who came across Florence's "alleged" invention through mentions in specialized

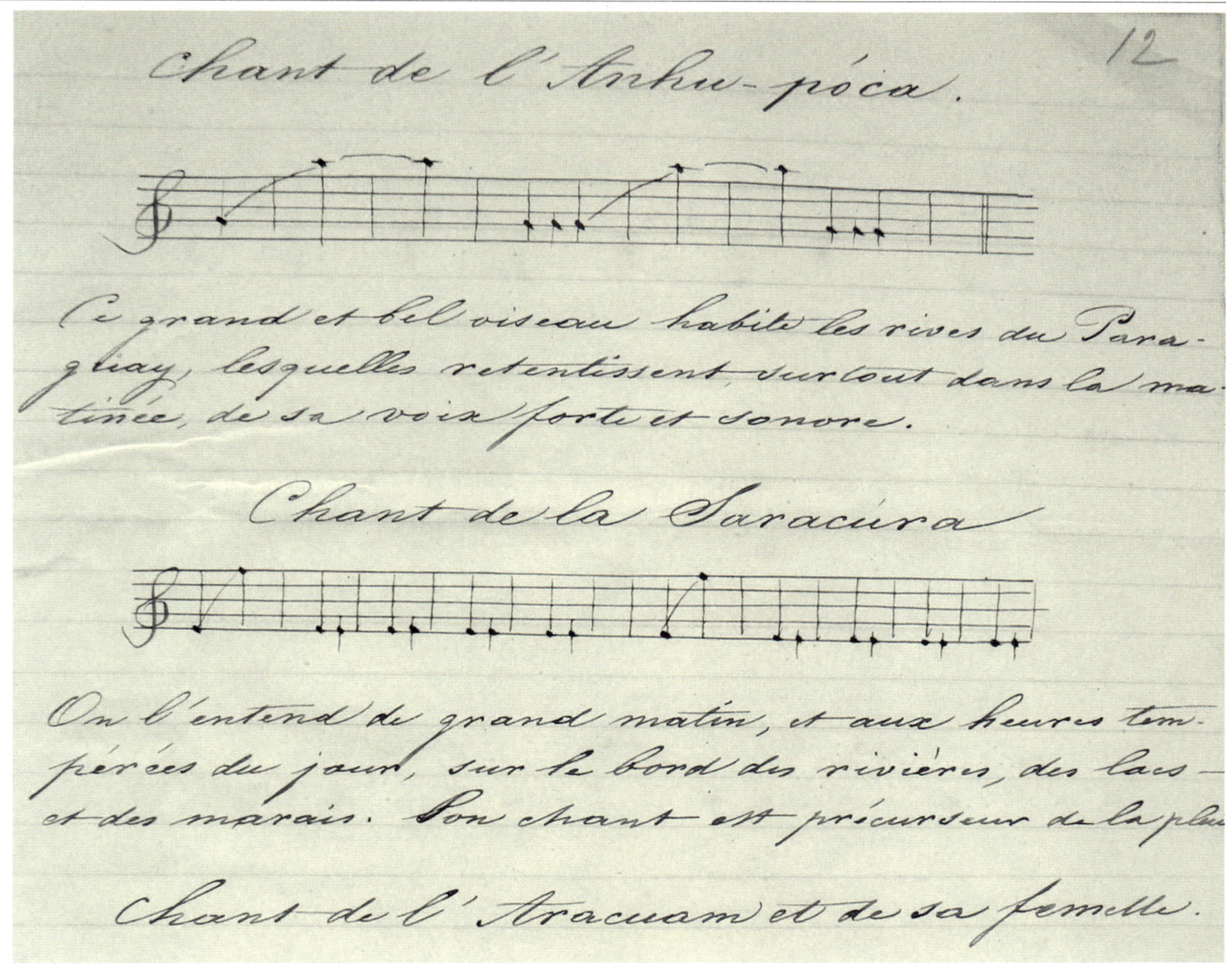

Page from Hercule Florence's manuscript *Voyage fluvial du Tieté a l'Amazone* (Fluvial voyage from the Tieté to the Amazon river), 1831, which included many examples of his *zoophonie* notations
Courtesy Archive of the Instituto Histórico e Geográfico Brasileiro, Rio de Janeiro, and Instituto Hercule Florence, São Paulo

Brazilian publications, began his research on what he called the "isolated discovery of photography in Brazil." To build his case Kossoy traveled to the George Eastman House in Rochester, New York, to test, with the aid of technicians, the notations made by Florence about his photographic experiments. His tests proved that Florence had indeed invented a photographic process in 1833. Around the same time his photographic discoveries were being at last acknowledged, his studies of Amazon sounds were also finding new supporters in the emerging field of bioacoustics, or animal communications. In 1978, the world-famous French ornithologist Jacques Vielliard was invited by the University of Campinas, on the outskirts of the city of São Paulo, in Florence's hometown, to establish what would become the most important bioacoustics lab in the Americas. Vielliard amassed an enormous collection of tropical sounds, creating the "Neotropical Sound Archive," and in 2005 set up a second archive called the "Amazonian Sound Archive," housed at the Federal University of Pará.

More recently, contemporary artists have found Florence a source of inspiration. In the nineties, German sound artist Michael Fahres, working with a group of artists from Russia, Germany, and Brazil, retraced Florence's journey with the Langsdorff expedition and reinterpreted his *zoophonie*. Italian photographer Linda Nagler is preparing a multimedia art exhibition around Florence's many artistic and scientific explorations for the New National Museum of Monaco in 2015. An Argentine trio including writer Pola Oloixarac, photographer Luna Paiva, and composer Esteban Insinger wrote a contemporary opera called "Hercule Florence in Mato Grosso," which will premiere in Buenos Aires this October. Perhaps Florence was neither a naturalist nor an inventor but rather a conceptual artist who was ahead of his time.

"I printed by means of sunlight seven years before photography was first talked about. I had already given it that name; however, all honors to Daguerre."

Natalia Brizuela is a professor at the University of California, Berkeley. She is the author of *Fotografia e império: Paisagens de um Brasil moderno* (Photography and empire: Landscapes of a modern Brazil) (Companhia das Letras, 2012) and the forthcoming *Uma literatura fora de si. Escrita e fotografia* (A literature beside itself: Writing and photography) (Rocco, 2014).

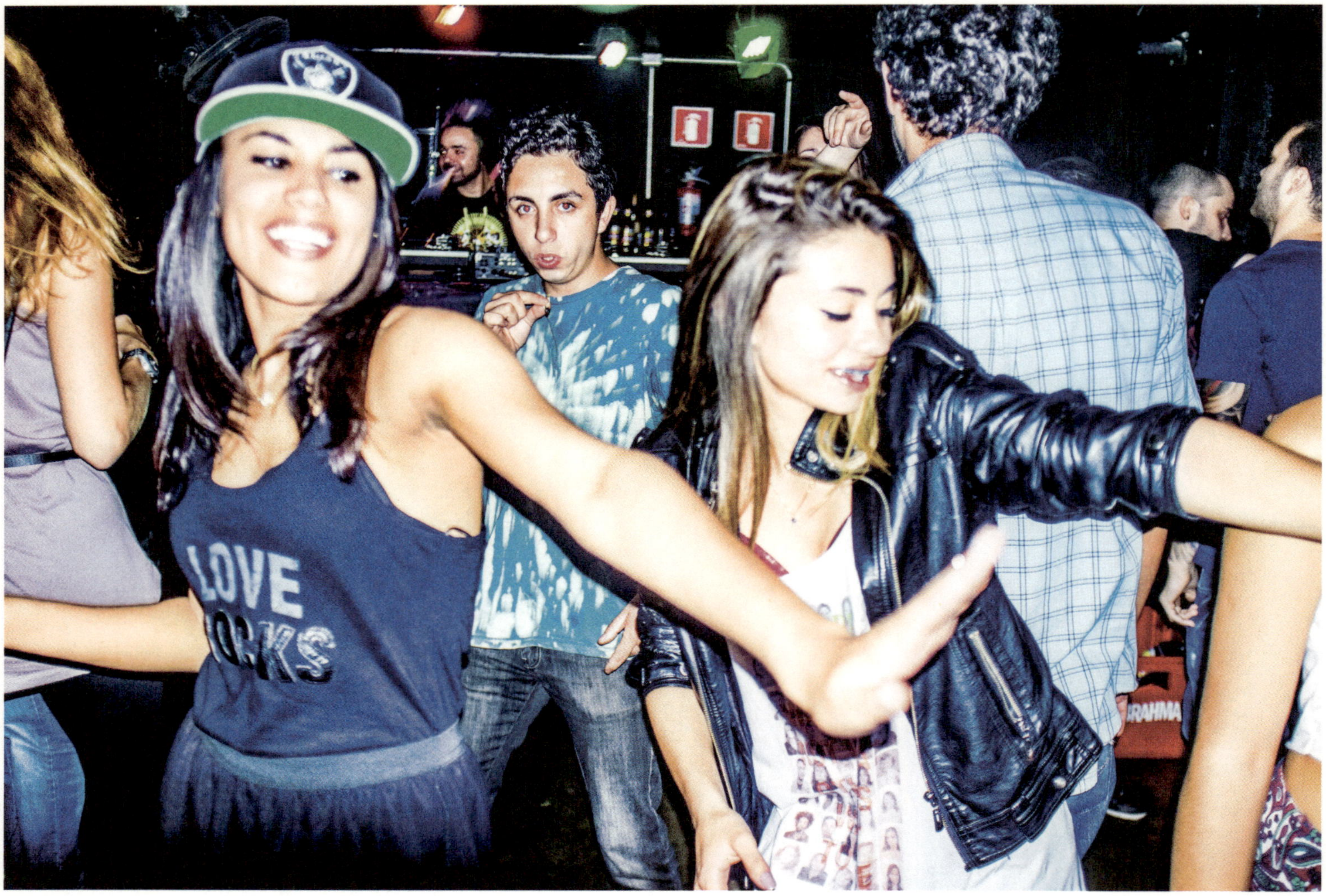

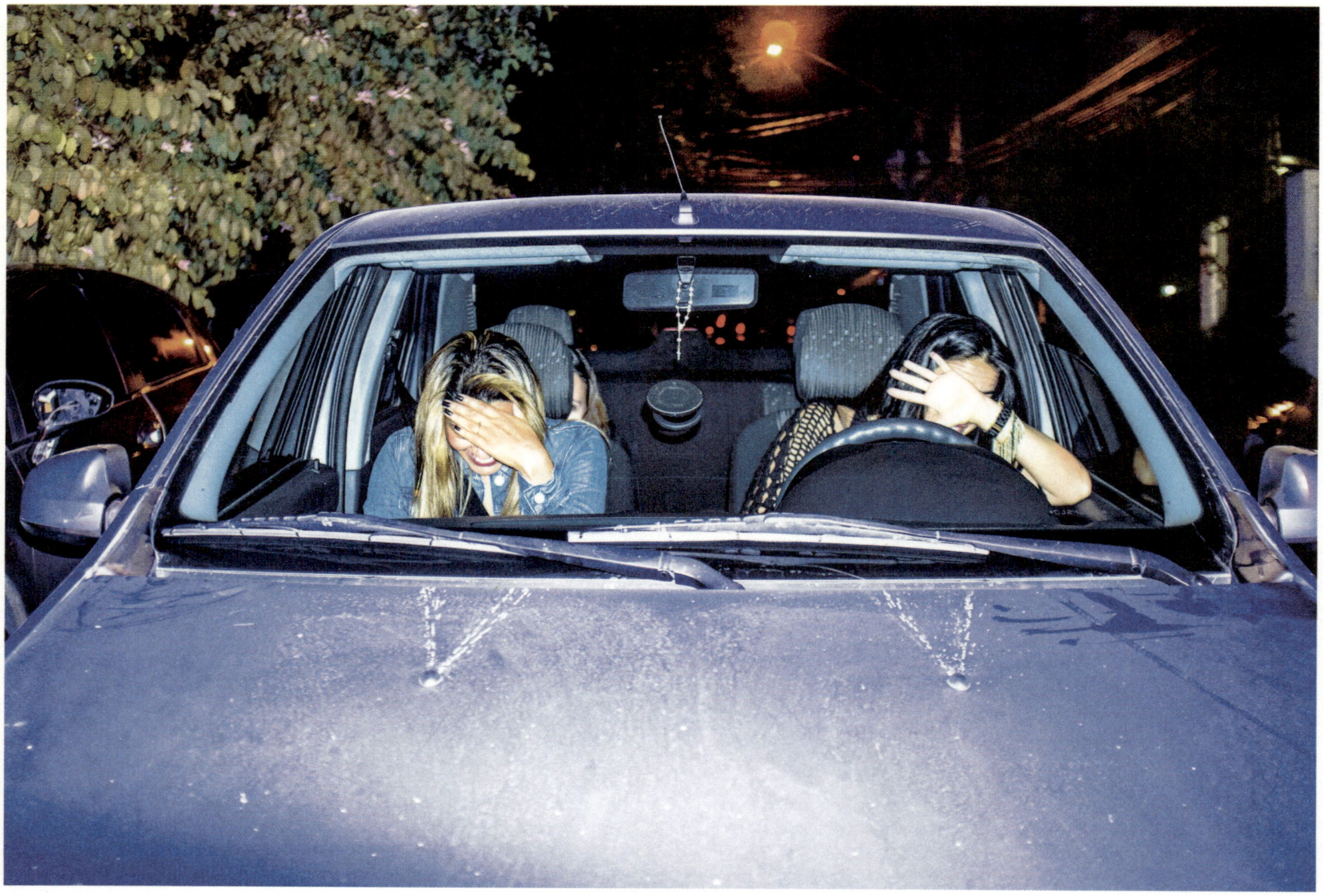

Photography collectives with diverse styles and philosophies are transforming São Paulo's media landscape through their documentation of last year's massive street protests and by exploring everyday life in the megalopolis.

Groupshot
Ronaldo Entler

In June 2013, mass demonstrations rocked Brazil. Protests against bus fare hikes, organized by the Movimento Passe Livre (Free Fare Movement), gained swift momentum, moving from one city to the next, absorbing other causes and attracting international attention. The demonstrations also triggered a media war. On one side, news reports highlighted scenes of protesters engaged in acts of vandalism. On the other, protesters captured excessive police violence. During this time, photography collectives played a key role, recording and supporting the protests. While the work of these groups, whose numbers have steadily grown over the past ten years, is hardly isolated to instances of political demonstrations, this particular moment of upheaval exemplified the collaborative impulse that fuels them.

Brazilian photography collectives are forging alternatives to image banks and news agencies. Even when their style veers toward photojournalism, or even commercial advertising, photography collectives' projects assume the form of social or political engagement. Generally made up of young photographers, they embrace social media and online networks and have little interest in traditional models based on solitary authorship.

The phenomenon is hardly unique to Brazil. Marked by their own aesthetic decisions and approaches, many such groups have formed across the globe, often united by specific collaborative projects. Such is the case with Blank Paper and Pandora (Spain), Kameraphoto (Portugal), Luceo (United States), Mondaphoto (Mexico), and Supayfotos (Peru). There are, however, certain historical precedents specific to Brazil, such as the photo clubs established in various cities in the mid-twentieth century, or the independent photography agencies that have sprung up since the 1970s—such as Fotocontexto, F4, and Ágil—and cultural initiatives such as Fotoativa, an important educational project founded in Belém do Pará in 1984.

Today's new collectives encompass a wide range of approaches but share a proclivity toward political confrontation. Their political engagement is reflected in how the groups have sought alternative models for managing and disseminating images and information. By mining social networks, they explore new paths for financial survival and dialogue with curators, critics, and other cultural producers. By banding together, these collectives assert a clear ideological and aesthetic identity and produce projects of great depth while also constructing spaces for the distribution of works not absorbed by the mass media. In some cases, they gain access to the art circuit or publishing and advertising markets, which are attracted by the gritty glamour of a language forged outside the mainstream.

Mapping São Paulo's collectives is no easy task. Many of these groups meet only sporadically and tend to be short-lived, but what follows is a selection of some of the most important collectives recently working in the city.

Cia de Foto

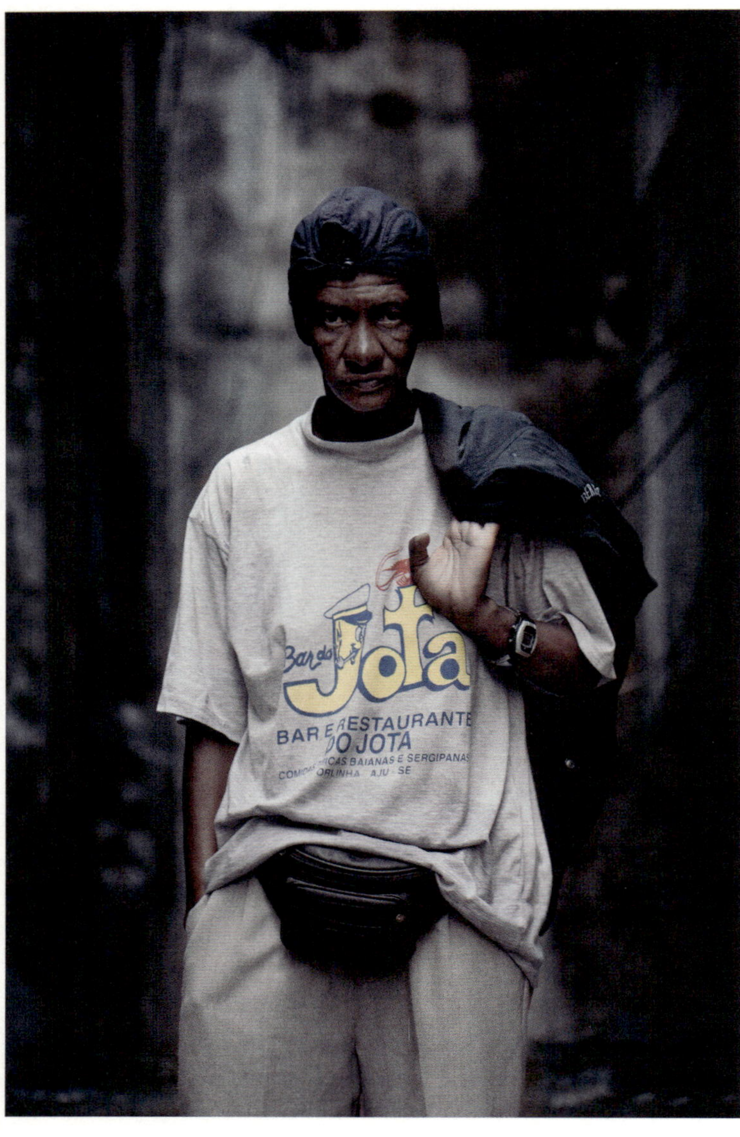

Above:
**Cia de Foto, from
the project *911*, 2006
(video still)**
Courtesy Galeria Vermelho,
São Paulo

**Cia de Foto stirred some
controversy by refusing ever
to provide an individual's
signature on any of the works
that it produced.**

Cia de Foto, whose name means photo company, was the most influential of these collectives and served as a model and inspiration for other groups in Brazil, but in late 2013, it caused a commotion by posting a brief message on its Facebook page announcing its dissolution.

Cia de Foto emerged in 2003, spearheaded by photographers Pio Figueiroa, Rafael Jacinto, and João Kehl, and later incorporated image editor Carol Lopes. Eschewing photographic pamphleteering, the group's presence within the framework of social debate was nonetheless apparent. One of its first projects, *911*, focused on the occupation of a building in downtown São Paulo by a group of squatting homeless families. A newer project, *Passe Livre*, addressed the bus fare hikes of 2013. In recent years, the group began to direct its attention to a range of diverse subjects, sometimes assuming a more poetic approach (though the subject matter remained political in nature). One example is *Marcha* (2011/2013), which recorded the daily commute of workers through one of the city's major train stations. By highlighting the dispersed yet unchanging nature of these commutes, the images suggest that masses of workers no longer represent a potent political force as they did in the past.

Cia de Foto was defined by its very structure as a collective and stirred some controversy by refusing ever to provide an individual's signature on any of the works that it produced. As many important public and private collections acquired the group's pieces, its structure grew to meet the demands of the market, and it led various art institutions to reformulate their own policies in order to acquire works of collective authorship. The group curated exhibitions, published books in experimental formats, and nurtured emerging artists. It also welcomed other collaborators. According to Pio Figueiroa, "It's been more thought-provoking to share and encourage people to debate ideas than to simply sign off on a completed work."

Several projects remain to be completed and the future of Cia de Foto's immense image archive now seems uncertain. Despite the group's breakup, Figueiroa has stated that he still sees collectives playing an important role in responding to the difficulties for professional development and to the lack of organization among Brazilian photographers.

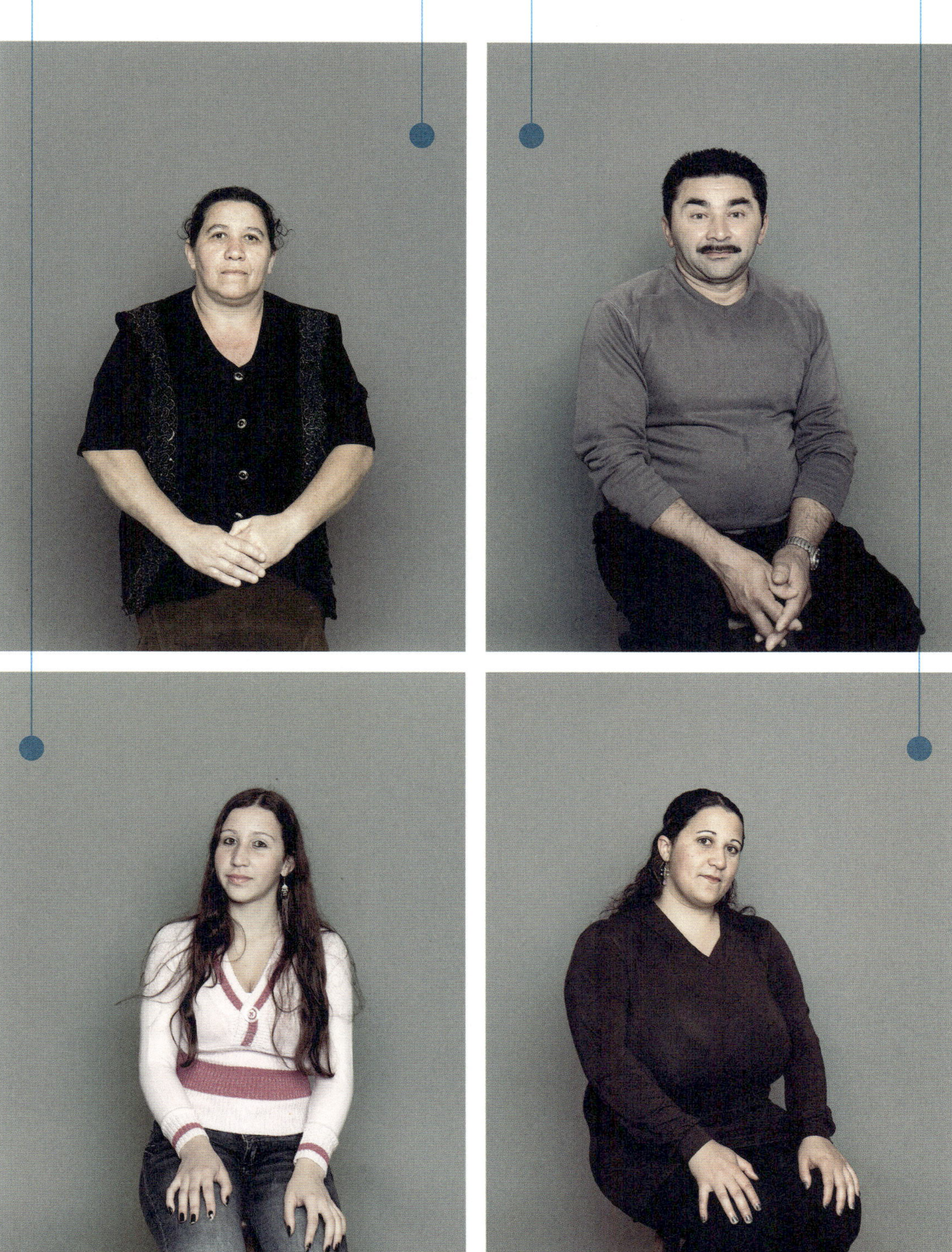

Garapa

Garapa takes its name from the Portuguese word for the sugarcane juice used to make, among other things, the distilled spirit *cachaça*. Formed in 2008 by photographers Rodrigo Marcondes, Paulo Fehlauer, and Leo Caobelli, the collective occupies an important role in Brazil's cultural scene and is devoted to experimenting with new narrative forms. While encouraging members to complete their own projects outside of the group, Garapa maintains a solid roster of jointly realized projects.

Morar (2009–11), the group's first effort, centered on the emptying and demolition of two contiguous buildings, *São Vito* and *Mercúrio*, during a somewhat suspect program of urban revitalization for the city's downtown. Some of the group's research was financed by crowdfunding, and the project made use of a wide range of techniques, from daguerreotype to video, and took a variety of forms: several exhibitions that included photographs and a short documentary, a tabloid-format publication, and a site-specific installation featuring portraits of former residents on the land where the two buildings once stood. According to Rodrigo Marcondes, the group's recent works have drawn on new partnerships, and while still maintaining a documentary approach, they also utilize certain fictional elements. In *Calma* (2013), a work that included the collaboration of artists Lana Mesic and Thomas Kuijpers, the collective followed the fictitious story of Rolf, a Dutchman who had come to São Paulo in search of his missing father.

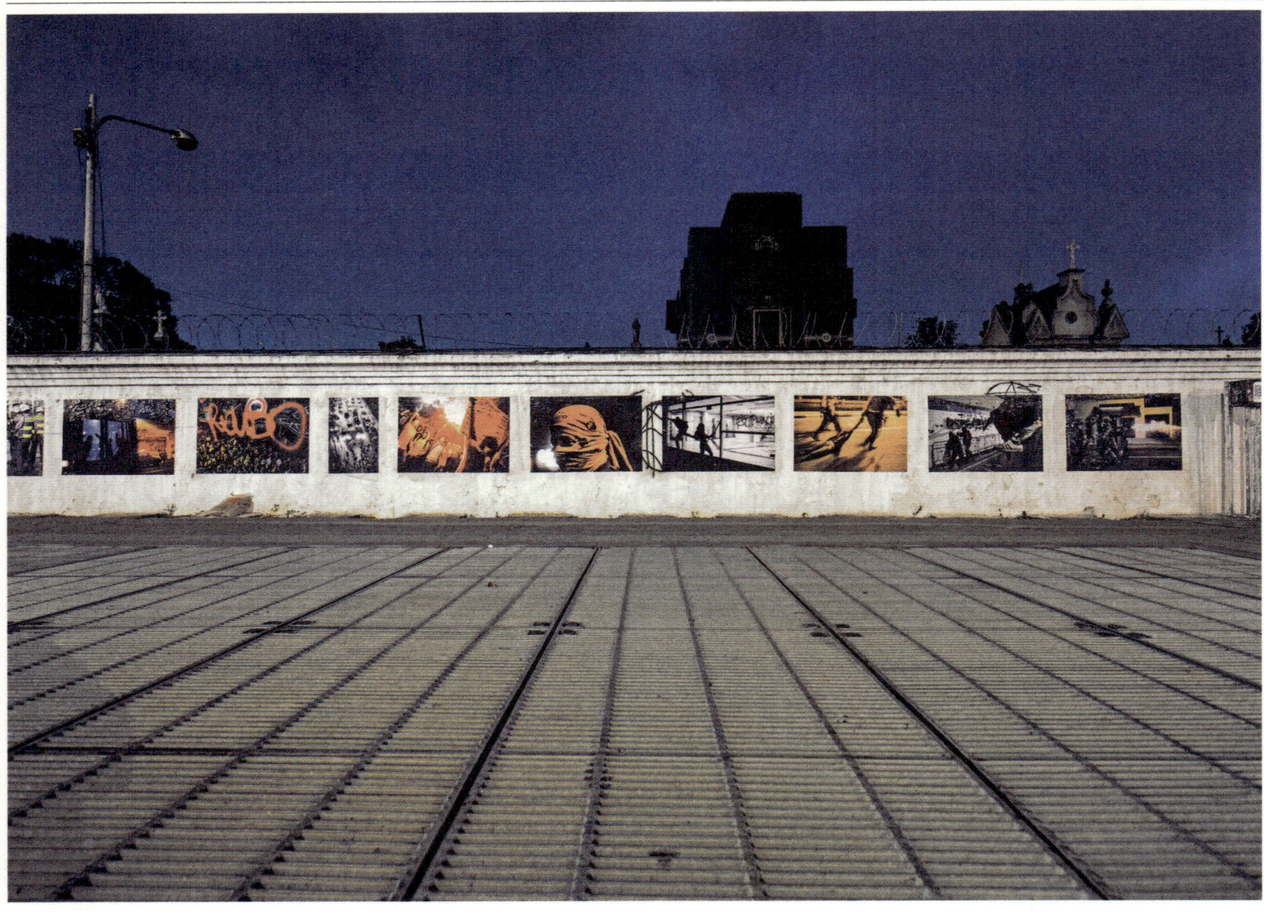

Above:
FotoProtestoSP installation
at Cemitério do Araçá,
São Paulo. Photograph
by Ignácio Aronovich
© Ignácio Aronovich/
Lost Art

FotoProtestoSP

One of the more stringent collectives to rise out of the unrest of 2013 is FotoProtestoSP. Its thirty members include several well-established veterans of Brazilian photojournalism, such as Maurício Lima, Marlene Bergamo, Fernando Costa Netto, Keiny Andrade, Ignácio Aronovich, and José Francisco Diório. Their manifesto radiates indignation with the country's political structure and asserts a desire to explore the critical power of photography beyond private media platforms and art institutions. "We understand the urgency of not letting inertia take control of society and, in order to visually display our indignation, we will take over the public or empty spaces in São Paulo with our photographs," their manifesto states.

Each member maintains his or her own working routine and no attempts are made to produce coverage specifically bearing a collective signature. According to Renato Stockler, one of the group's members, its objective is to occupy the city's leisure spaces and to remind residents of the power people have when they unite around a common cause. "It's about giving back to the street what the street initially gave to photographers," Stockler says. One of FotoProtestoSP's most important actions involved wheatpasting two walls in downtown São Paulo with large-format photographs of the protests. Despite its relative newness, the important names attached to the group and the dramatic imagery produced have drawn much attention to their initiative.

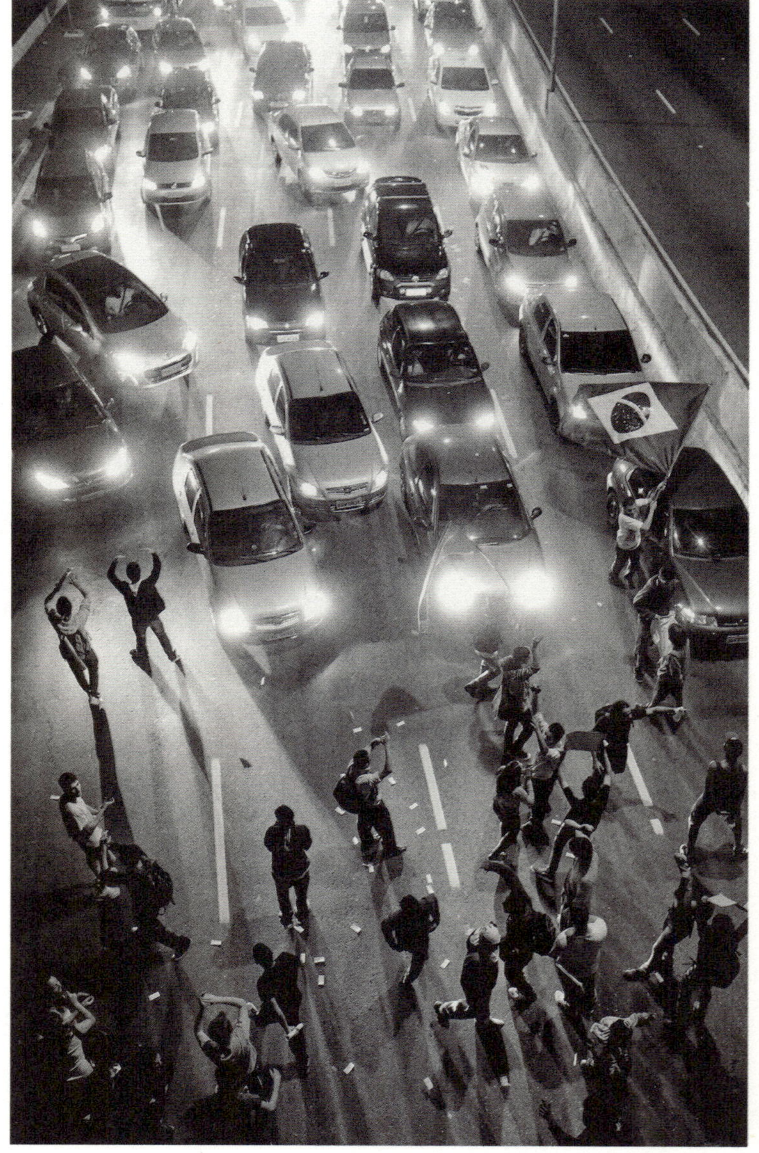

SelvaSP

SelvaSP, meaning São Paulo jungle, formed in 2012 with an entirely aesthetic objective: the revitalization of street photography. The group's manifesto recalls the work of classical photographers and questions why critics have decided to view this genre as archaic. The collective, which still considers itself in a formative phase, currently has twelve members: Gabriel Cabral, Victor Dragonetti (Drago), Leo Eloy, Francisco Costa, Syã Fonseca, Gustavo Gomes, Paulo Marinuzzi, Rafael Mattar, Lucas Mello, Gustavo Morita, Padu Palmério, and Hudson Rodrigues.

According to Gabriel Cabral, despite the group's coverage of the 2013 protests, their photo essays are defined more by trying to capture everyday life in the city—neighborhood identities and the gestures and expressions of people on the street—than by urgent reporting on fast-breaking events. SelvaSP produces tightly edited photo essays, not the news.

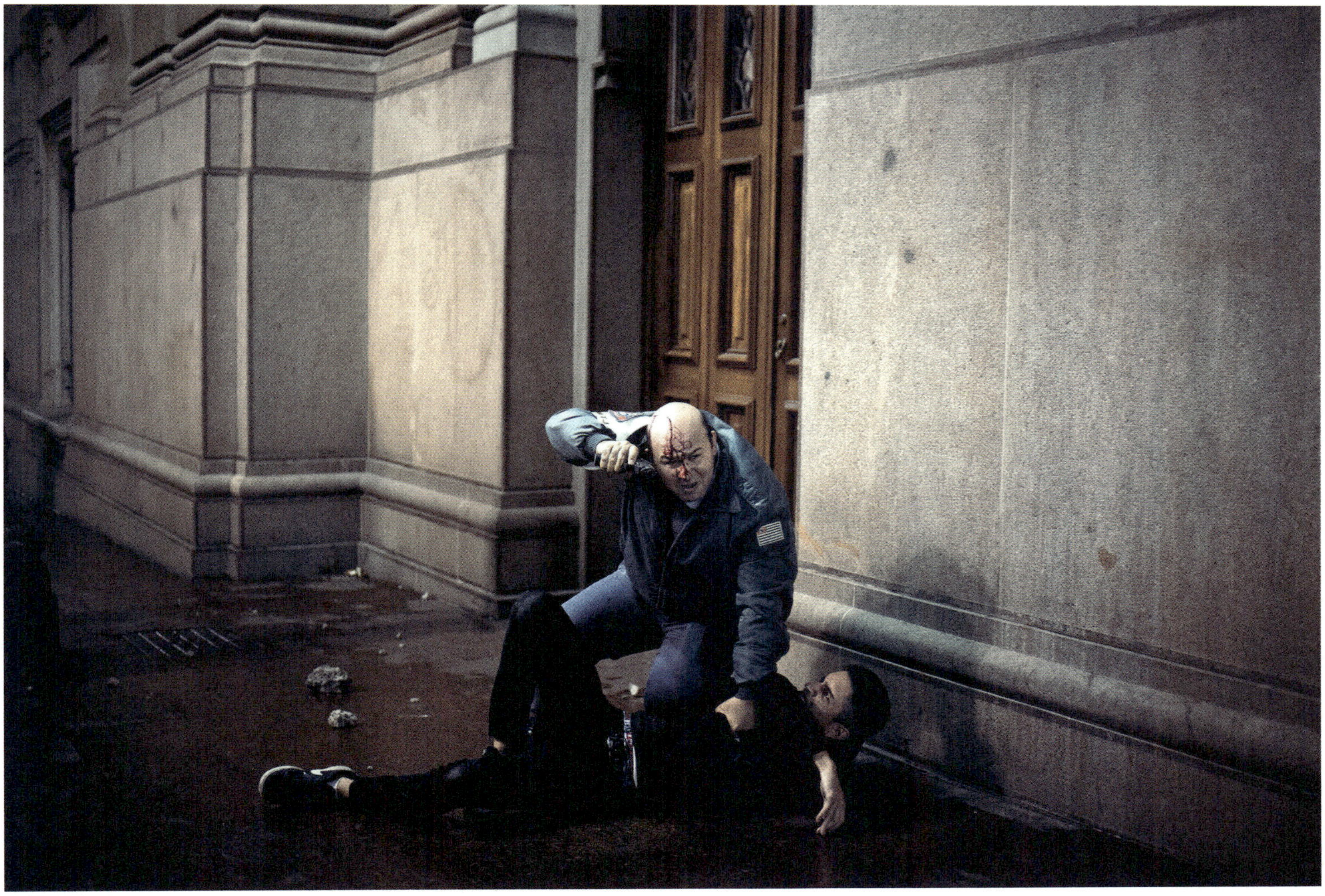

Above:
Drago, A hurt military police officer fends off attackers during the second protest against the bus-fare hikes in São Paulo, June 2013
© Drago/SelvaSP

Right:
Gustavo Gomes, from the series *Plástico* (Plastic), 2013
© Gustavo Gomes/SelvaSP

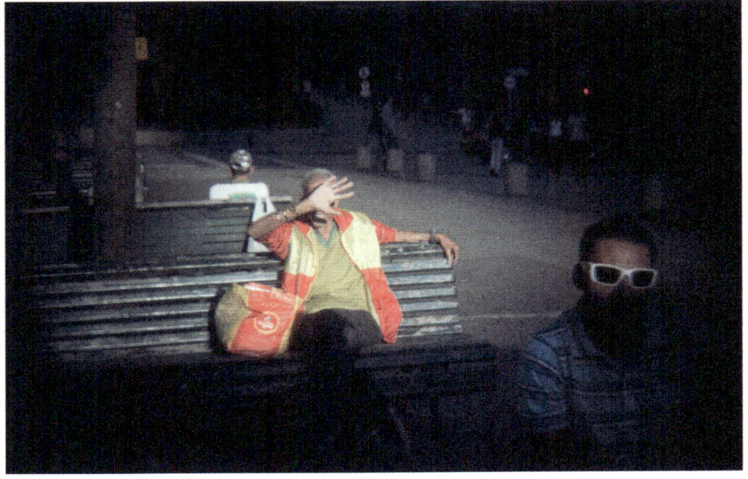

Mídia Ninja

"We're not looking to be impartial," Vilela asserts, "what distinguishes us from the major platforms is the transparency with which we present points of view."

During the 2013 protests, Mídia Ninja became one of the most instrumental collectives to provide on-the-scene coverage: Several videos posted on Twitcast reached as many as one hundred thousand viewers. With a huge portfolio documenting conflict situations, they were able to confront major news providers whose coverage had been critical of the protests, forcing some to adjust their content and provide a more nuanced portrayal that included not only scenes of vandalism on the part of protesters but also scenes of police violence.

Ninja (a Portuguese acronym for Independent Narratives, Journalism, and Action) was formed in 2011 as a sideline of Fora do Eixo, a collective network created in 2005 to organize independent music festivals in several Brazilian cities. Part of Mídia Ninja's know-how and strategy is a result of its work with these festivals. While Bruno Torturra, Pablo Capilé, Filipe Peçanha, and Rafael Vilela are some of the members who most often appear in public to discuss their projects, the collective estimates that there are nearly one hundred regular members and a network of as many as two thousand collaborators who can be mobilized across the country. Although known for their use of camera phones, many collaborators have, in fact, had solid audiovisual training.

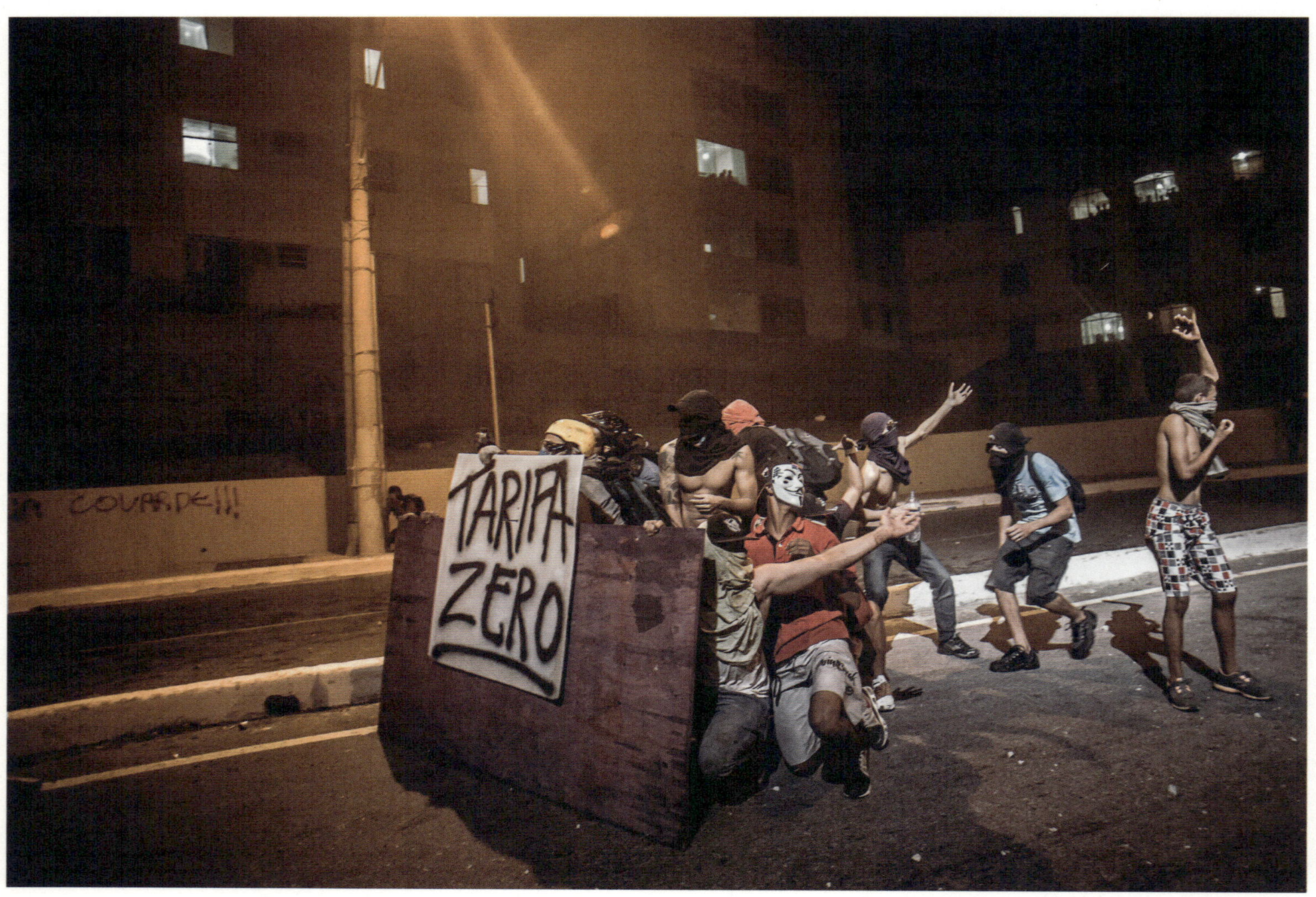

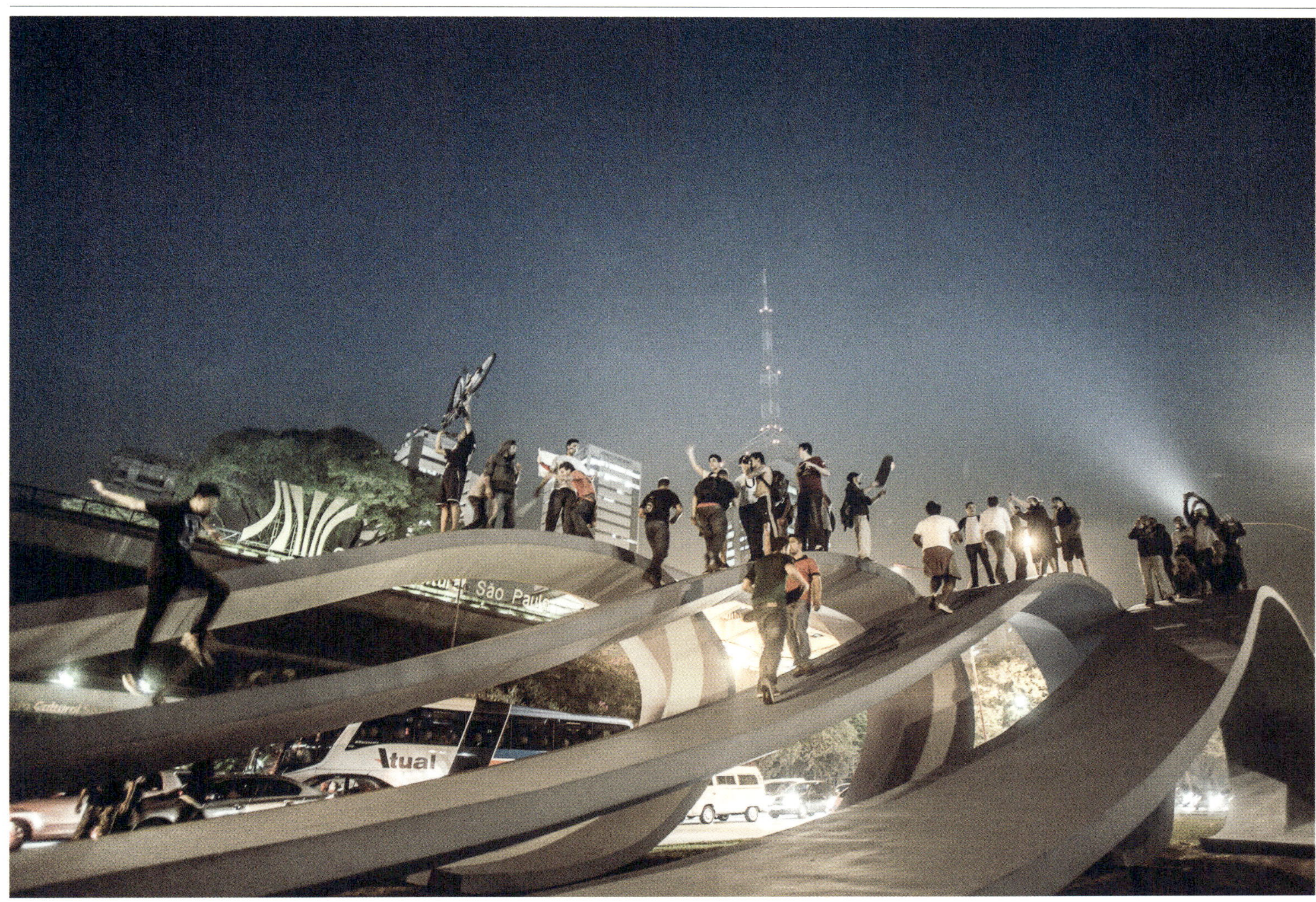

Mídia Ninja, Monument
occupied during popular
protests, 23 de Maio
Avenue, São Paulo, 2013,
part of the project *Ruas
de Junho* (June Streets)
Courtesy Mídia Ninja

Though made under a banner of independent journalism and media activism, work by the collective members has often been featured by mainstream news outlets, where it has been the subject of debate: Critics question whether their informal coverage qualifies as legitimate journalism. According to Vilela, Ninja's projects have been funded primarily by social organizations that support the same causes. "We're not looking to be impartial," Vilela asserts, "what distinguishes us from the major platforms is the transparency with which we present points of view." The group's images are available for free downloading on Creative Commons and have been published in newspapers around the world. Aside from the alternative channels that they explore, the works produced by Ninja have also begun to exert a presence within the art circuit and are often featured in photography exhibitions and collections.

Mídia Ninja is an evolving project. Its core membership recently relocated to Rio de Janeiro from São Paulo. With the World Cup approaching, Rio will be packed with tourists and journalists, as well as militants keeping an eye out for the social unrest that is often unleashed by such major events—and the collective will be well-positioned to witness, record, and disseminate.

It would be difficult to conceive of these collectives as part of a broader, cohesive movement, or to suppose that the future of photography is necessarily headed in the direction of collective authorship. Many of the groups have been temporary, and others are still too new to assess their impact. Nevertheless, these collectives have demonstrated their power. Restlessness is one of the unique qualities of any group formed by diverse points of view and desires. They have proven that it is possible to reinvent photography during times of crisis.

Ronaldo Entler, a researcher and photography critic, is a professor at the School of Communication of Armando Alvares Penteado Foundation (FAAP), in São Paulo, where he is also the graduate coordinator of the school's masters of photography program.

Bookending the City

Cassiano Elek Machado

Since the nineteenth century, photographers have used the book form to portray São Paulo's environs. Recent titles continue this tradition by deploying a range of approaches, from the typological to the sculptural.

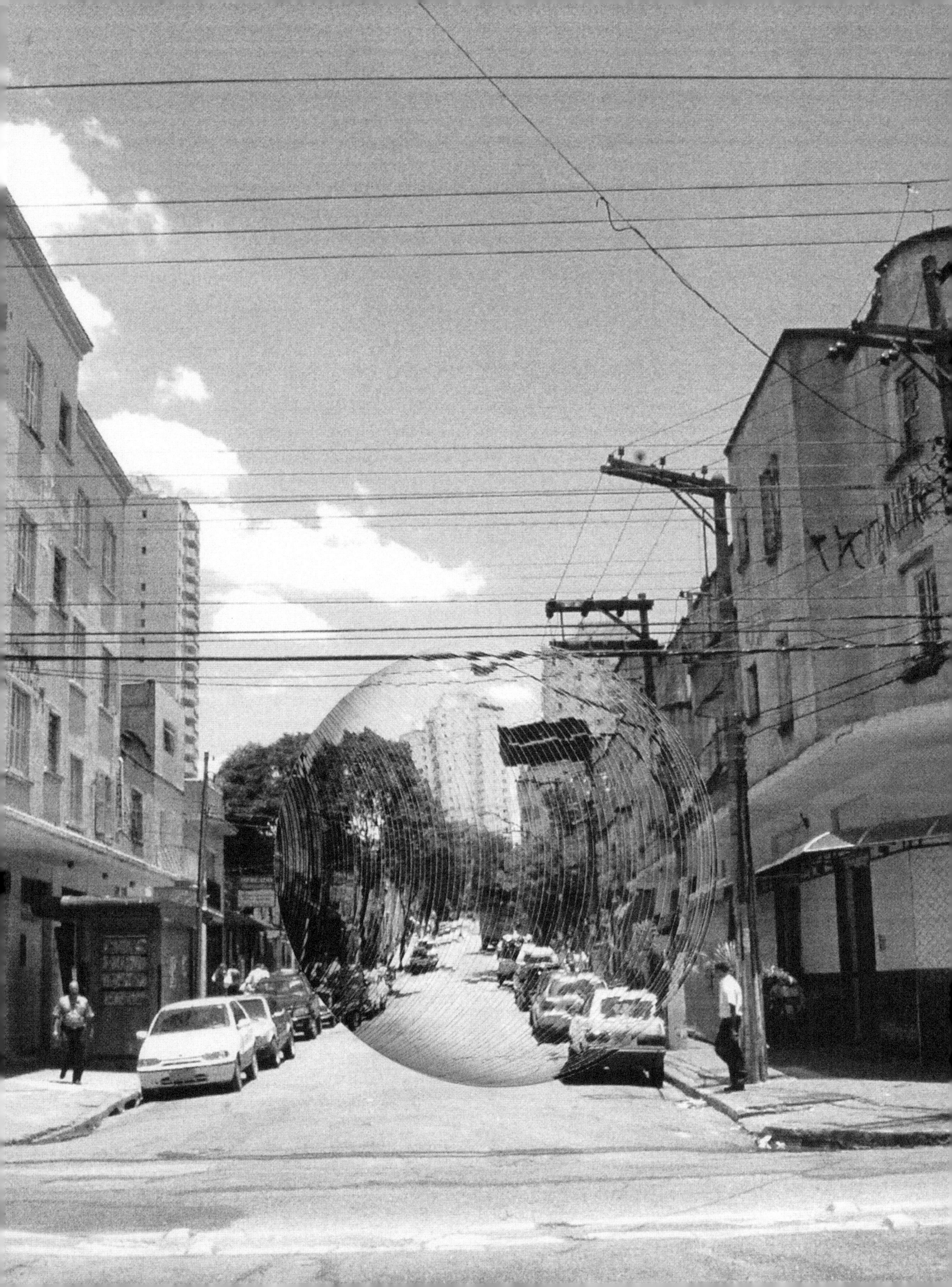

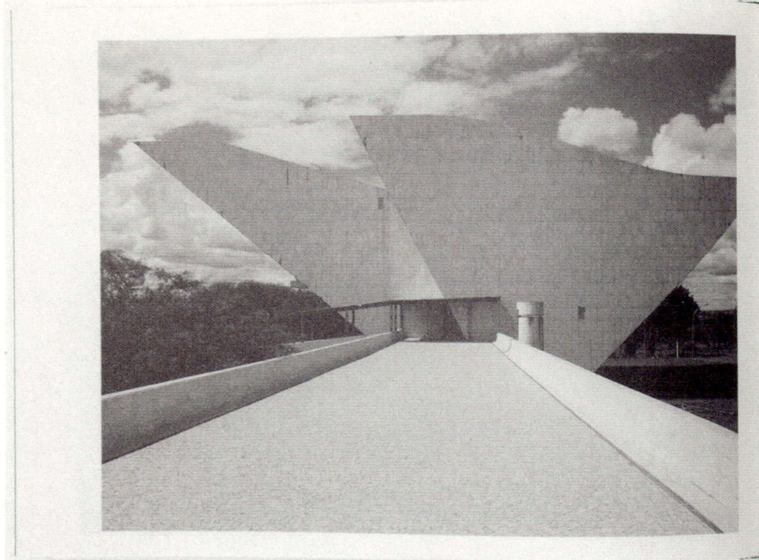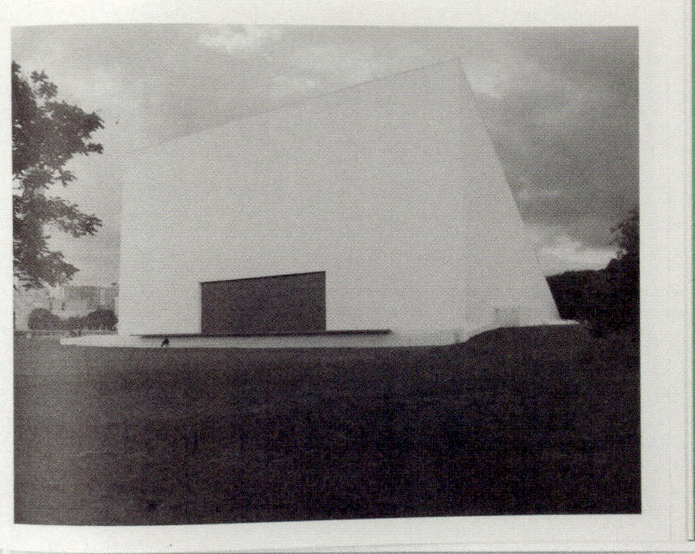

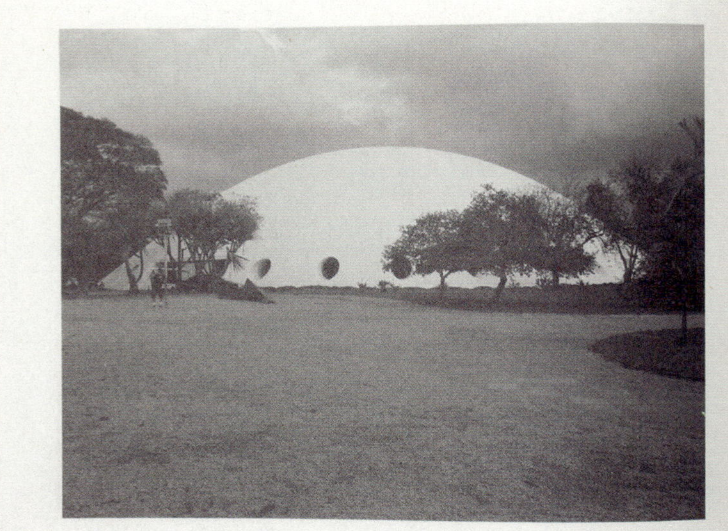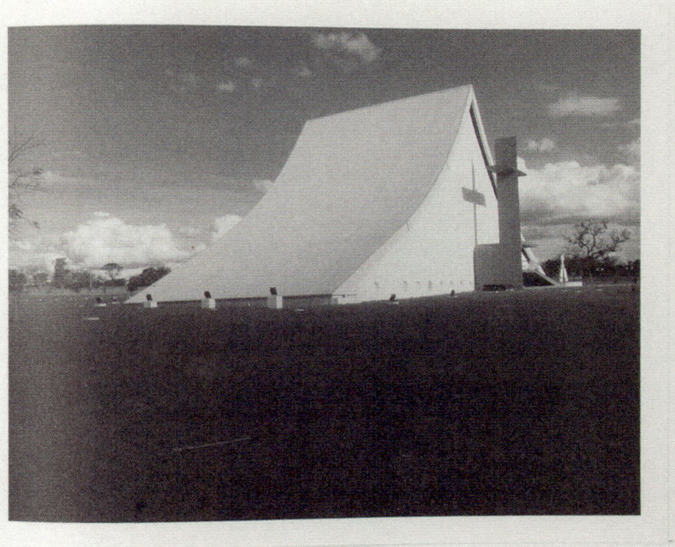

Erik van der Weijde,
O. Niemeyer, 2012
Courtesy the artist

Within cities like São Paulo there exist countless worlds that can be peeled away, layer by layer, to reveal hidden lives. Photobooks have become precious records of the city's nuances and conflicts, the flux of its inhabitants, and its constituent parts—lampposts, houses, buildings, street signs, all rising from the asphalt.

The poet Manuel Bandeira wrote, "They're going to demolish this house / But my room remains, / Not as an imperfect form / In this world of appearances: / It will stay for an eternity / In its books, in its pictures, / Intact, suspended in air!" These lines easily come to mind while viewing the books of Dutch photographer Erik van der Weijde, who currently resides in Natal, in northeast Brazil. His artistic project is far-reaching, and in his countless photobooks, scrapbooks, and zines, he hoards an impressive quantity of memories from the many places he's visited on his travels.

The Beetle, known as the Fusca, for example, which Volkswagen manufacturers in Brazil stopped making in July 1996, rolls out intact, "suspended in air," in the pages of the booklet *Type 1*, which van der Weijde published in 2013 under his own imprimatur, 4478ZINE.

While he dedicates time to documenting Fuscas, or the odd metal structures used for holding bags of garbage on Brazilian street corners, van der Weijde also documents famous buildings designed by Oscar Niemeyer. The resulting photobook, *O. Niemeyer*, is an elaborate typology of the architect's creations that, in the artist's images, have the freshness of a thing that has just been built.

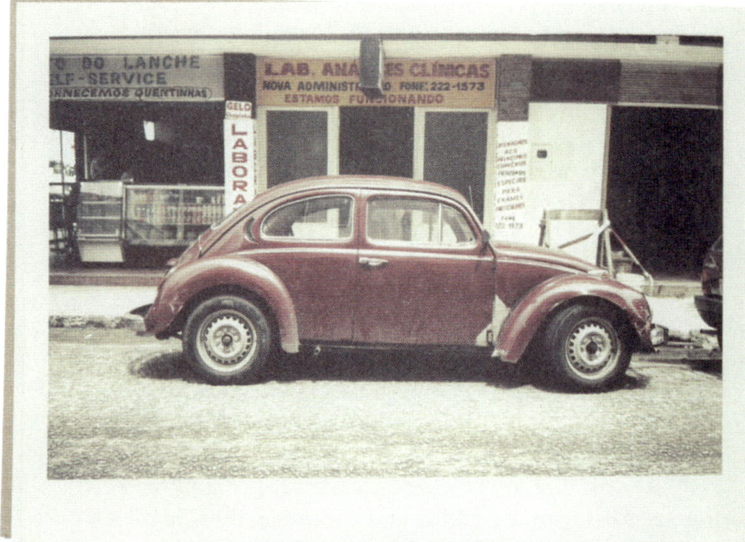 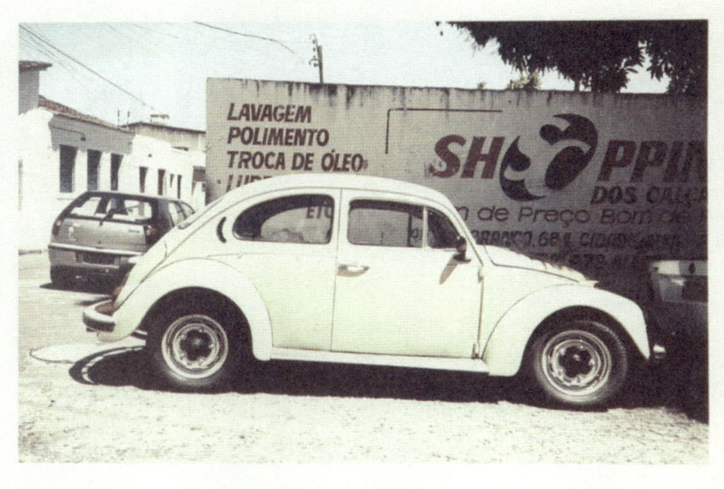

There are no figures in the Niemeyer photos; there are no drivers in the VWs, no garbage collectors hauling off the trash bags from the metal structures. People are rarely featured in van der Weijde's Brazil photobooks, but when they do appear, they are the protagonists. Such is the case in *Av. Paulista*, a photobook in the form of a brochure, made up of thirty-six black-and-white photos of women walking down the sidewalks of São Paulo's best-known avenue.

In these images, the background is barely visible: van der Weijde's camera is squarely fixed on the derrieres of women passing by. We don't see their hair, or their faces, and, for the most part, not even their feet—it's thirty-six pairs of thighs and glutes. Besides documenting the physical endowments of these women, within the frame van der Weijde also manages to freeze their gestures, their ways of dressing (usually squeezed into tight pants); he even captures their haste.

Time is also condensed in multiple ways in Brazilian photographer Lucia Mindlin Loeb's work. In a recent photobook by this São Paulo artist, we see a portal opening onto a random street corner. Notably, there are many characteristic elements of São Paulo: the chaos of power lines that slash across the greater part of the skyline; the "eclectic" architecture with townhouses in the foreground and "modern" buildings in the background; graffiti tags with crude lettering, elongated and unintelligible; uneven sidewalks, replete with cracks; the corner bar, the newsstand, a few trees spiking up from the gray streets. Another image, a graphic intervention from the artist, creates a whirlpool in the center of this São Paulo microcosm. In one of Argentine writer Jorge Luis Borges's most famous stories, "The Aleph," a character finds an unassuming place in Buenos Aires—a cellar—to be the exact location in the cosmos in which all the variety of the universe is concentrated. "What eternity is to time, the Aleph is to space," Borges later wrote in a commentary on the story.

Loeb promotes her own "alephs," her suspensions in space, with modest resources: collages of hundreds of layered and slightly shifted individual images that create an illusory effect. She has marked the epiphanies that are within our reach at any time of the day, and anywhere in the city. Loeb's work shares points of interest with some other representations of São Paulo produced by an artist currently making waves on the Brazilian scene. Originally from the state of Paraná, Odires Mlászho has resided in São Paulo for decades and includes in his labyrinthine investigations of language and memory a series that redefines spaces emblematic of the megalopolis: Ibirapuera Park, or the Copan building. (It is not by chance

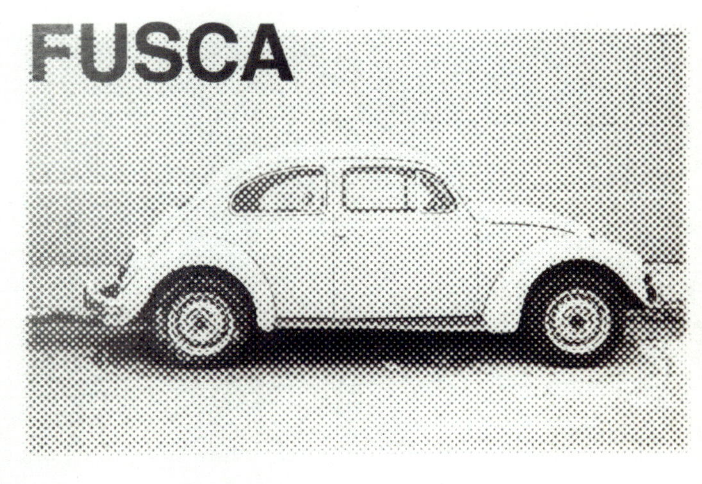

Erik van der Weijde,
Foto.zine nr.5–Fusca, 2013
Courtesy the artist

Photobooks have become precious records of the city's nuances and conflicts, the flux of its inhabitants, and its constituent parts—lampposts, houses, buildings, street signs, all rising from the asphalt.

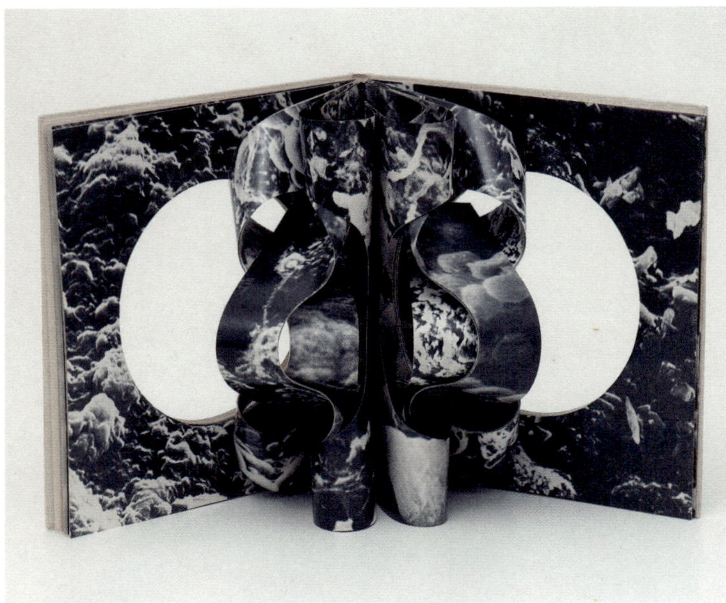

that both spaces have been transformed by Oscar Niemeyer.) Like Loeb, Mlászho uses simple resources—scraps of paper cut with scissors and combinations of the fragments of these images—to produce work that reflects on the chaos of the city as well as its eternal possibility of reinvention. As he demonstrated in the 2013 Venice Biennale, Mlászho has dedicated himself over the past decade to a universe equally dear to Loeb: that of books (at times intervening in well-known volumes), which in his case function as both a support and an object of art.

Also on the lineup of books-as-objects, a recent representative from São Paulo has been getting attention: Claudia Jaguaribe. One of the country's foremost photographers and author of photobooks such as *Aeroporto* (Airport), an investigation of the "non-places" where one waits while en route, and *Entre Morros* (Between hills), a trip through the most impossible angles in Rio de Janeiro, last year Jaguaribe completed a tour de force through the gigantism of São Paulo. *Sobre São Paulo* (Over São Paulo) is a printed, accordion-style book, roughly twenty meters long, that unfolds as a long sequence shot throughout the city. Photographed from helicopters in oblique view or taken from balconies (rather than from above, as in the lovely pictures by Cássio Vasconcellos gathered in the book *Panorâmicas* [Panoramics]), the images were subtly spliced together on the computer, creating a panel that softens the vision of what Caetano Veloso, in his classic song about São Paulo, calls "the hard concrete poetry of its street corners."

Jaguaribe's work evokes, in its own way, one of the most interesting portraits ever made of the city. Valério Vieira was one of the first big names in creative photography in the country. In 1922, in conjunction with the celebration of one hundred years of Brazil's independence from Portugal, Vieira produced a work titled "Panorama of São Paulo," the second or possibly third of his panoramic cityscapes. The panel, which depicts the city's downtown area in 180 degrees, was sixteen meters long and was considered at the time the largest printed photograph in the world.

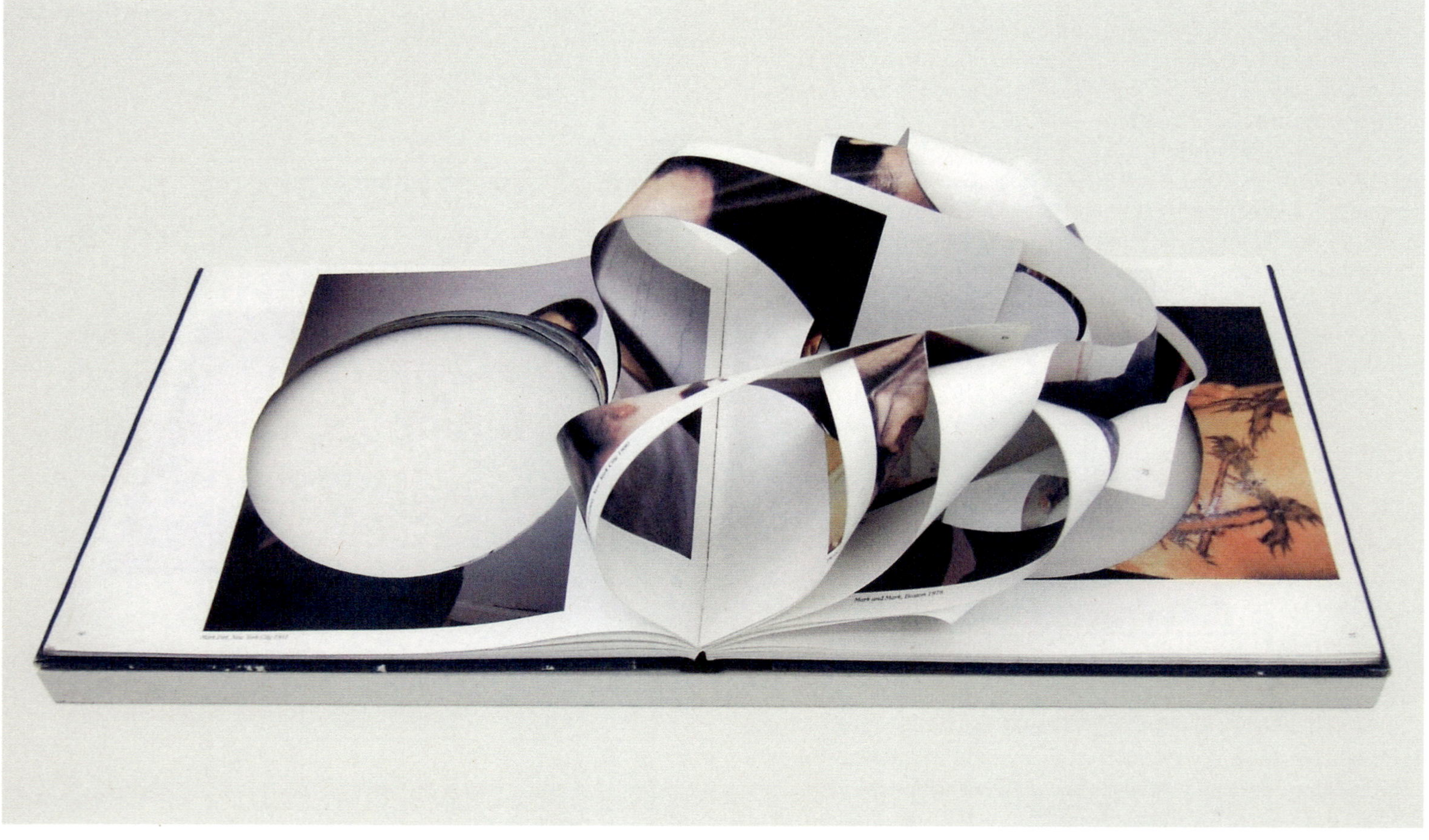

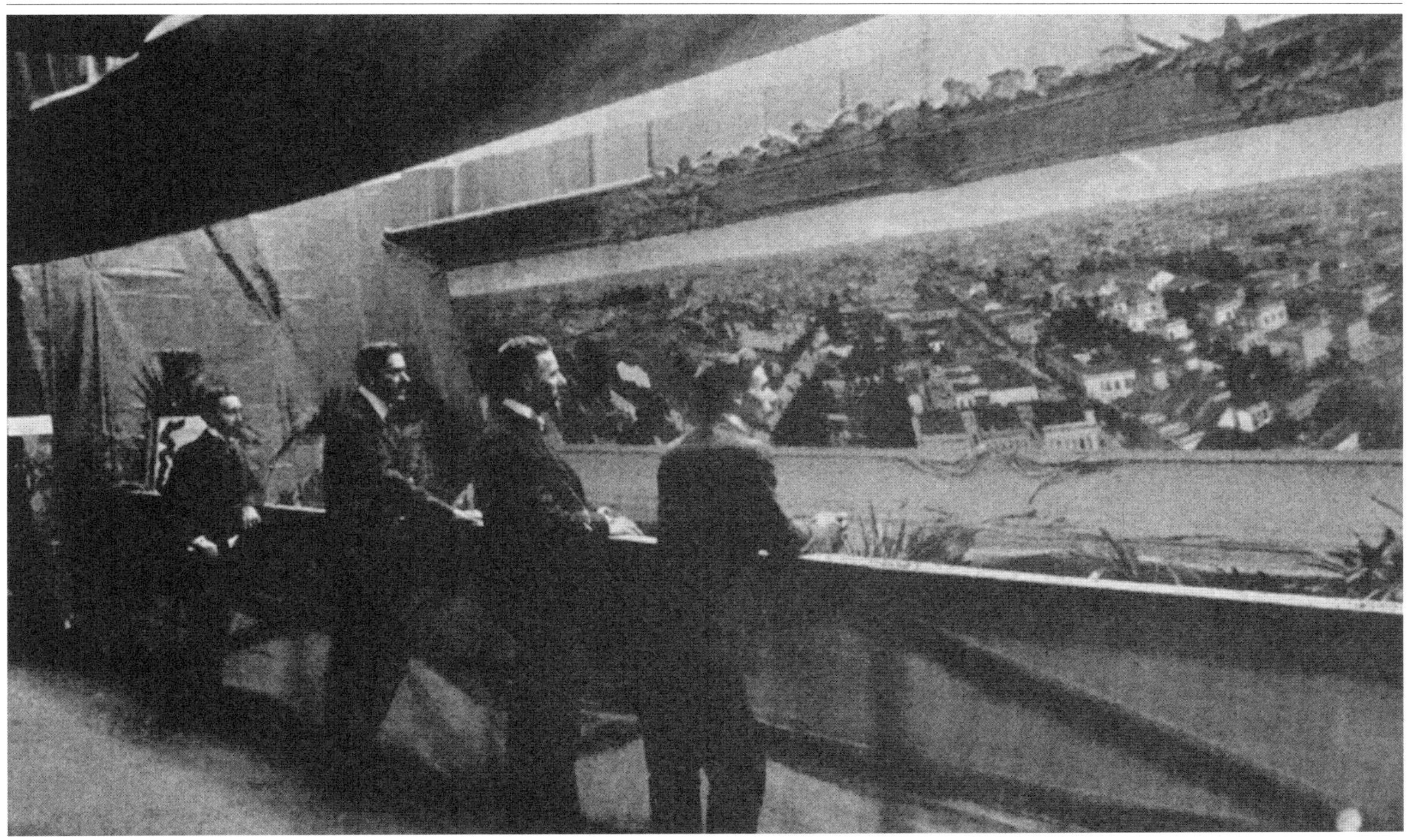

Installation view of
Valério Vieira's 1905
panorama of São Paulo,
on display at the Salão
Progredior (Progredior
Salon), São Paulo.
Photographer unknown
Courtesy Arquivo Histórico
da Inspetoria Salesiana de
Nossa Senhora Auxiliadora,
São Paulo

Loeb promotes her own "alephs," her suspensions in space, with modest resources: collages of hundreds of layered and slightly shifted individual images that create an illusory effect.

Before Vieira, there weren't many who dedicated themselves to creating panoramas of São Paulo. While the city's roots stretch back to 1554, a little more than fifty years after the arrival of the Portuguese to the lands that would later become Brazil, until the second half of the nineteenth century, the current gigantic metropolis called São Paulo was no more than a village. Even though diverse painters and early pioneers of photography portrayed the city throughout those periods, it was a native of Rio de Janeiro—a *carioca*, Militão Augusto de Azevedo—who first dedicated himself to systematically documenting São Paulo's transformation into a modern city in his *Álbum comparativo da Cidade de São Paulo 1862/1887* (Comparative album of the city of São Paulo 1862/1887). Other photographers in the twentieth century would follow—Aurélio Becherini and Guilherme Gaensly in the twenties, and later Thomaz Farkas and German Lorca in the forties and fifties, to cite only a few who produced their own explorations of the city. The echoes of this tradition have grown louder, as these recent works by Loeb, van der Weijde, Jaguaribe, and Mlászho reiterate: In cities such as São Paulo, there are countless worlds, profusions of them. They are quick and ephemeral, but photobooks come close to achieving the impossible task of capturing them.

Cassiano Elek Machado is editor-at-large for the daily newspaper *Folha de São Paulo*. Previously he was editorial director at the publishing house Cosac Naify and a reporter for the cultural magazine *piauí*. He lives in São Paulo.

A new network of independent exhibition venues, residencies, and galleries has emerged in São Paulo, reshaping the landscape for photographers.

Support Structure

Silas Martí

"Only now do I understand how this place works—you start to feel it with your body," says Fernanda Brenner, founder and director of Pivô, a gallery and artist residency that opened a year ago. She is sitting on a sofa that just arrived, a gift from an architect, as she watches artists and staff go about their business, carrying crates and works of art around this gigantic empty floor of the Oscar Niemeyer–designed Copan, a towering residential building, home to thousands in downtown São Paulo. "The most urgent thing this city needs is spaces for people to meet, to become more involved with what they're doing."

Pivô is helping to fill the gap, leading the way in the burgeoning art and photography scene of South America's biggest metropolis. Spaces like this once-abandoned floor, along with other (generally smaller) studios across town, in the artsy Vila Madalena district and in former industrial areas like Barra Funda, now make up a growing network of alternative studios, galleries, and residencies that support emerging photographers by mounting exhibitions and publishing books that promote their work.

Opposite:
Views of Pivô, an independent art space inside the Copan building, São Paulo, 2014
Photographs by Ricardo Bassetti

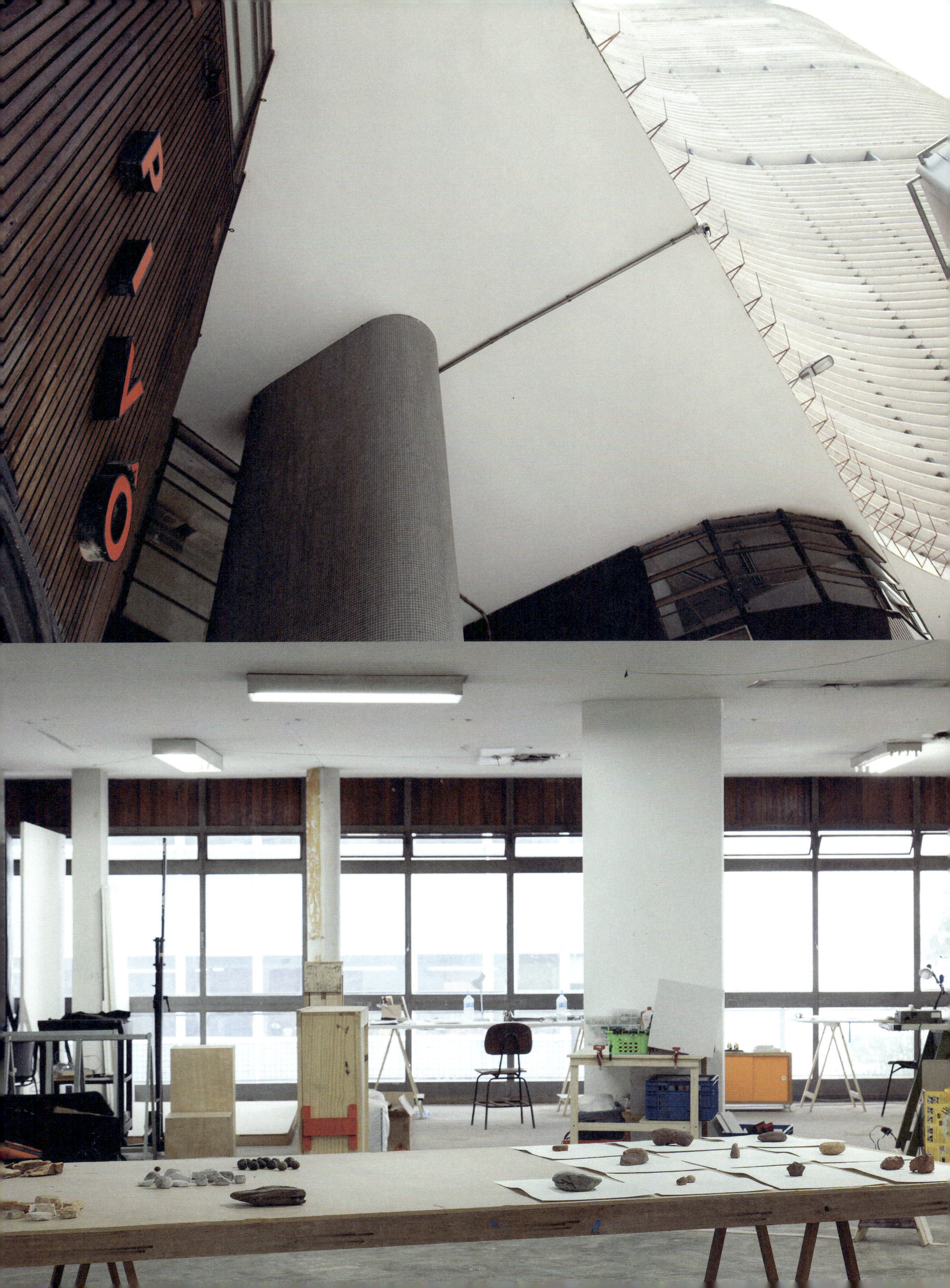
PILÓ

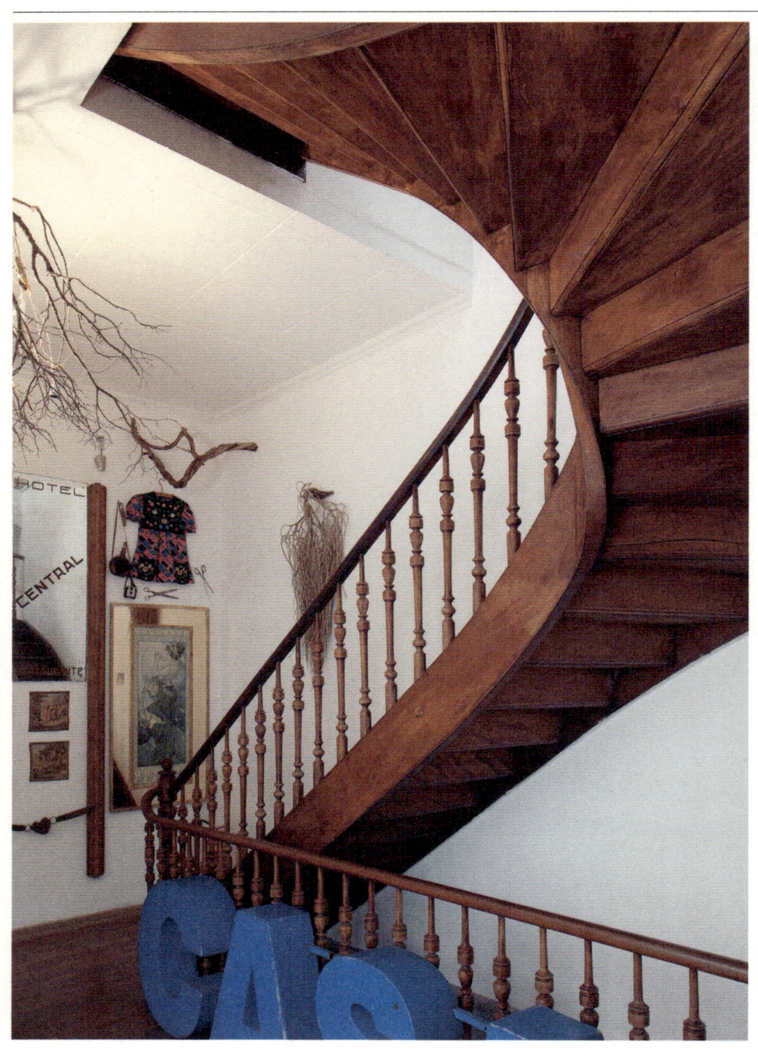

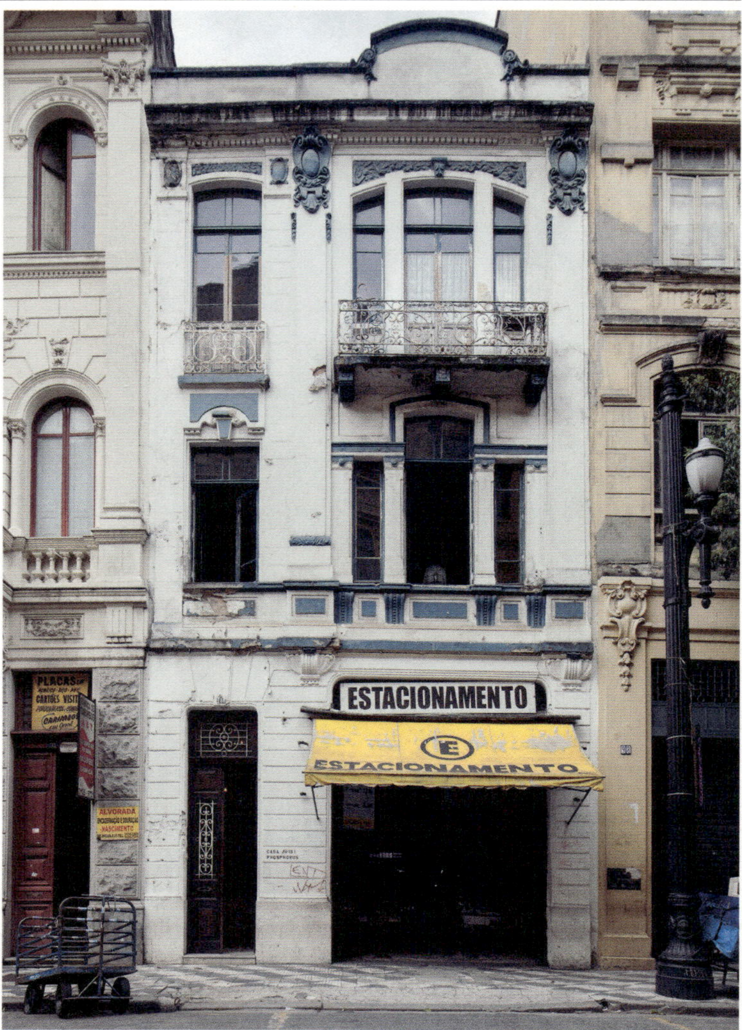

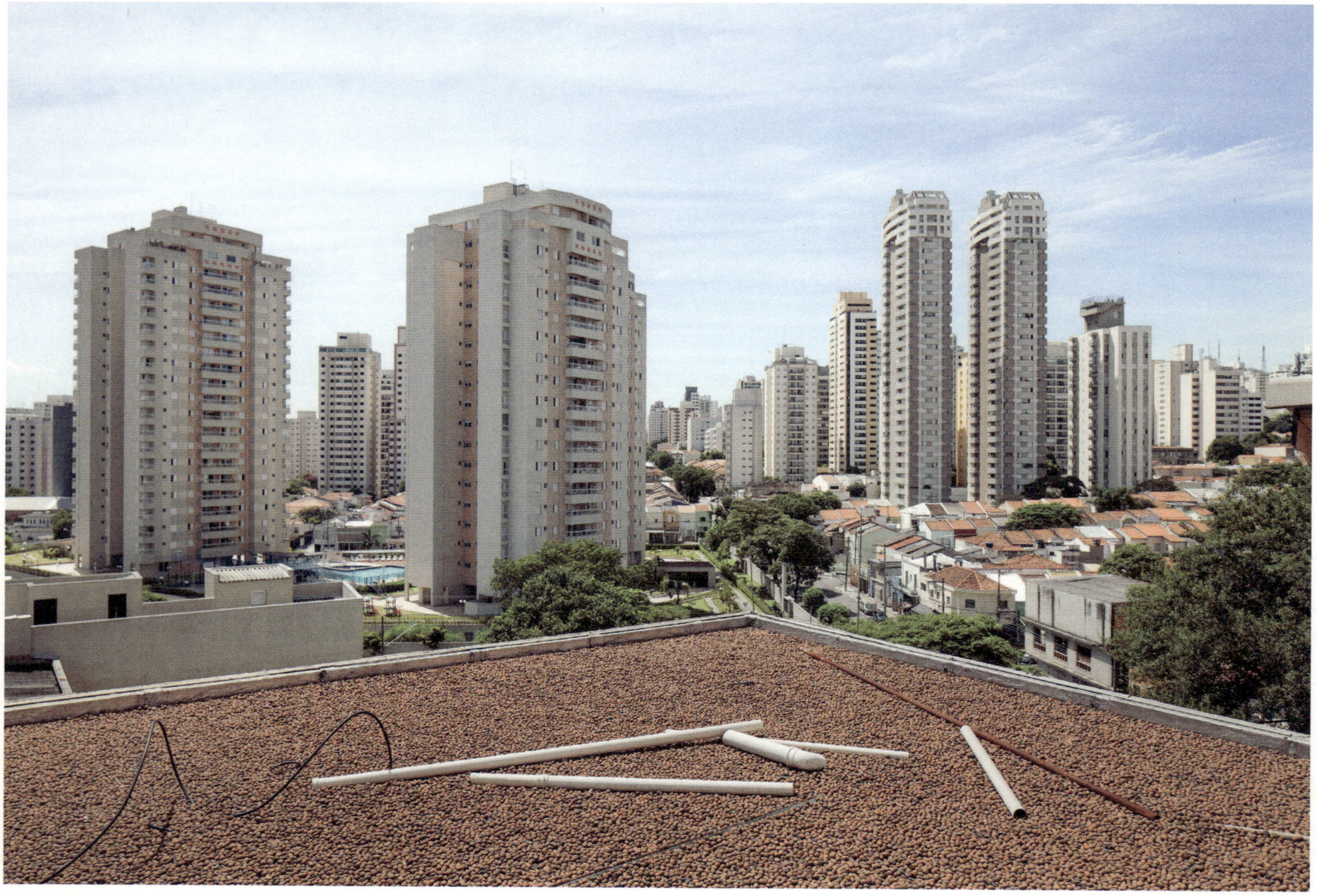

Brenner, a twenty-seven-year-old artist who has devoted
the past three years of her life to this massive undertaking, has
secured just enough funding to keep Pivô open for another year,
a victory for any independent space in Brazil. She says now
the place will be able to welcome up to twenty artists at a time,
with a new library and a whole floor dedicated to research. "It's a
support structure for artists," she says. "That's the true vocation
of this place."

While photography is not its specific focus, two recent
projects put Pivô at the forefront of the scene. Luiza Baldan's
latest series, in which she photographed the "guts" of Copan,
as Brenner puts it, resulted from a time the artist spent living in
that very building, four floors above the gallery, and documenting
her every step—an allusion to the fact that Copan is one of the
most photographed buildings in the country. Another was Letícia
Ramos's hybrid project, in which a photographic series she
made in Antarctica gave way to a performance, film, and a book,
all developed within the walls of Pivô. "It was a project that
evolved here," says Brenner. "It's expanded photography."

Not far from Pivô, toward the heart of the city, is Phosphorus,
a space concerned mostly with installation-based projects.
Occupying an old house built in 1890, just steps away from the
Pátio do Colégio, a Jesuit school whose inauguration in 1554
marked the birth of São Paulo, this independent venue is devoted
to temporary exhibitions of works created and developed on site.
In another example of expanded photography, Maria Montero,
a former exhibition producer and curator who founded the
space, has invited the artist Raquel Uendi to develop her work
at Phosphorus, a mix of sculpture and photography in which
pictures appear to merge with layers of broken glass.

The next project at Montero's gallery will also involve a
photographer. She plans to host Dalton Paula's first São Paulo
exhibition in the coming months. A fireman and artist who lives
in Goiânia, in central Brazil, he has created a series of photographs,
videos, and performances in which he discusses the thorny issue
of race in a country that prides itself on its ethnic diversity. This
will be the first in a sequence of shows Montero wants to stage
that don't adhere to the space's mission, since they aren't directly
connected to São Paulo. But three years after Phosphorus opened,
its founder is ready to grow and take on new challenges.

In a similar spirit of embracing change, the artist collective
Luzia just moved to a new space in Vila Romana, a neighborhood
on the west side of São Paulo that has become a new hub for
artists because of its cheap studio spaces. Their new venue isn't
as spacious as the warehouse they used to occupy in the same
part of town, but it burned down in a fire, and they were forced
to move. The small rooms of the top floor of an apartment block
now serve as headquarters—and an informal beer brewery—
for the group of three photographers. Luzia's work is gaining
recognition for its guerrilla photographic interventions—they
enlarge pictures to fit entire walls, then paste them in tunnels and
along sidewalks. One of their projects involved photographing
the improvised architecture of Brazilian slums and posting them
on blank façades in more privileged areas of town.

"We are really using the city as a gallery," says Paulo
Pereira, one of the artists in Luzia. Pedro Matallo, also in the
group, defines their work as "a philosophy of life," meaning that
photographing and displaying their work around town gives
them a reason to wake up in the morning. Matallo says he and
his friends decided to found Luzia because they missed "talking
more about life instead of theories and academic concepts."

Indeed, real life trumped ivory-tower theories throughout
São Paulo this past year, with millions of people taking to the
streets in a massive wave of protests against corruption. A little
gallery above a popular bar in Vila Madalena saw the uprisings as

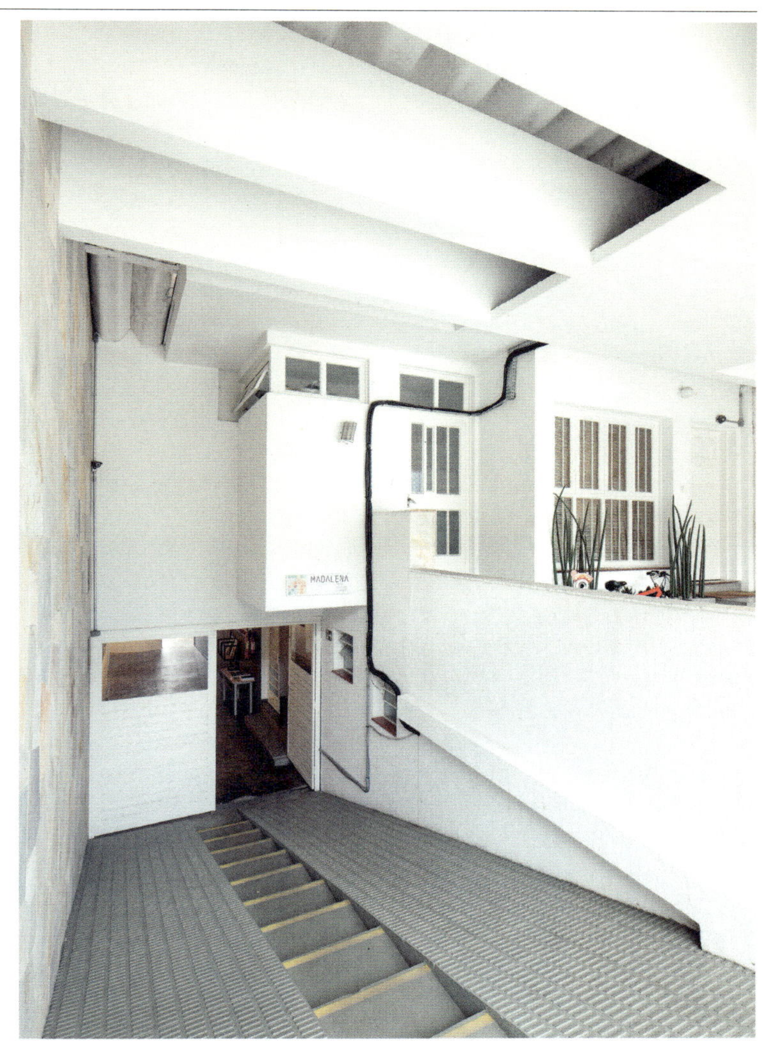

Entrance to Estúdio
Madalena, a hybrid studio
space and venue in the Vila
Madalena neighborhood,
São Paulo, 2014
Photograph by Tuca Vieira

"The most urgent thing this city needs is spaces for people to meet, to become more involved with what they're doing."

Opposite, top:
Views of Phosphorus,
an art space in the center
of São Paulo, 2014
Photographs by
Ricardo Bassetti

Bottom: Rooftop of
the Luzia collective
headquarters in
the Vila Romana
neighborhood,
São Paulo, 2014
Photograph by Tuca Vieira

a chance to expand their activities and created a group of twenty-eight photographers who documented nearly every moment of the riots around town. Doc, the two-year-old space that until the protests only represented photojournalists, became a prototype and hub for photography done in real time on the streets of the city, and is hosting a series of workshops by Magnum Photos this year.

Like Luzia, the Doc crew also displays their work on walls all over the neighborhood. "We really occupy the streets here," says Fernando Costa Netto, Doc's founder and director. "And it seems people have gotten past the strangeness of a little gallery hidden above a bar and now see us as an influential space for photography. Whenever someone thinks of this kind of work, our telephone rings."

A few blocks away, telephones are also ringing off the hook at Estúdio Madalena. This hybrid studio space (which doubles as a big production company) is responsible for staging the Paraty em Foco festival, an annual event at the old colonial town outside Rio de Janeiro known for organizing a series of major exhibitions in the houses around town and for workshops with some of the most recognized names in photography worldwide, such as Cristina De Middel, Rinko Kawauchi, and Pieter Hugo. They also organize courses and edit books suggested by their students—such as *Desaudio*, Lucas Lenci's vibrant depiction of seventeen silent urban and rural landscapes around the world—encouraging and embodying what founder and curator Iatã Cannabrava calls a "living body of people and their actions." If an idea worth publishing comes up in the classroom, Cannabrava offers their aptly named "John Malkovich room"— a space with a low ceiling that houses all the printing and editing equipment—for artists to work.

These titles, when finished, end up in the library that today has about nine hundred books available for consultation. "Our idea is to welcome researchers and photographers," says Cannabrava. "We have all the rare stuff, everything that's being talked about now and sometimes things that will soon become famous." Working on all fronts, from curating to book editing, Cannabrava says the Estúdio Madalena model has given them great agility and efficiency in a scene often hindered by the bureaucratic system of grants and endowments in the country. "This is an excellent moment," he says. "We managed to pull together the institutions, the businessmen, and the art collectives."

While Estúdio Madalena and Doc have championed more traditional models anchored in exhibitions and books, Pivô and Phosphorus, together with a string of new galleries, such as Fauna, Fass, and Ímã, are introducing new ways of supporting and exhibiting photographers in São Paulo's rich artistic landscape. There is a clear opposition between a more traditional documentary school of photography—which takes after the work of figures like Sebastião Salgado, known for his dramatic black-and-white photographs of natural and social landscapes around the world—and a more experimental approach, mainly influenced by the bold work of Miguel Rio Branco, a virtuoso of color whose deeply saturated images often depict underground characters from various places, including Brazil's Bahia region and Tokyo. But between the detached and austere aesthetic of the documentary-oriented and the more visceral energy of the experimental crowd, there seems to be a place for everyone in this new wave of photographic spaces in São Paulo.

Silas Martí is a journalist and art critic based in São Paulo. He is the staff writer for visual arts and architecture at the *Folha de São Paulo* newspaper.

Pictures

Caio Reisewitz,
Casa Rua Santa Cruz
(House on Santa Cruz
Street), 2013
© Caio Reisewitz and
courtesy Luciana Brito
Galeria, São Paulo

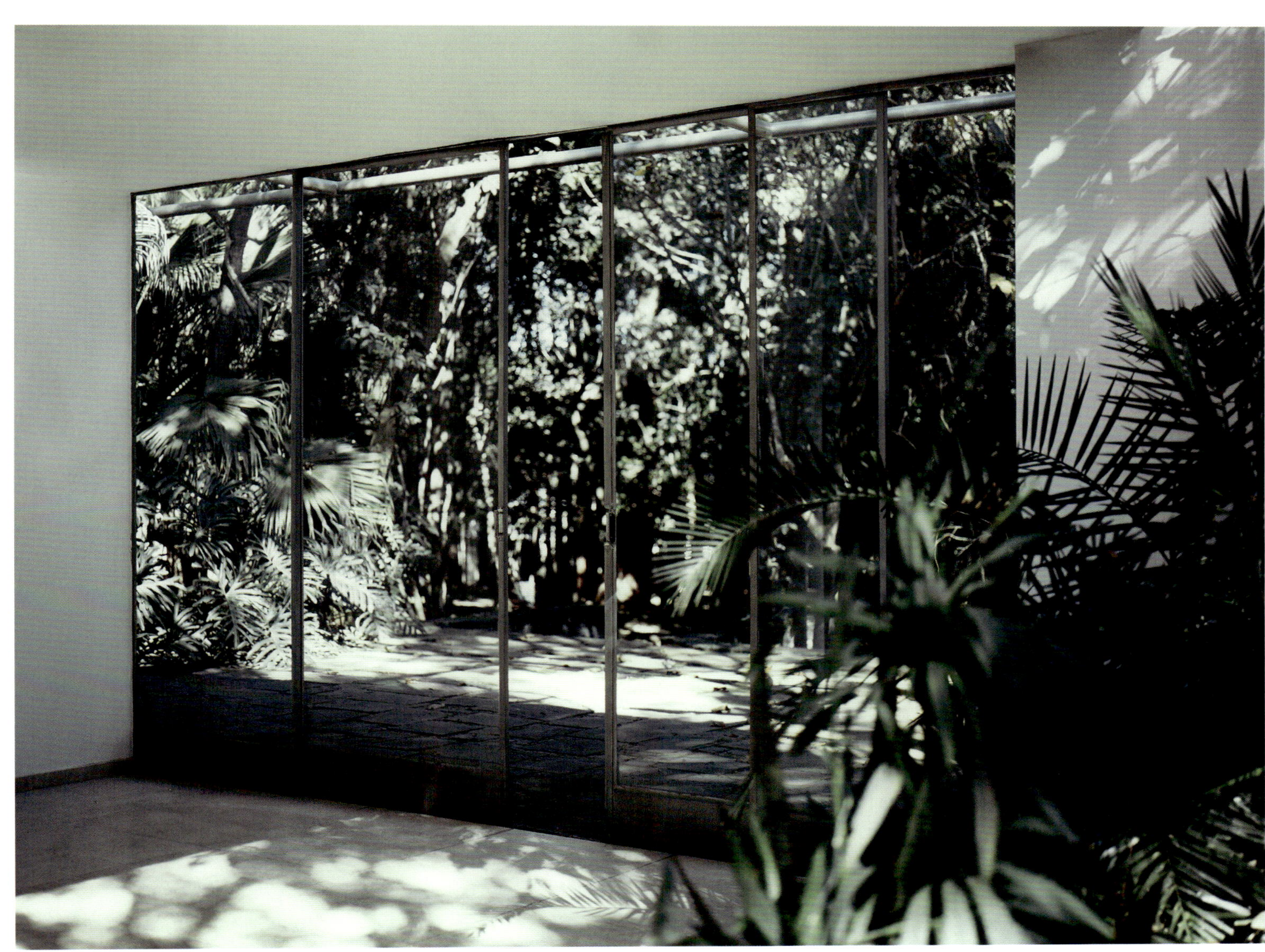

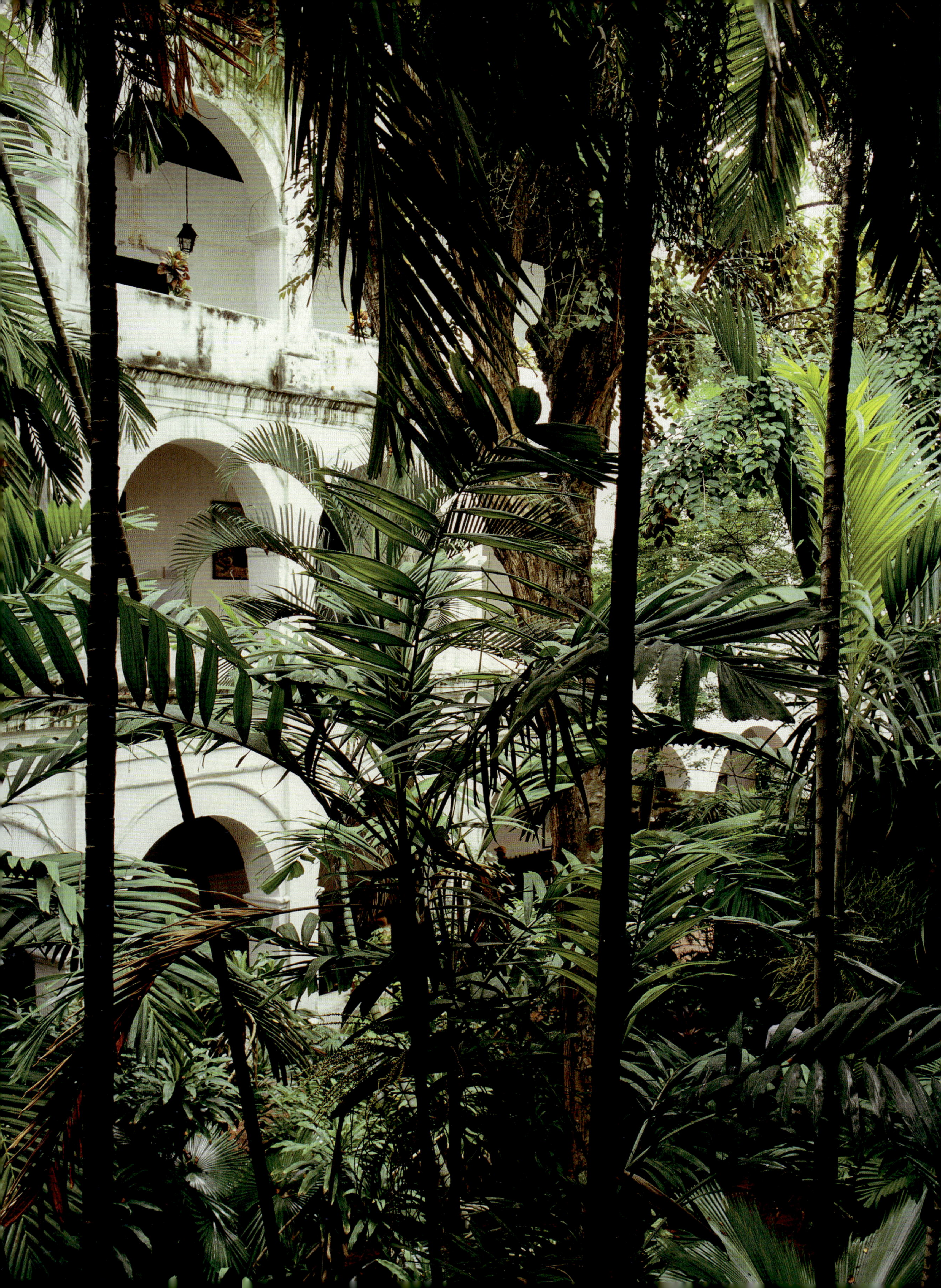

Since returning to São Paulo in 1997 after studies in Germany, Caio Reisewitz has won an international reputation as one of Brazil's most significant photographers. His admiration for members of the Düsseldorf School such as Thomas Struth, Candida Höfer, and Andreas Gursky is evident in the meticulous accuracy of his monumental color photographs, yet his concentration on the landscape and architecture of Brazil lends his work a distinctive and immediately recognizable character. Reisewitz's images offer a sustained reflection on the struggle between primeval nature and the voracious human appetite to exploit it that has marked Brazil's history since colonial times. The title he chose for his presentation in the Brazilian pavilion at the 2005 Venice Biennale, "Threatened Utopia," signals the key preoccupation of his work.

The dense rainforest settings of many of Reisewitz's photographs have led some viewers to assume that he specializes in scenes from the Amazon region. In fact, most of his landscape photographs are made within a few hundred miles of São Paulo, a silver-white skyscraper city surrounded by an immense, verdant tropical forest. Reisewitz regards the still-extensive remnants of the Mata Atlântica (Atlantic Forest) that once filled Brazil's east coast as a natural wonderland, and he marvels that it is virtually unknown to São Paulo's twenty million urban dwellers. The relation of city and country-side in Brazil today could be described as one of close physical proximity and surprising psychological distance.

Often Reisewitz's photographs recall the extraordinary abundance of Brazil's natural environment and the history of its domestication for cropland, ranching, and mining. *Boituva* (2008) presents a close-up view of a patch of the famous red clay soil that eighteenth-century colonists discovered to be ideally suited for coffee cultivation. In *Cubatão II* (2003), we look down on a ribbonlike highway slicing through an otherwise pristine vista of mountain forests. *Itaquaquecetuba* (2004) shows a green hilltop set ablaze as part of a land-clearing operation. Such images register the current state of Brazil's breakneck quest for economic development and pinpoint the global environmental dangers posed by the wholesale destruction of Brazil's forests.

Reisewitz's work has recently moved in surprising new directions, notably in a series of small, handmade photo collages that extend his exploration of the tension between the city and the countryside. Visually more playful than his view-camera photographs, these works sometimes contain lyrically curving cutouts that echo the exuberant visual rhythms found in Brazilian modernist art and architecture of the 1960s. These collage experiments have led Reisewitz to new ways of conceiving his view-camera photographs. His latest large-format works often employ a dense visual layering, as in *Santuário San Pedro Claver III, Cartagena de Índias* (San Pedro Claver III monastery, Cartagena) (2007), in which elusive architectural details can be glimpsed through a tangled skein of tree branches and plant forms.

The city in the forest, and the forest in the city—this is the metaphor that currently drives much of Reisewitz's work. It underlies his photographs of Brazil's iconic modernist residences, such as that of the 1928 Casa Modernista by émigré Russian architect Gregori Warchavchik, *Casa Rua Santa Cruz* (House on Santa Cruz Street) (2013), and of the 1951 Glass House by Lina Bo Bardi, both located in São Paulo. It is probably most evident, however, in his photograph *Casa Canoas* (Canoas House) (2013), which provides a fresh look at the legendary minimalist-style house that Brazilian architect Oscar Niemeyer built for himself in 1951 on the outskirts of Rio de Janeiro. As Reisewitz portrays it, the glass-walled house all but disappears amid the luxuriant vegetation that presses in on all sides. At the same time, the building's elongated and sensuously curving white roof seems to reach out to embrace the forest. In images like this, Reisewitz holds onto the hope that nature and human culture may yet share common ground in Brazil.

Caio Reisewitz

Christopher Phillips

Christopher Phillips, a curator at the International Center of Photography in New York, organized the exhibition *Caio Reisewitz*, on view at ICP from May 16 to September 7, 2014.

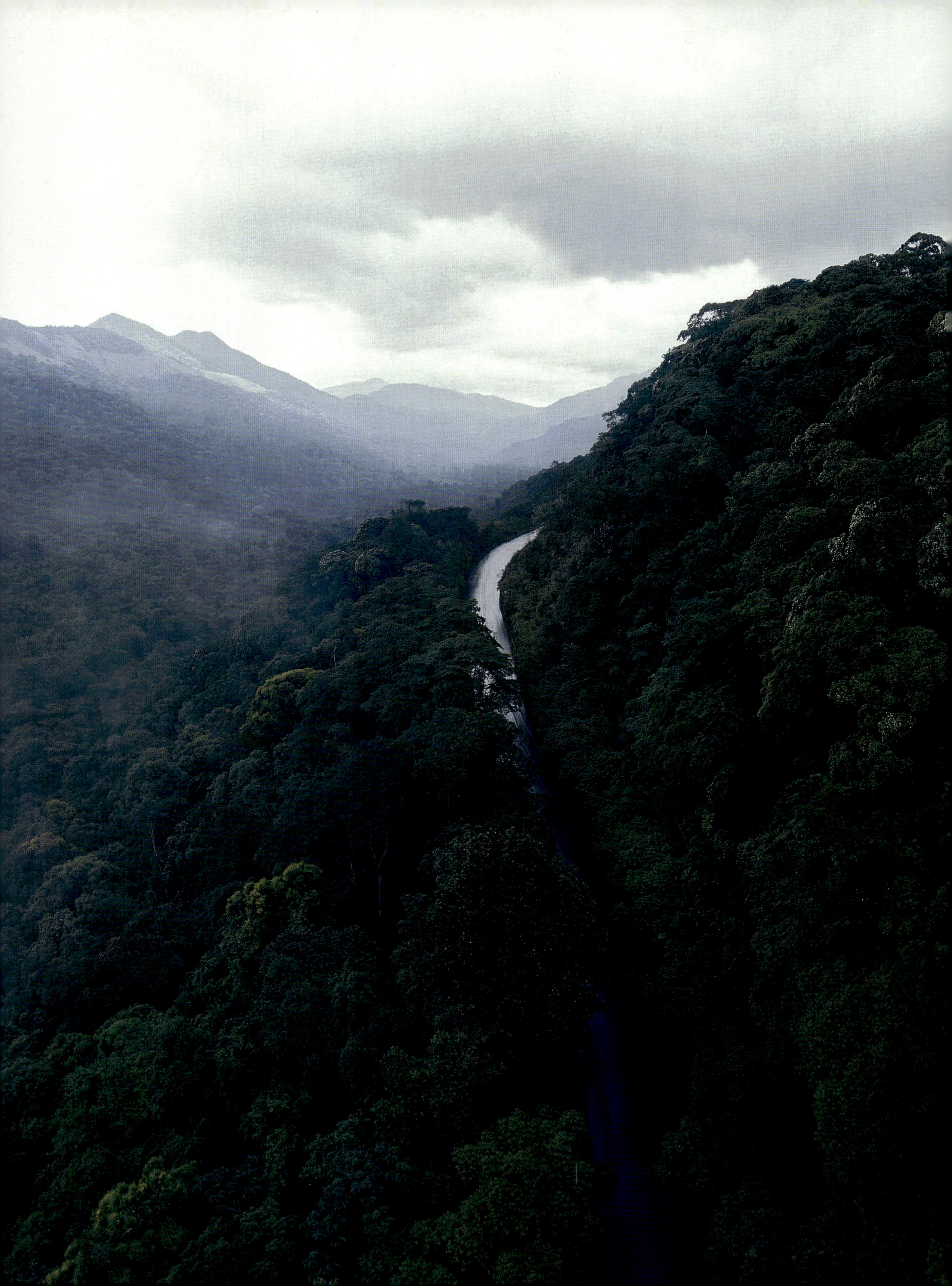

Opposite:
Cubatão II, 2003

This page:
Itaquaquecetuba, 2004

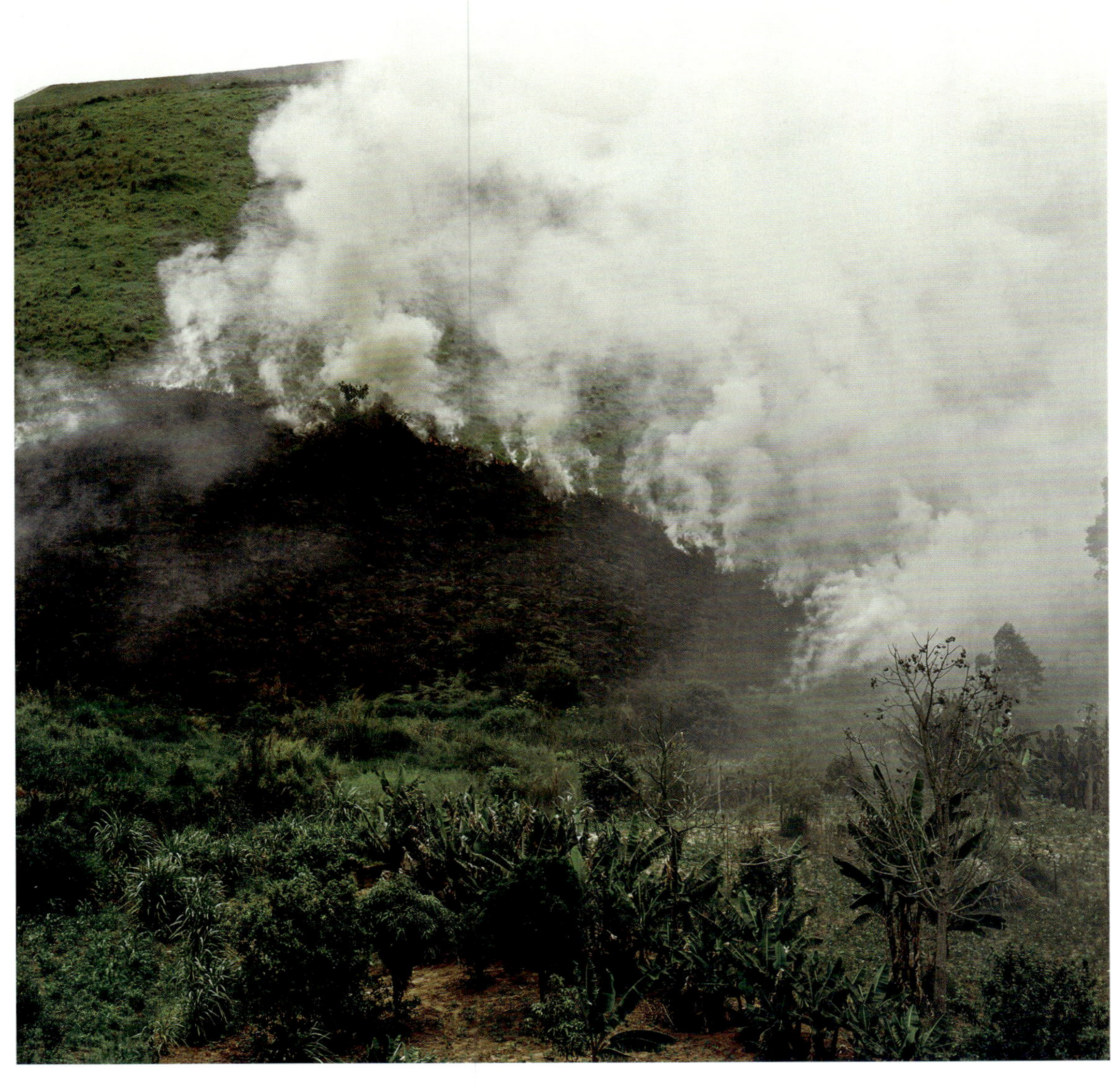

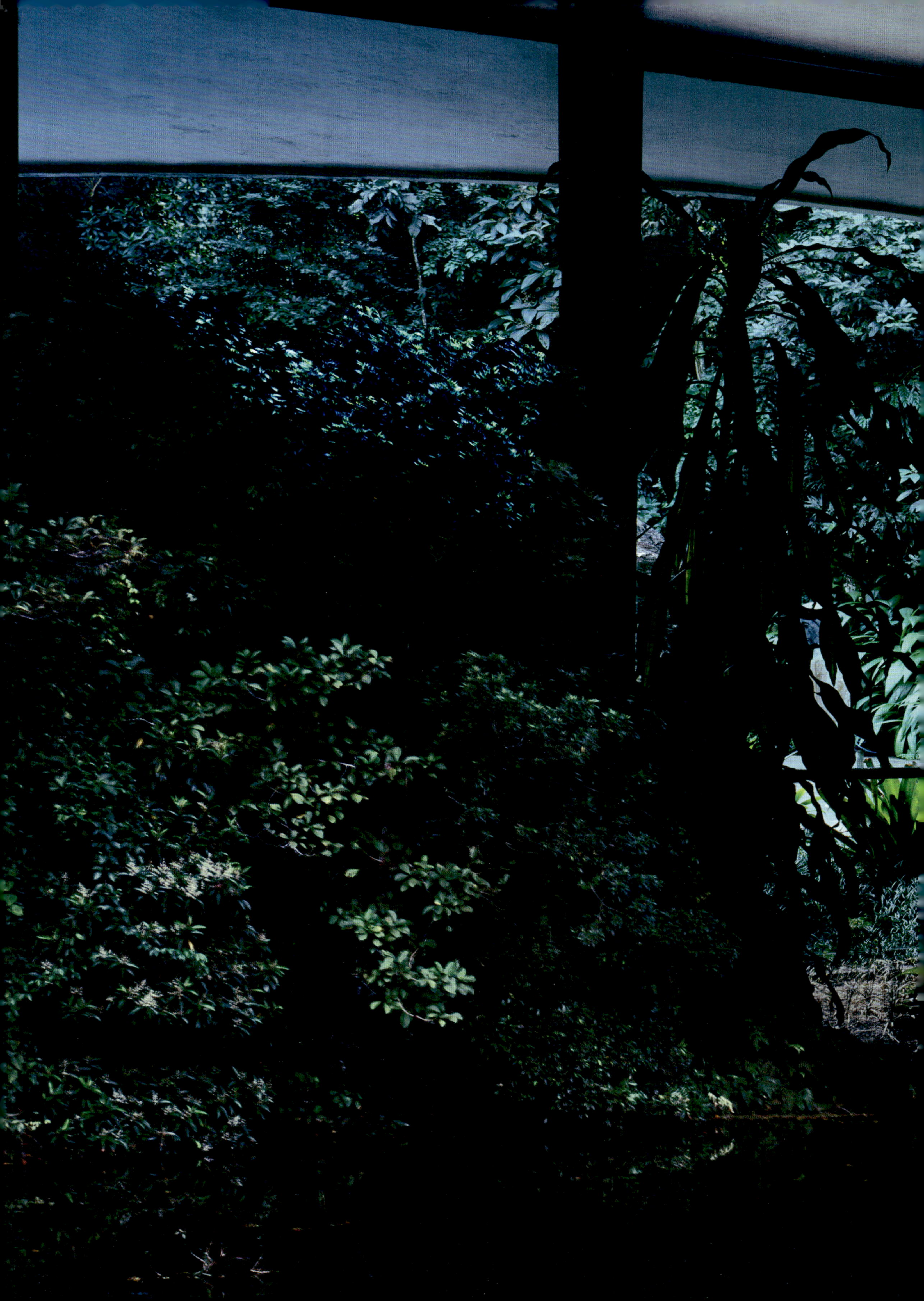

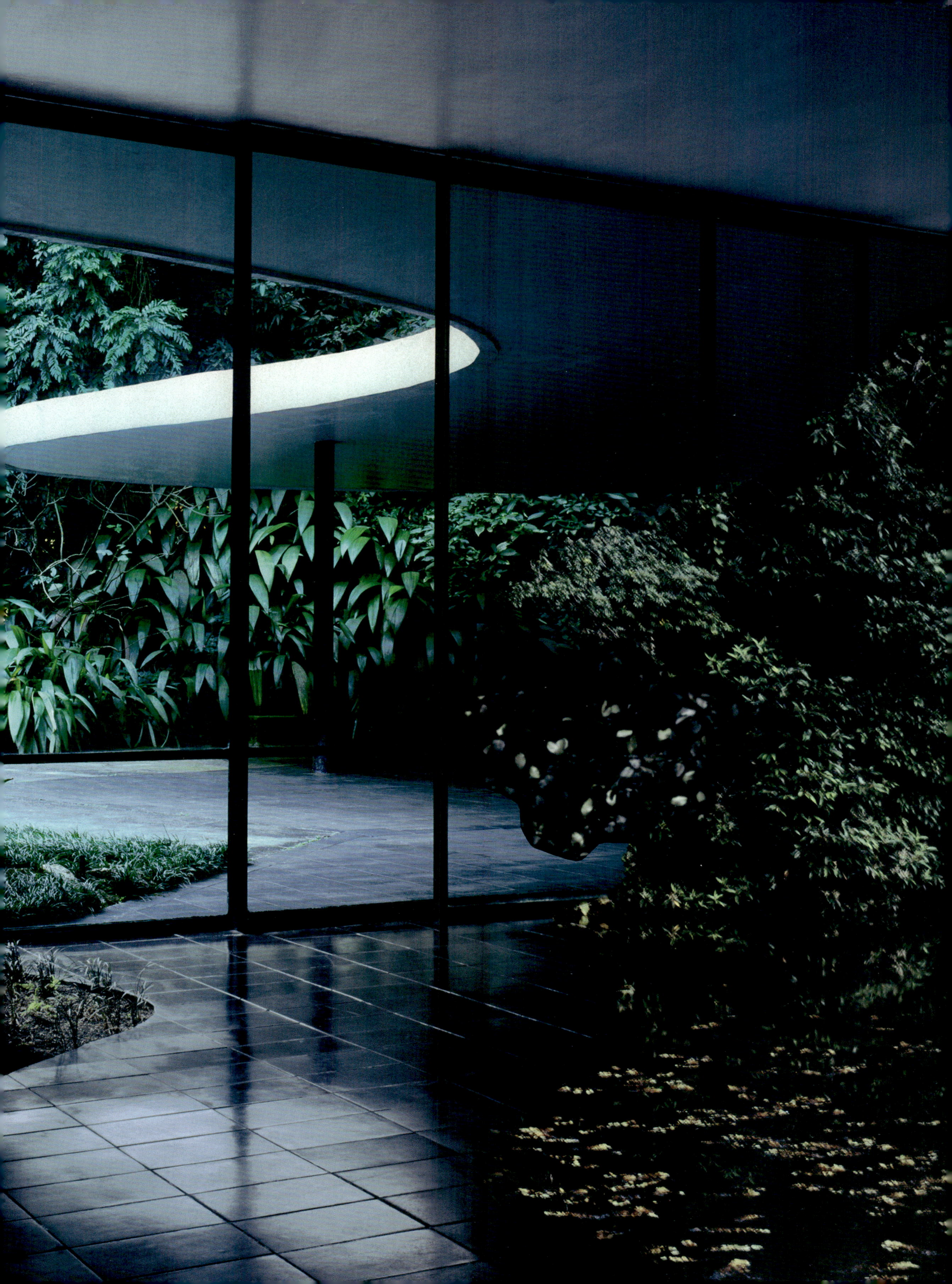

Previous pages:
Casa Canoas
(Canoas House), 2013

This page:
Diadema, 2004

Opposite:
Boituva, 2008
All photographs
© Caio Reisewitz and
courtesy Luciana Brito
Galeria, São Paulo

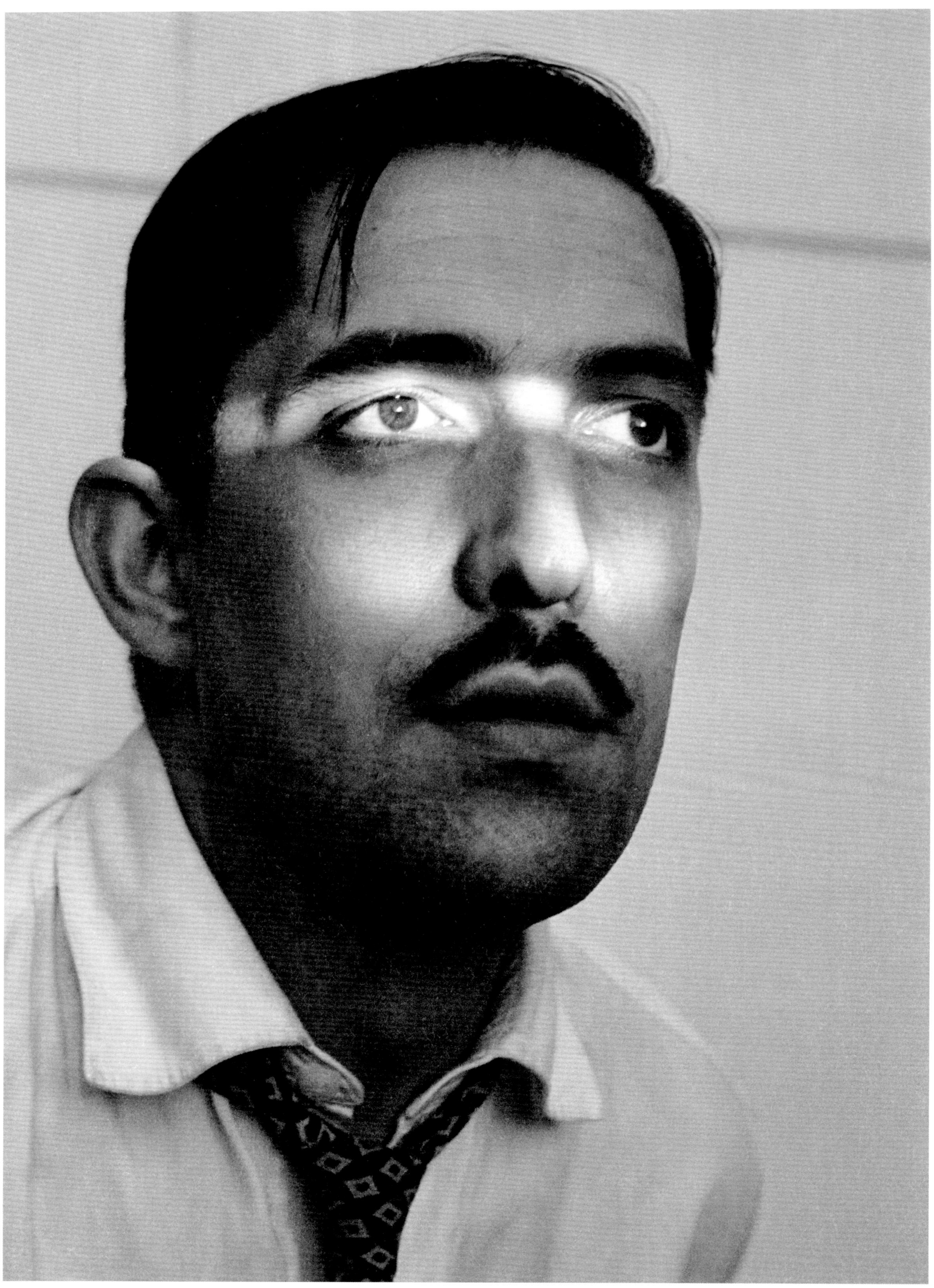

The photographs of Geraldo de Barros do not represent an exact mirror image of the city of São Paulo, yet they do echo, as few others have, the vertiginous growth of the metropolis after 1945. The repeated insertion of shafts of light superimposed in his *Fotoformas* seems to reflect the constant movement of bodies and the accelerated pace that began to characterize the city in modern times.

A painter and designer linked to Brazil's Concretist art movement, de Barros devoted himself to photography during two periods of his professional career: Between 1946 and 1951 he created his *Fotoformas* (Photoforms), which evolved from his own discovery of modern art; and between 1996 and 1998, during the final years of his life, he immersed himself in his archive of family photographs to develop the series *Sobras* (Leftovers). The *Fotoformas* series represents a pivotal landmark in the history of modern photography in Brazil. Aside from pioneering the use of abstract photography, de Barros also developed a range of technical procedures combining superimposition, cropping, montage, and the scoring of negatives. Created in tandem with his work in painting, engraving, and design, his *Fotoformas* also reveal an impressive and varied range of references, which include Paul Klee, Picasso, Moholy-Nagy, Mondrian, Max Bill, Jean Dubuffet, and Brassaï. His investigative spirit reflected the rapid internationalization of São Paulo's art scene, which was fostered by the inaugurations of the São Paulo Museum of Art (1947), São Paulo Museum of Modern Art (1948), and the São Paulo International Biennial (1951), institutions that helped to quickly transform the city into Latin America's main cultural center. The *Fotoformas* also positioned Brazilian photography at the cutting edge, in line with various developments in postwar Europe, such as the German group Fotoform headed by Otto Steinert.

The mechanical and reproducible nature of photography opened de Barros's eyes to the utopian possibilities of fusing art and industry through design. After his initial experiences with photography, he began focusing his efforts on painting and furniture design. During the 1950s, he began designing furniture at Unilabor, a socialist cooperative outfit that had tremendous commercial success. In the 1960s and '70s, he created furniture and advertising campaigns for his own factory, Hobjeto, which went on to become one of the foremost furniture enterprises in Brazil. Applying many of the concepts espoused in the 1920s by the Bauhaus school, de Barros produced modules that could be assembled to suit customers' needs. The modular format was central to his own poetic vision and can be seen in the repetition of various elements in his photography and painting. His commitment to the streamlined methods needed for the mass production of objects of impeccable aesthetic standards never impinged on his own very demanding creative processes.

De Barros returned to photography in the late 1990s, due in part to a series of local and international exhibitions that brought his *Fotoformas* images out of storage, where they had remained for decades. After suffering a series of strokes that greatly limited his movements, he astonished the art world with the appearance of his *Sobras*, images based on personal archival photography. The artist once again demonstrated his connection with contemporary trends at a time when photography began to emerge as a medium that questioned the very nature of its identity. With the help of an assistant who cropped and mounted fragments of negatives, he created black-and-white swaths that were intended to represent memory lapses, thus liberating his work from any documentary function while also resembling engraving or design. His *Sobras* images reflect the artist's ability to reinvent photography and himself in the process.

Geraldo de Barros

Heloísa Espada

Heloísa Espada is an art historian and curator. She is organizing a retrospective of Geraldo de Barros's photographs that will be presented at the Instituto Moreira Salles, Rio de Janeiro, in October 2014.

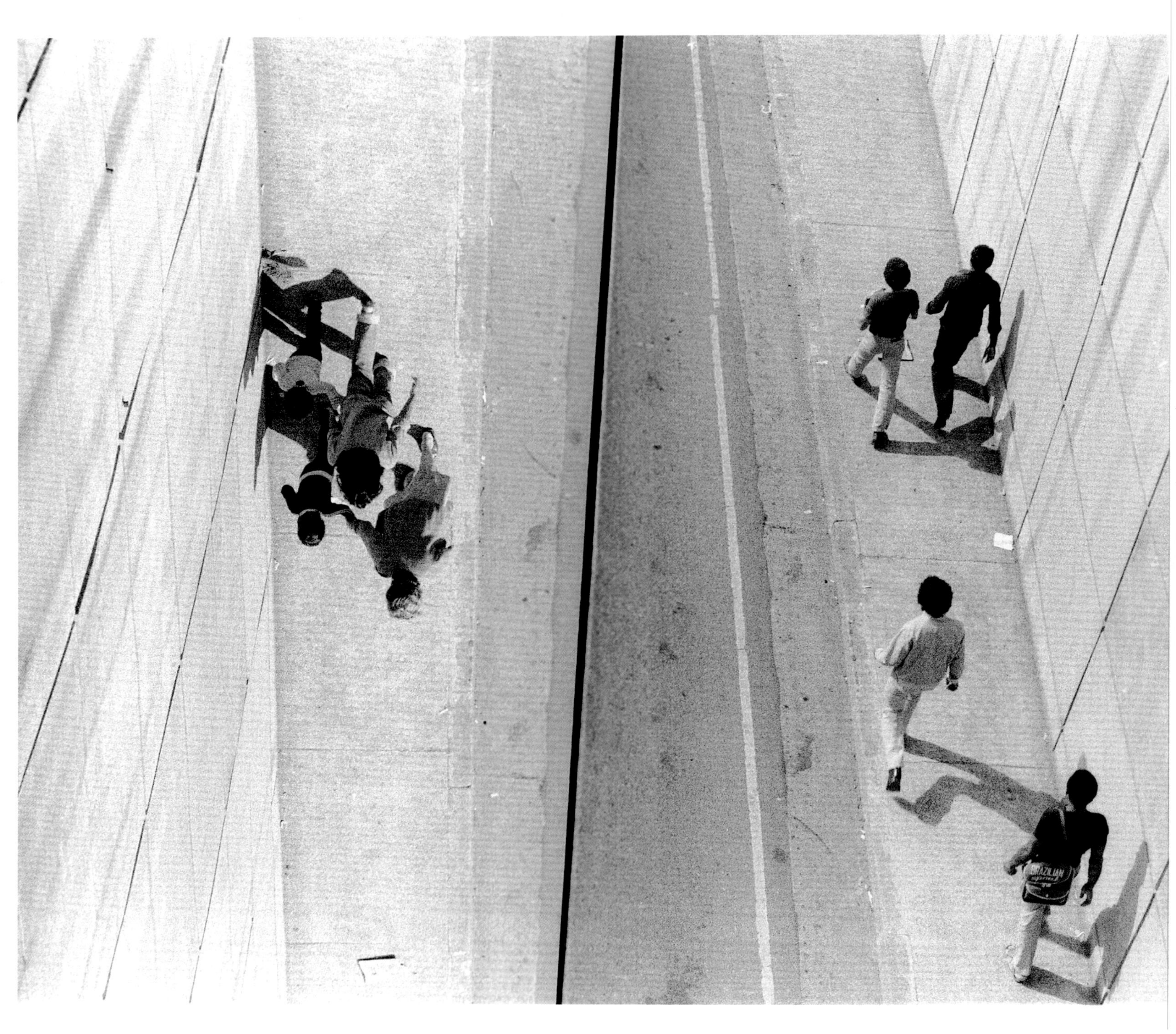

Sobras (Leftovers), 1996–98

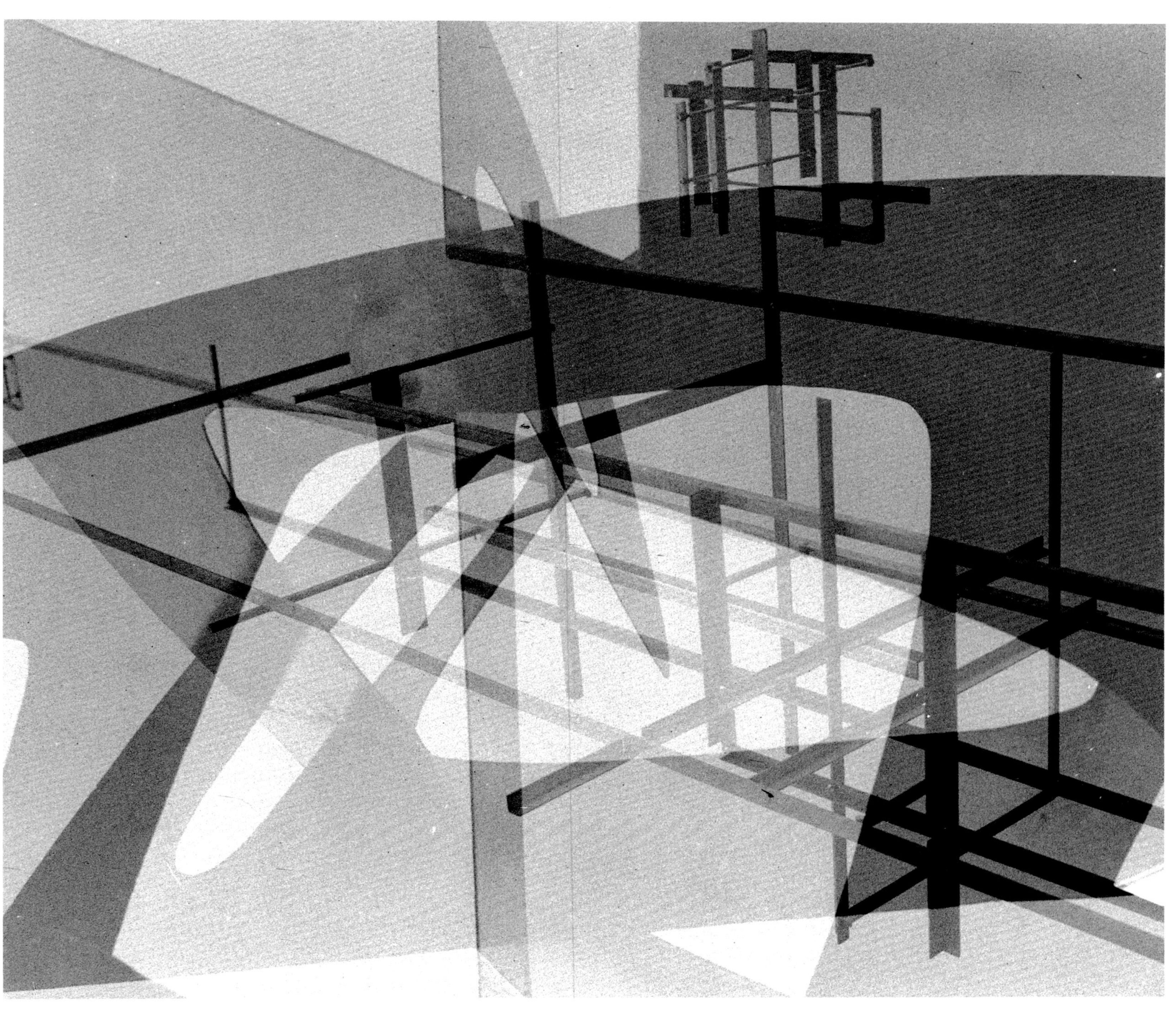

Fotoforma (Photoform),
1949

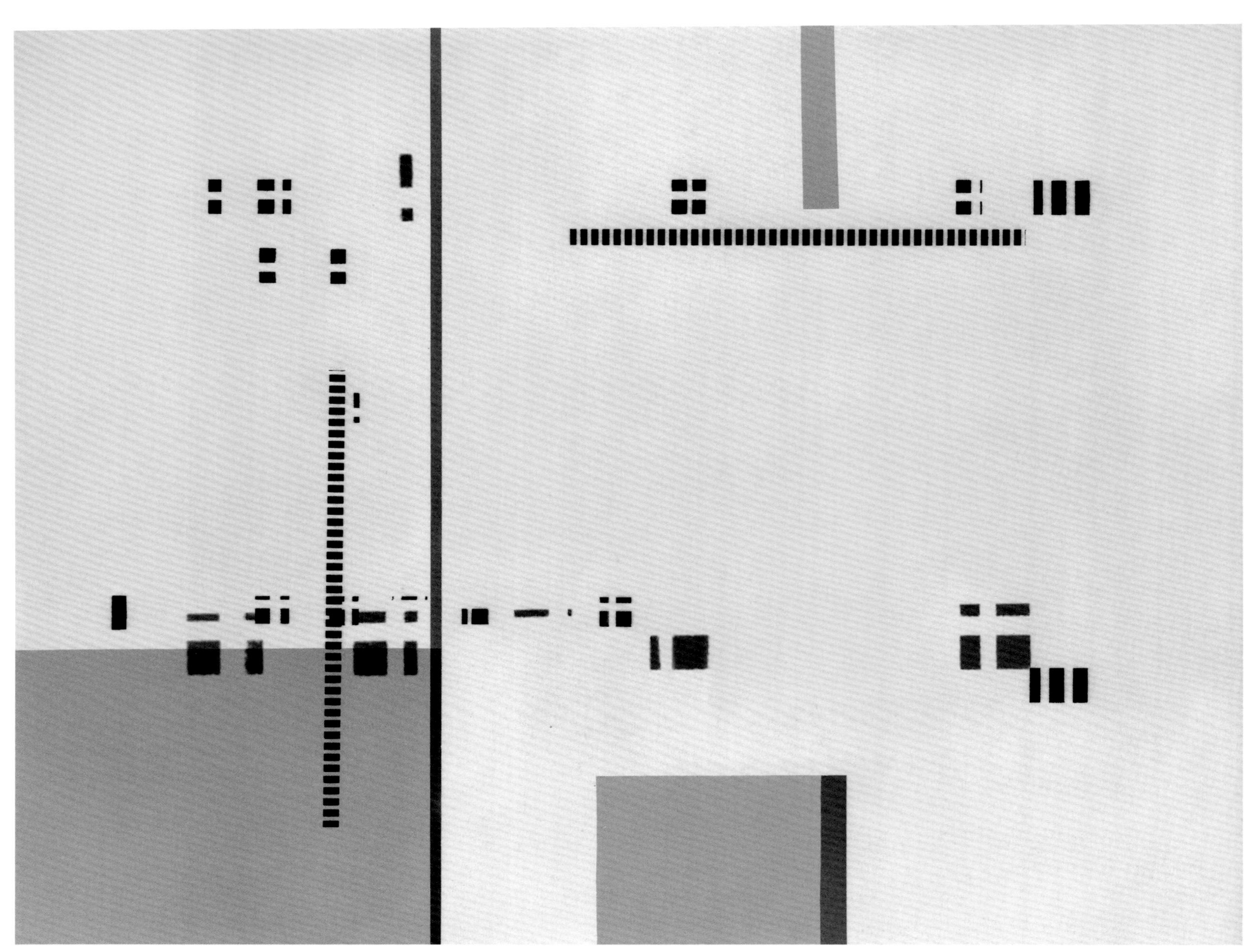

Fotoforma (Photoform), 1949

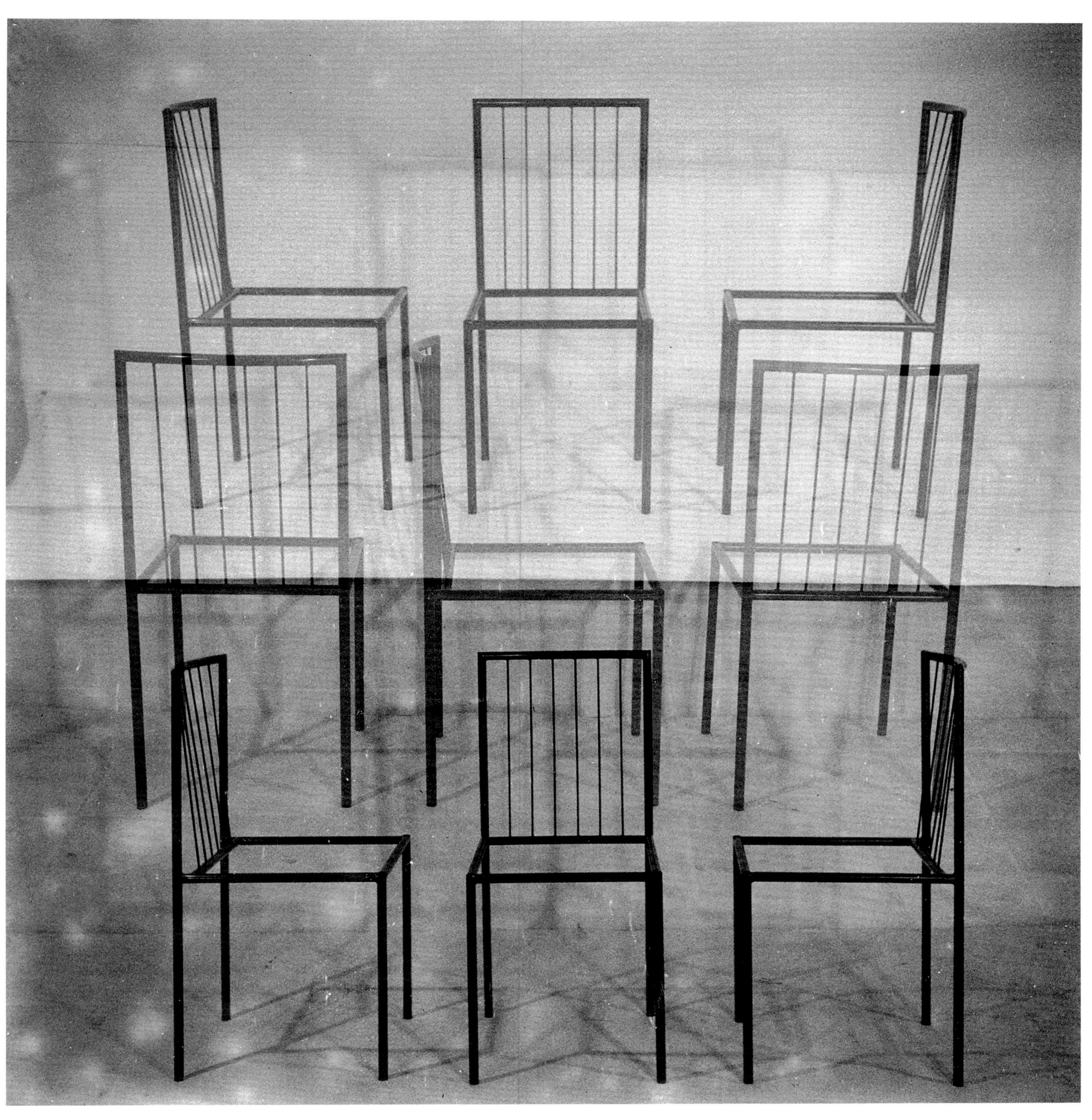

Sem título (cadeira Unilabor) (Untitled [Unilabor chair]), 1954–55

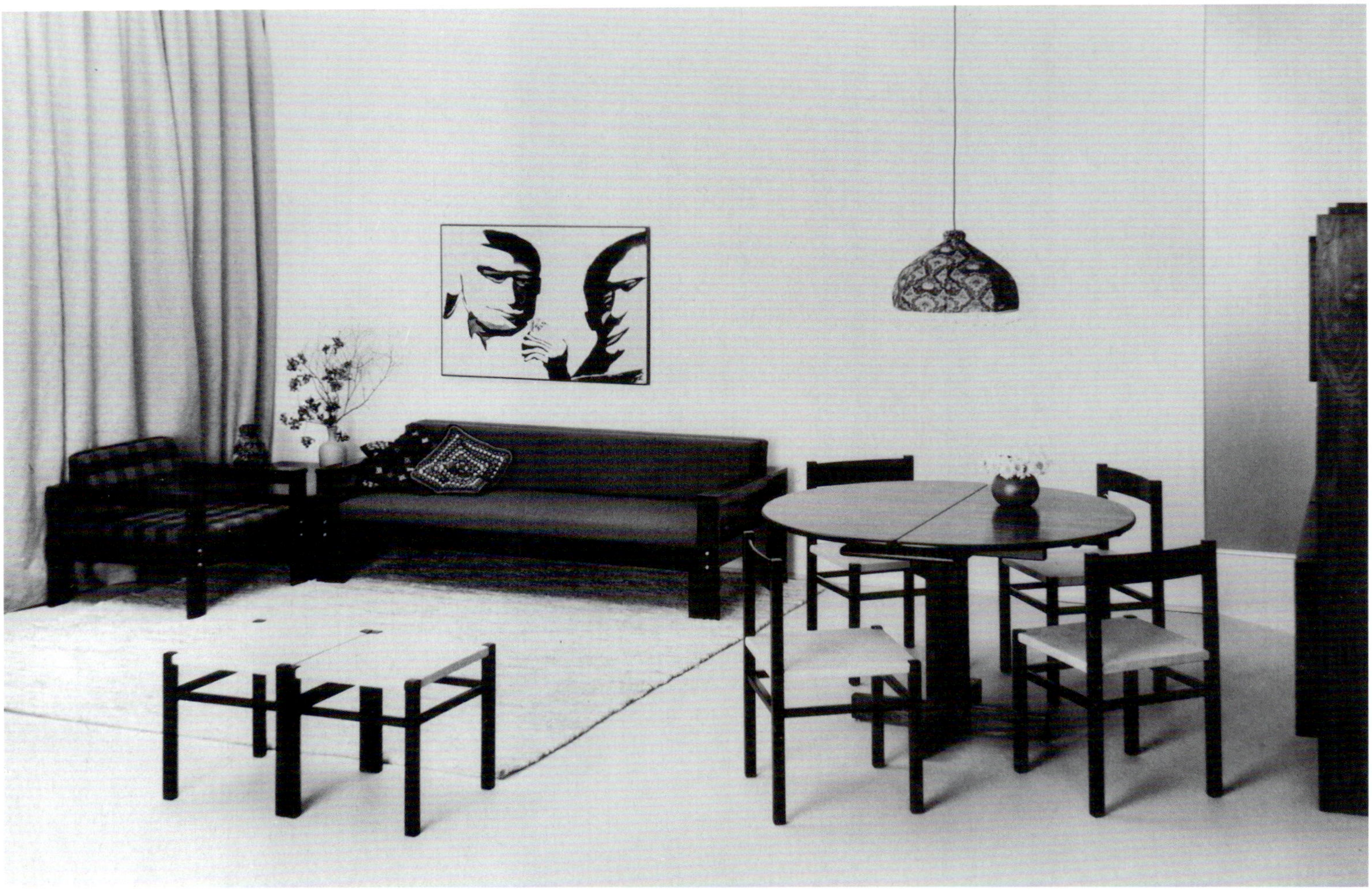

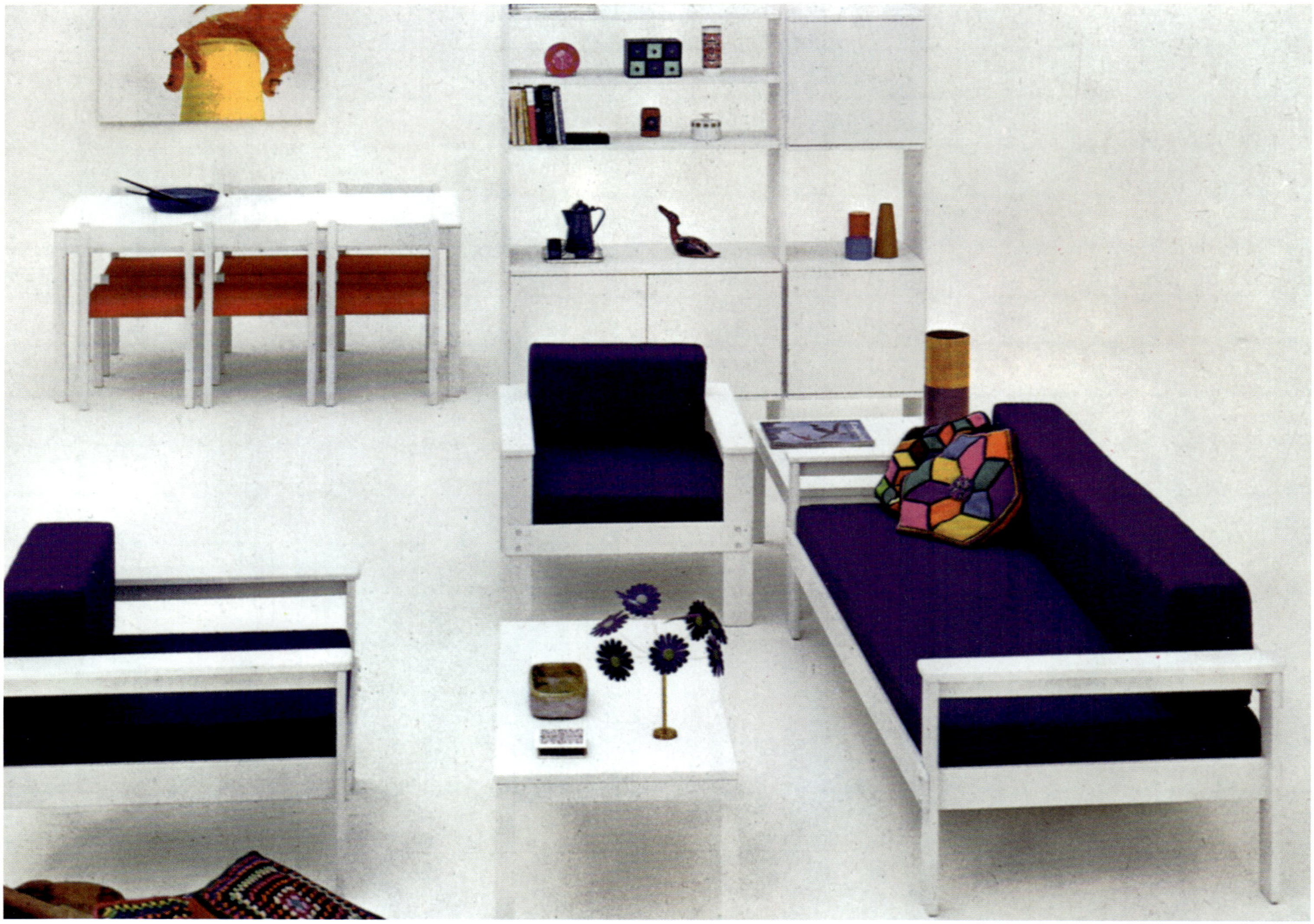

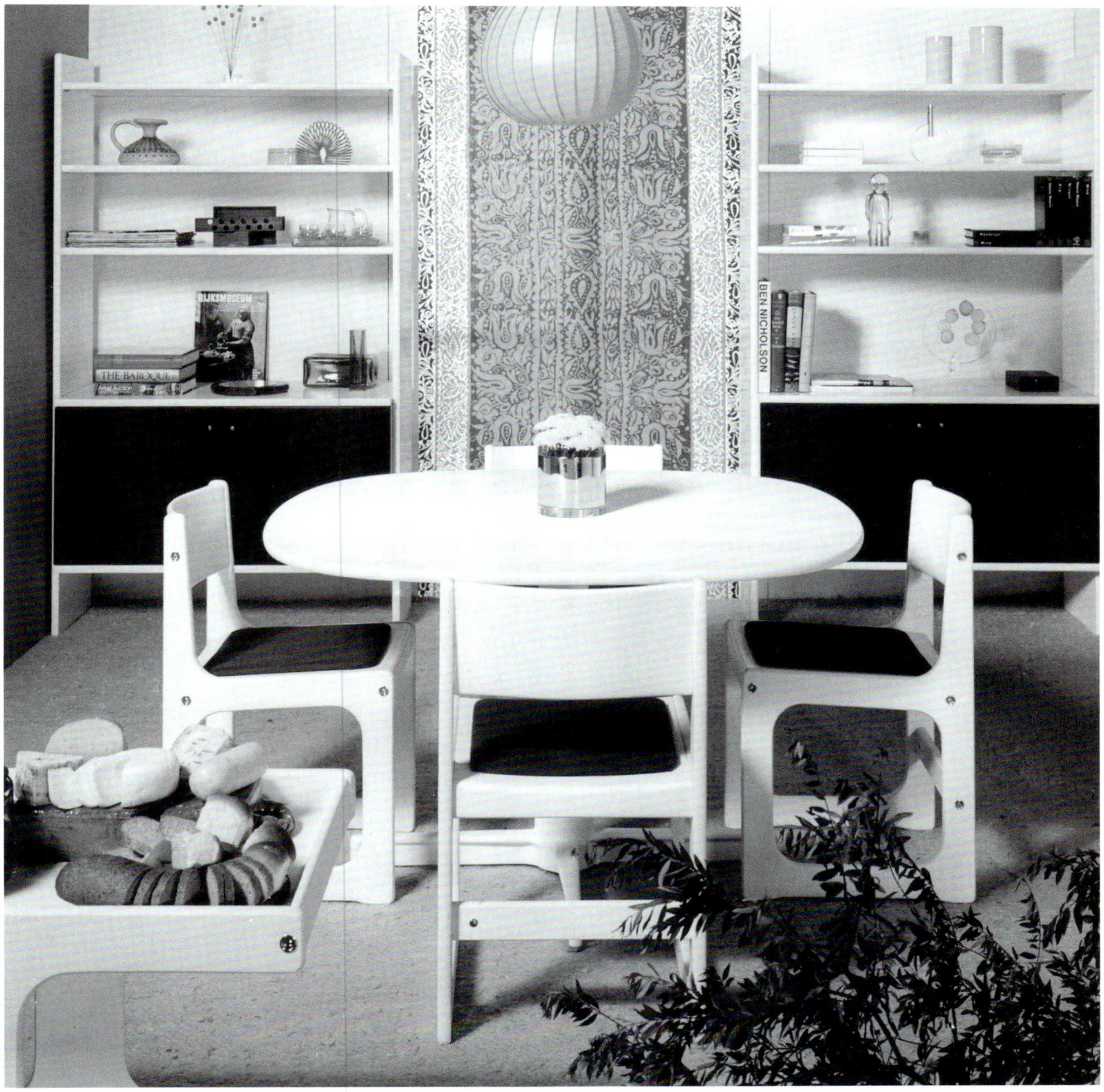

Opposite and right:
Spaces decorated
with Hobjeto furniture
and a painting by
Geraldo de Barros, 1960s.
Designs by Geraldo
de Barros

Opposite and right:
Lithographic color
reproductions of
photographs used
as Hobjeto magazine
advertisements, 1960s.
Designs by Geraldo de
Barros, photographs by
German Lorca.

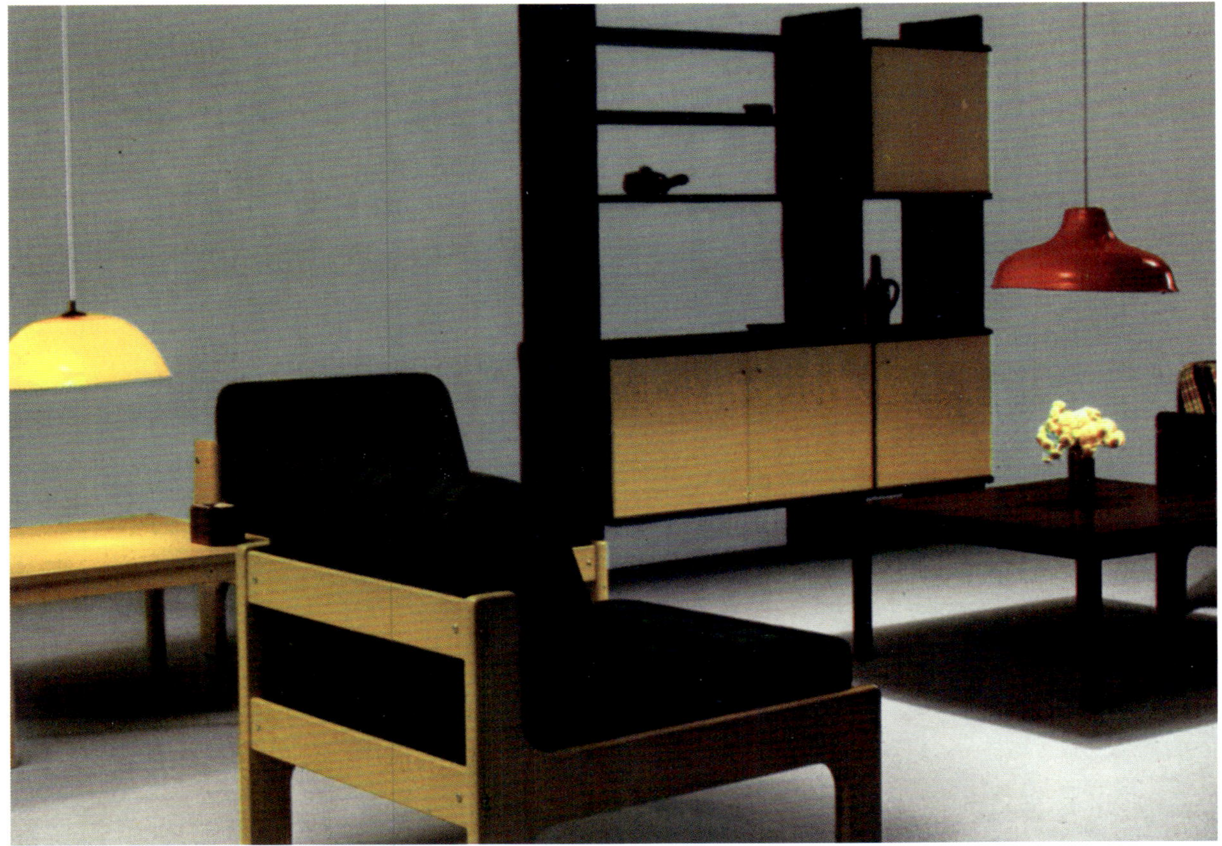

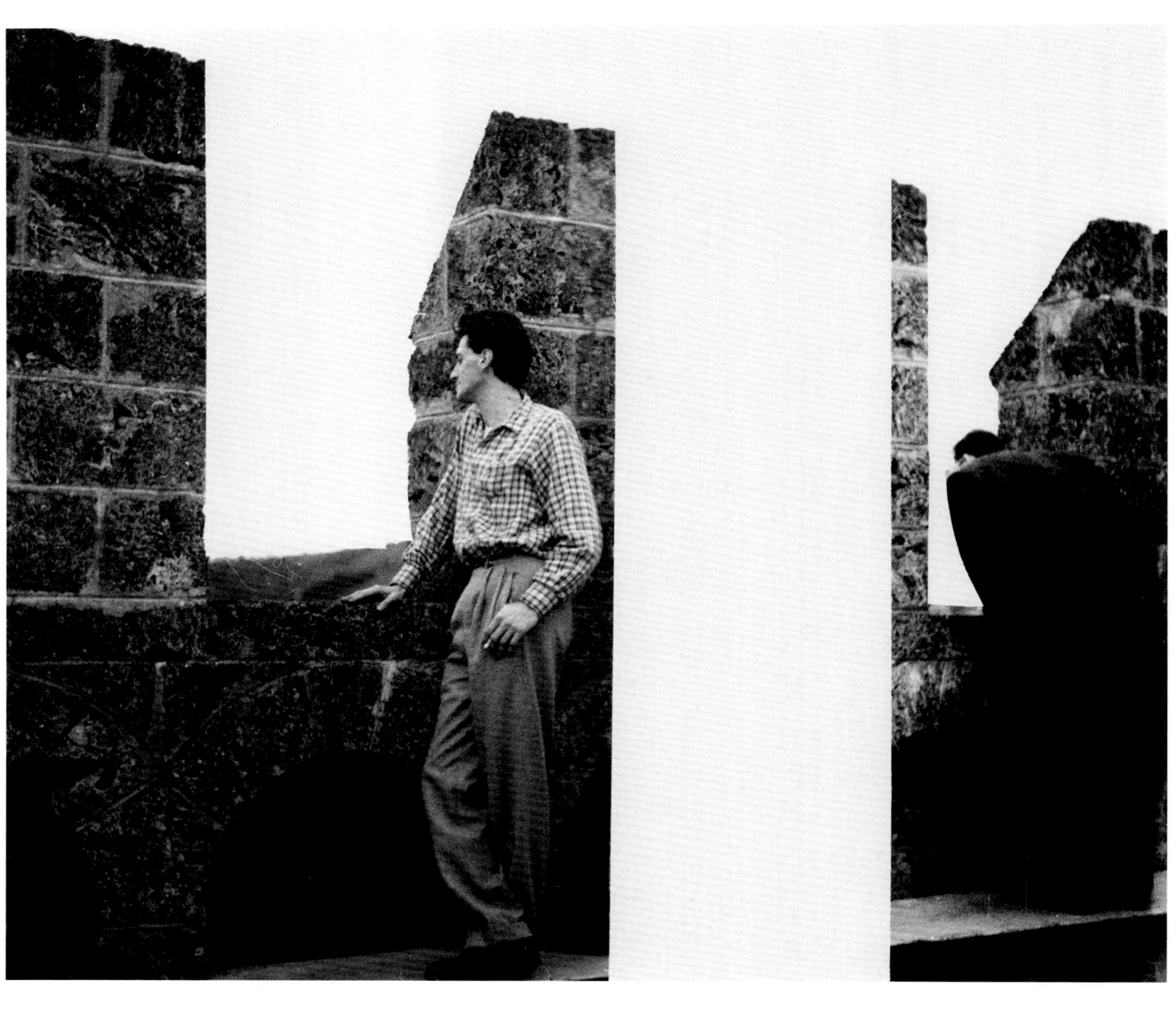

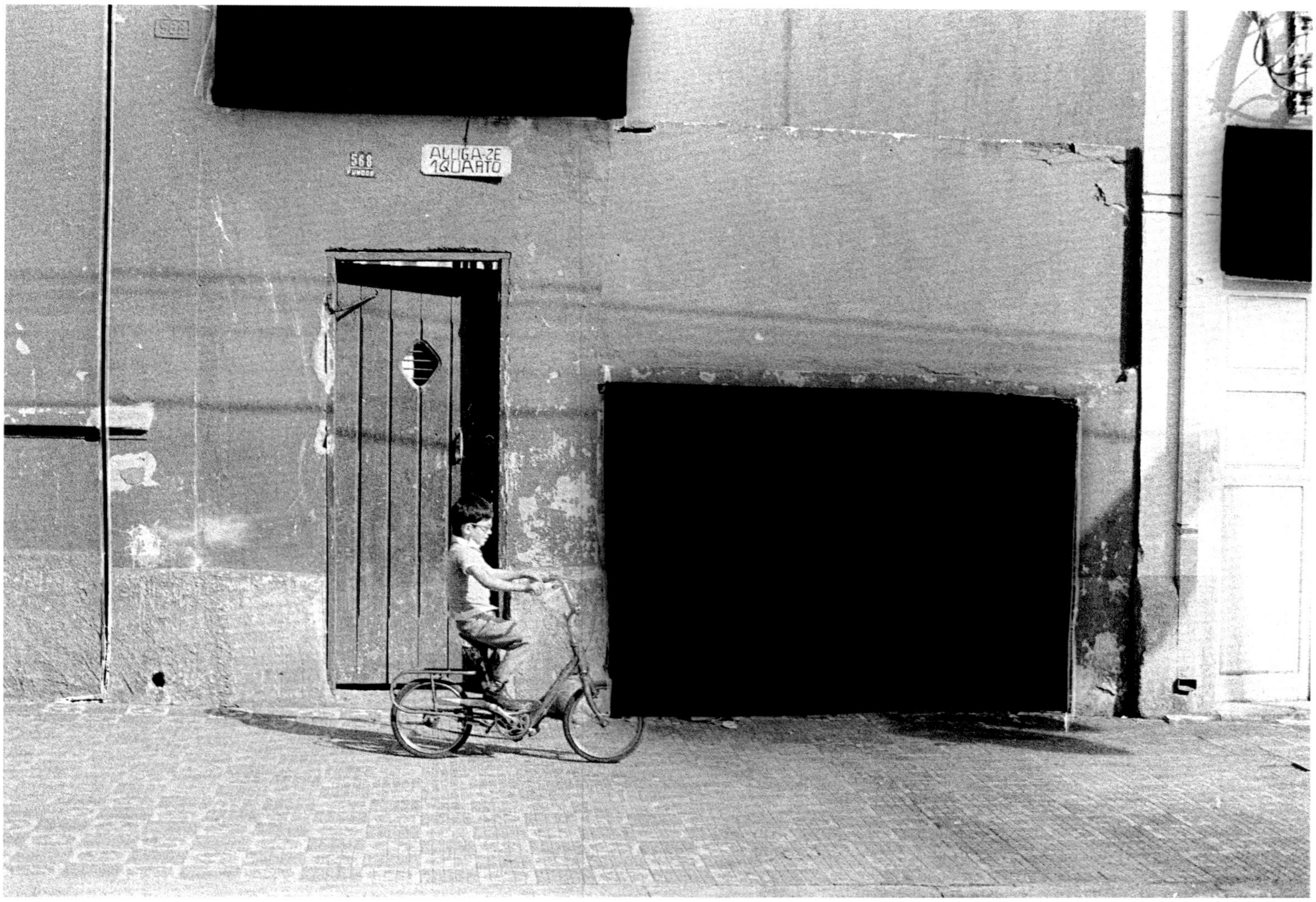

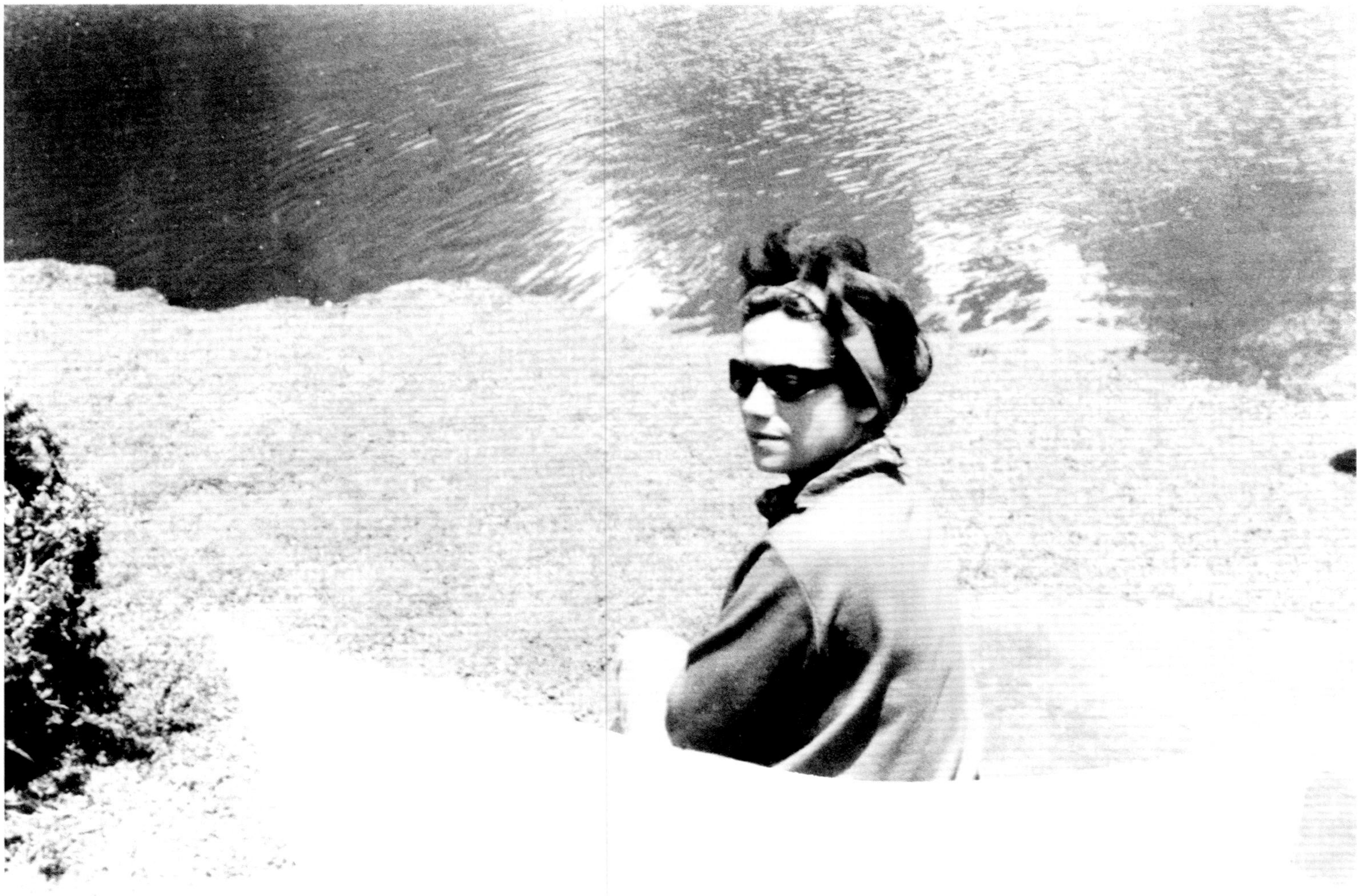

Since the early eighteenth century, Afro-Brazilian performance groups known as Maracatu have descended onto the streets of Recife and other cities in the interior of Brazil's northeastern state of Pernambuco during Carnival and other festivals. There are two groups: the urban form, the Maracatu nação (nation), devote their dancing and singing—set to the mesmerizing rhythms of the musical style called *batuque*—to the coronation of the *Rei do Congo* (King of the Congo). Their rural counterparts, the Maracatu rural, have their origins in the sugarcane mills, an environment with a history of authoritarianism and oppression.

The name Maracatu derives from an amalgam of sources—maracas, the American Indian percussion instrument; *catu*, which means "beautiful" in the Tupi language; and *marã*, Tupi for "war" or "confusion." Their complex background is also evident in the processional standard-bearer of the Maracatu nação, who dresses in the style of Portugal's Louis XV and is followed by an entourage of ornately styled performers and representations of religious imagery, centering around a dead queen attended by various courtesans. The layered imagery of this ritual performance, which has metamorphosed over centuries, reflects a fusion of African, indigenous, and European elements.

Today, these groups have become seamlessly incorporated into the popular festivities of Pernambuco and involve the participation of all types of people, regardless of racial origin or socioeconomic background, in a nation that still suffers from discrimination and segregation. During Pernambuco's Carnival, Maracatu groups are distinguished by a unique dance style characterized by formalized frolicking and a subtle choreography of mythic origin related to the dances of the syncretic religion known as *Candomblé*. Brazilian author Mário de Andrade described this unique dance as follows: "Intoxicated by the percussion, the dancers proceed almost lethargically, slightly reeling on each quarter note, with an almost undetectable trot, and without any visibly formal footwork."

The generally hypnotic nature of a Maracatu procession contrasts with the frenetic rhythm of other dance groups participating in Carnival, most notably the fiercely syncopated Frevo, whose musical style also originated in Pernambuco. The Frevo and the Maracatu reflect a sense of momentary collective elation. For a few days of the year, they don lavish costumes, spend their scant savings to enjoy themselves in the festivities, and parade proudly through the streets of the city. Official government tourist photography often turns to these festivities to highlight the "gold" of Brazilian racial democracy.

Bárbara Wagner became interested in what lies beneath this false gold veneer and began documenting the dancers' rehearsals. Her series on the Maracatu offers a portrait of the people who make up the "joyful" faces of this northeastern Brazilian group as they practice their dance. The photographs delve into who the *maracatuzeiros* actually are when they are not involved in festival performances and how their days are spent in the run-up to Carnival and afterward. The series looks beyond those brilliantly colored costumes and the atmosphere of celebration flowing almost anarchically through the darkened streets to reveal the dancers as they wait to share their tradition with others for a few moments.

Bárbara Wagner
The Maracatu

Agnaldo Farias

Agnaldo Farias is a critic, curator, and professor of architecture and urbanism at the College of the University of São Paulo.

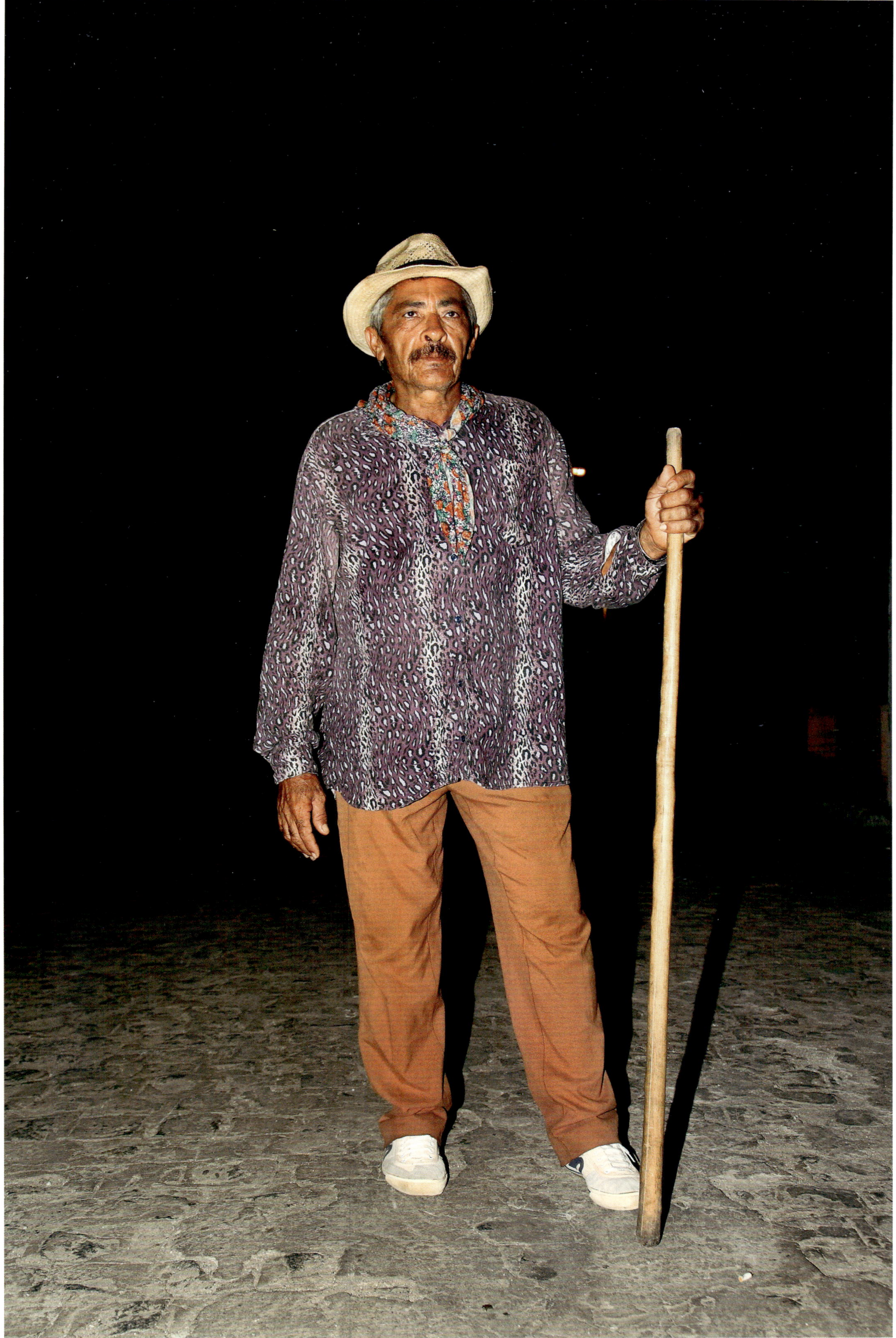

Estrela Brilhante (Shining
Star), 2008

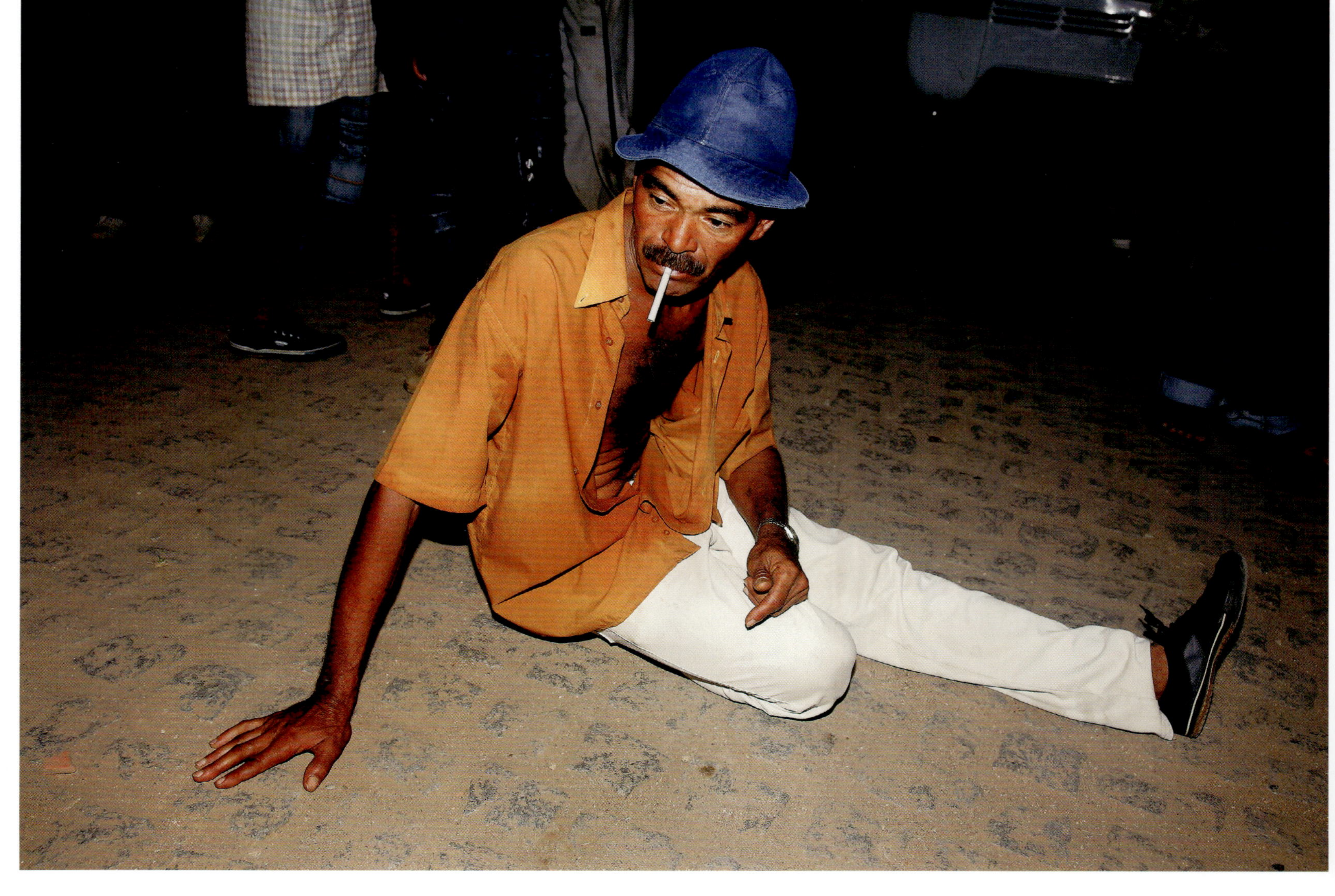

Cambinda Brasileira
(Brazilian cambinda),
2009

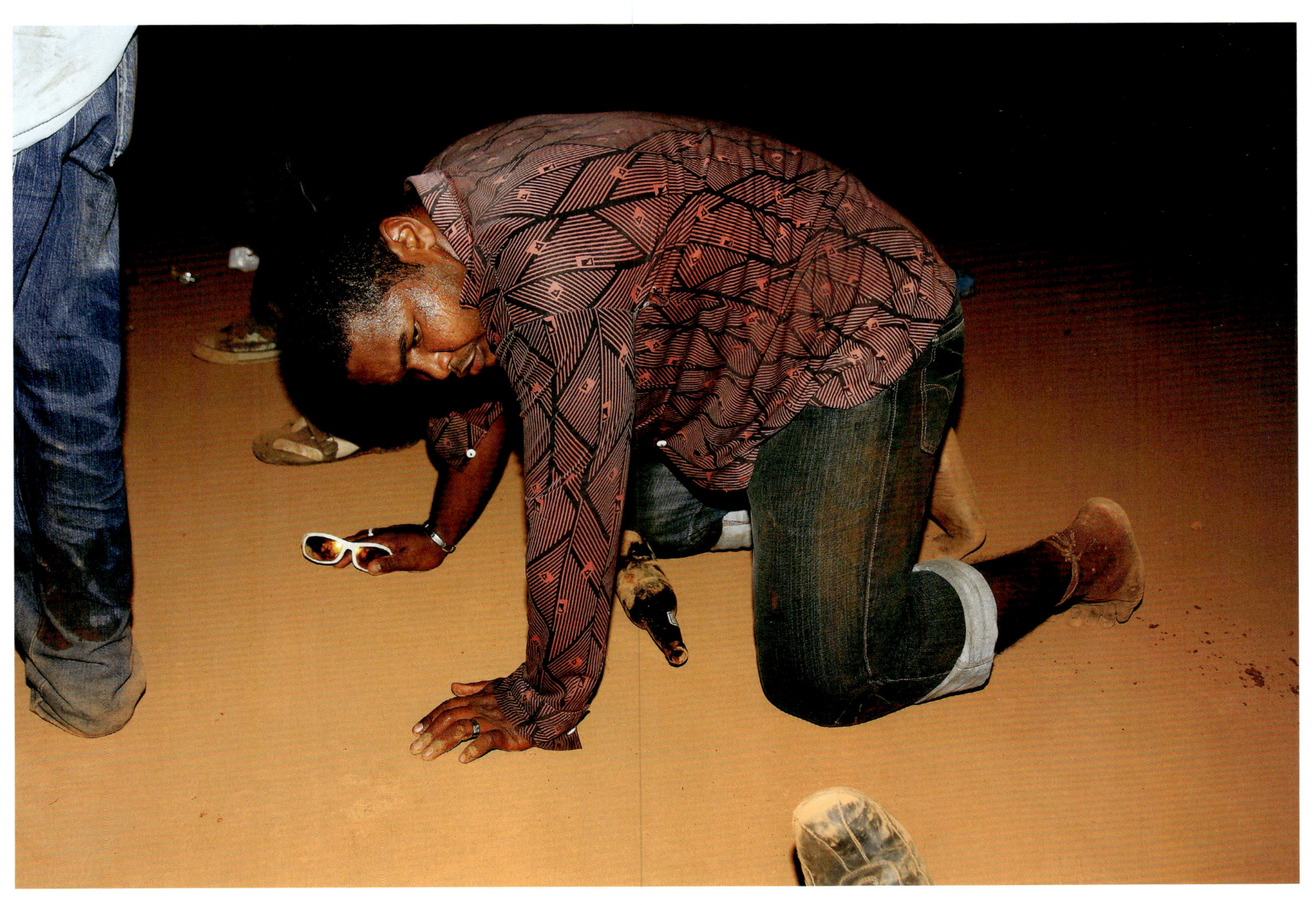

Cambinda Brasileira
(Brazilian cambinda),
2009

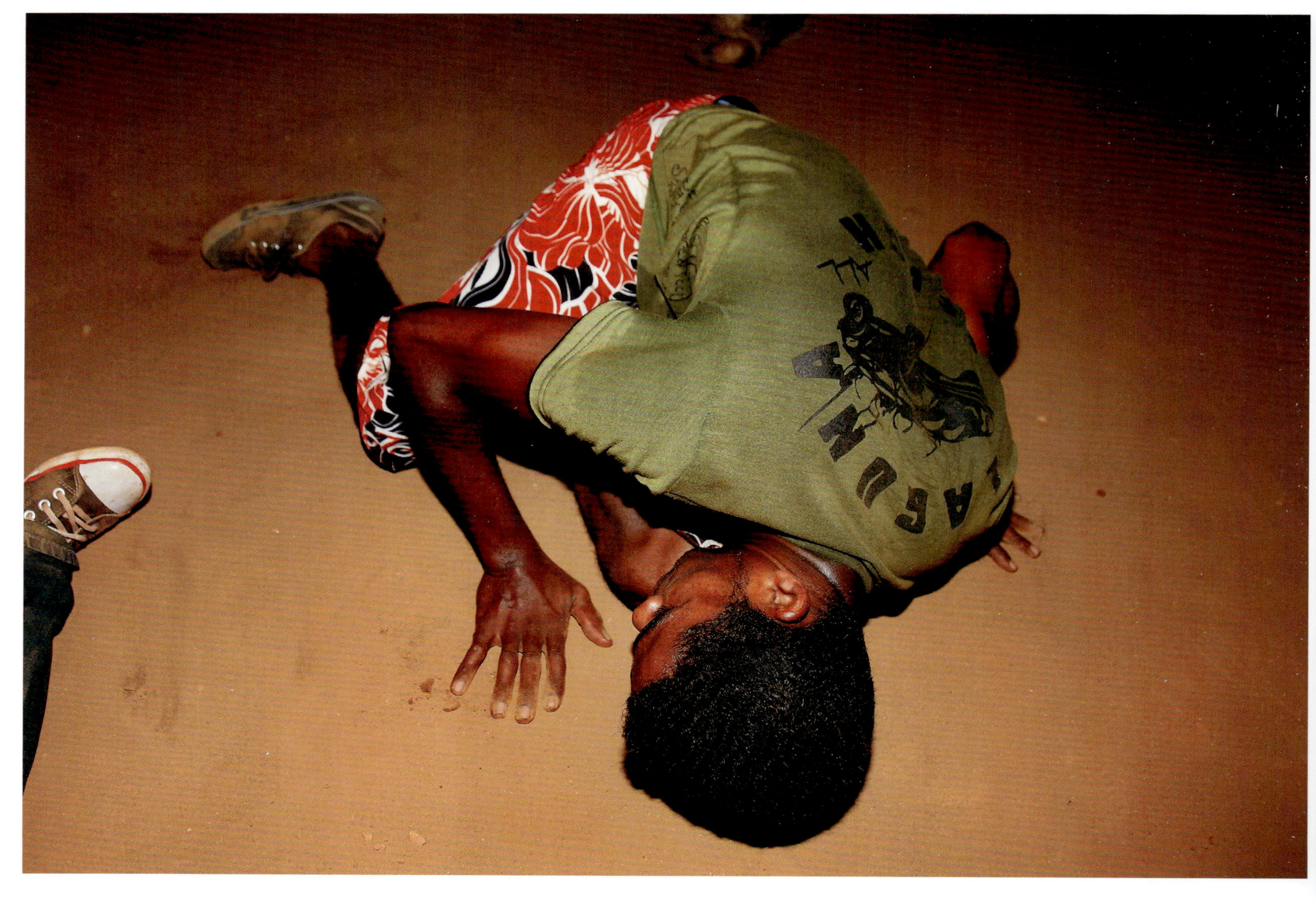

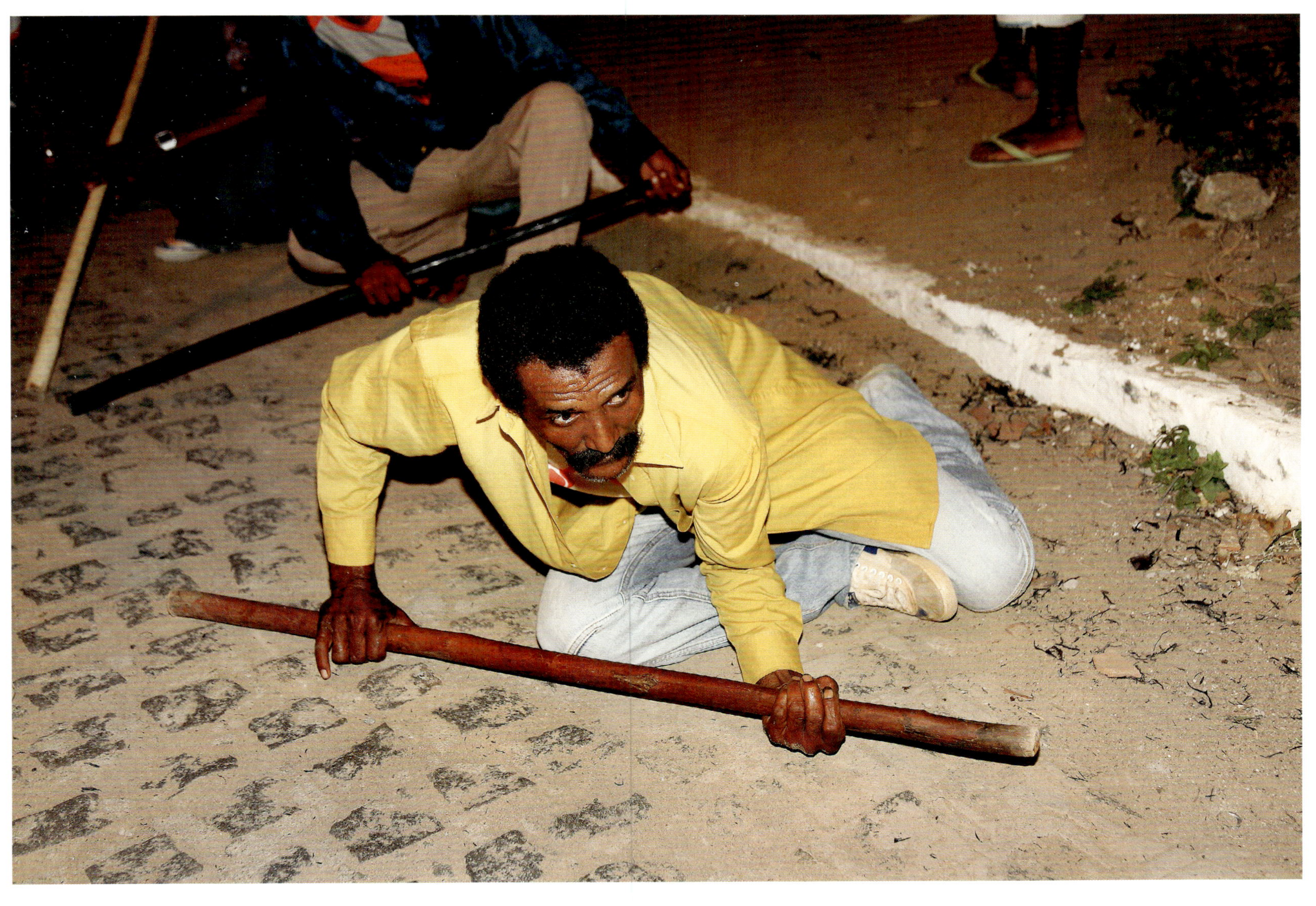

This page:
Cambinda Brasileira
(Brazilian cambinda),
2009

Opposite:
Águia Dourada
(Golden Eagle), 2010
All photographs courtesy
Galleria Extraspazio, Rome

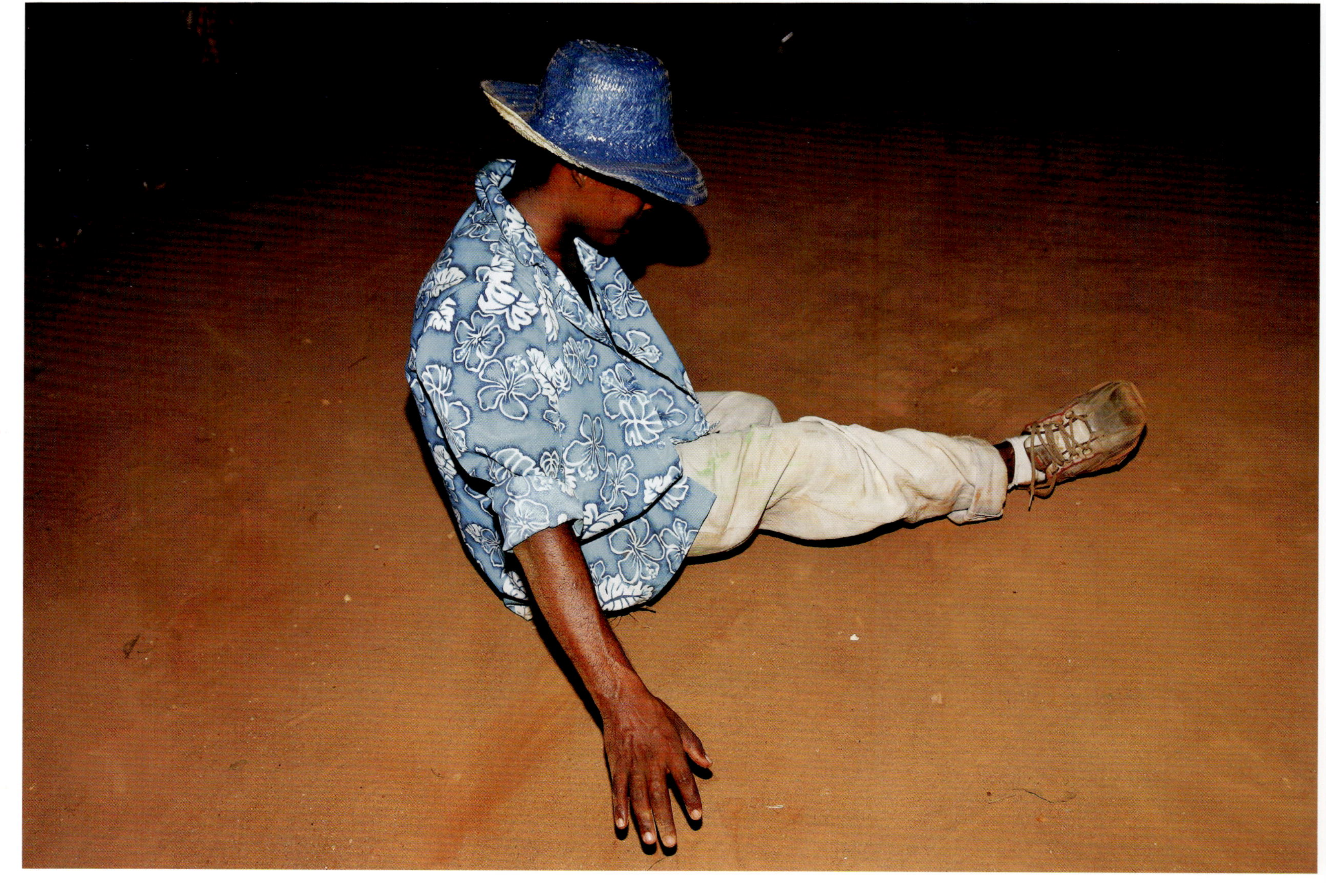

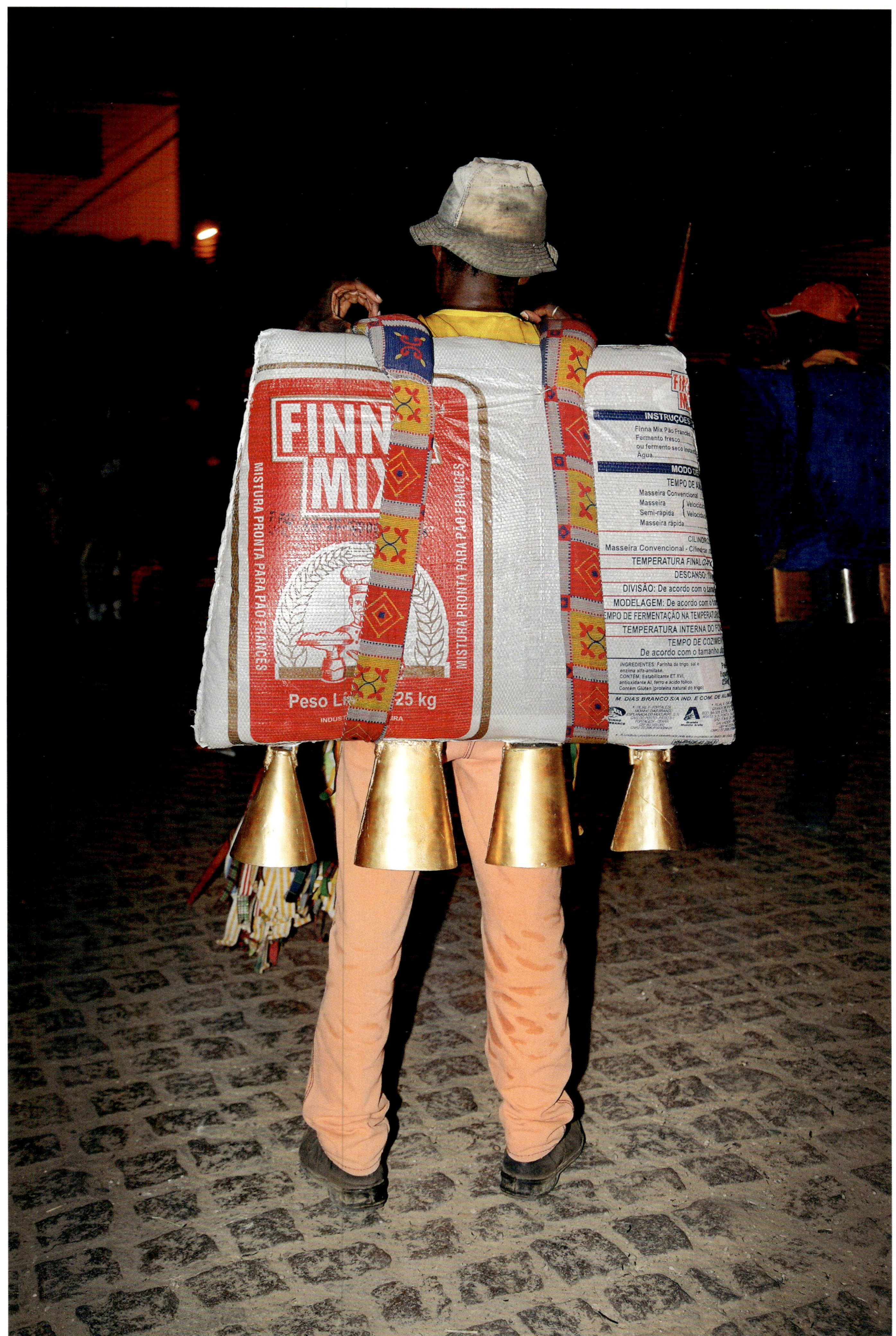
FINNA
MIX
MISTURA PRONTA PARA PÃO FRANCÊS
MISTURA PRONTA PARA PÃO FRANCÊS
Peso Líq. 25 kg
INSTRUÇÕES

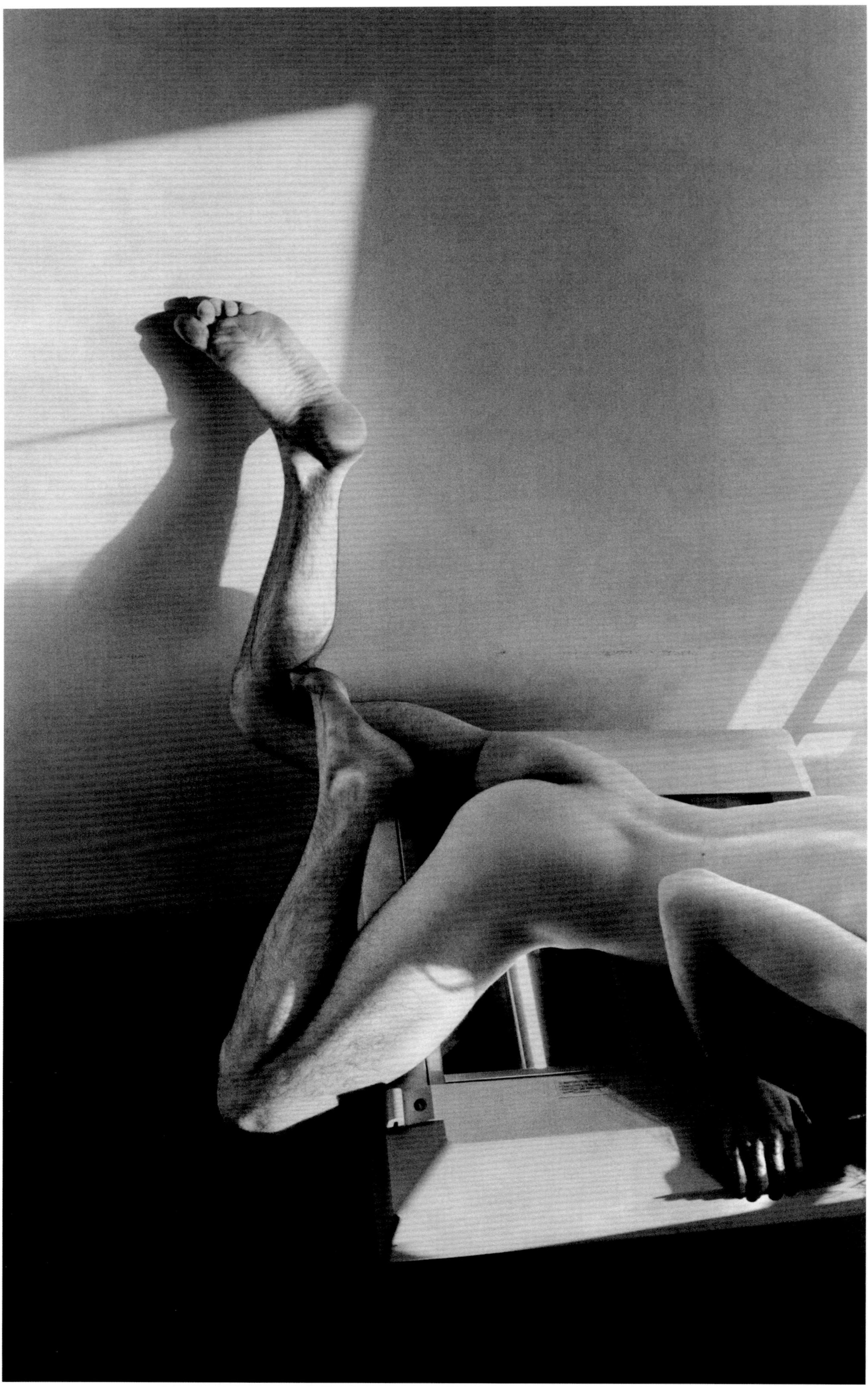

Hudinilson Urbano Jr. was an extraordinary figure in the cultural and artistic milieu of São Paulo. He studied art at Fundação Armando Alvares Penteado (FAAP) in São Paulo but was quickly forced to leave when his father discovered that he was studying art, not industrial design. He then worked for a local television station and as a postal worker. Delivering mail inspired him to become a participant in several mail-art networks (art sent through the postal service), fostering international communication between artists in the late 1970s and early 1980s, during the height of repression under Brazil's military regimes. After becoming known for his innovative graffiti (and for pioneering the use of stencils in an urban context, along with artists such as Alex Vallauri), he formed the collective *3nós3* with Mario Ramiro and Rafael França in 1979.

For the next four years this intrepid group carried out conceptual public interventions such as bagging a number of monuments throughout the city; stretching oversize banners across entire avenues, thereby clogging traffic; or obstructing the doors of twenty-nine exclusive commercial galleries in São Paulo with tape. To document these and other interventions, *3nós3* notified television and radio stations, hence devising prototypes for what would later come to be known as media art. Hudinilson Jr. was also one of the first artists to make Xerox art, photocopying nude body parts to create viscerally intimate images.

His work was included in major exhibitions, such as the 1st Havana Biennial (1984), the 18th São Paulo Biennial (1985), and the 3rd Bienal de Mercosul (2001), yet it was his *Cadernos de referência* (Reference notebooks) that caught the attention of those who became aware of his oeuvre in recent years. Since the early 1980s, Hudinilson Jr. compulsively collected and compiled everything that crossed his path, including private items such as letters, photographs, and phone numbers of associates, and publicly accessible documents such as newspapers, business cards, invitations to exhibitions, and male erotic magazines. Eagerly appropriating material and collaging it into annual diaries or other bound books, such as wallpaper sample catalogues, he often worked on several notebooks at once, and updated or reworked notebooks from previous years.

The notebooks read like Warburgian atlases of the artist's own personal universe: leafing through the pages, distinct analogies develop between the depiction of rhinoceroses, panthers, Greek statues, architecture, athletes, actors, singers, dancers, artworks given to him by friends, his own annotations, and myriad male figures posing for the camera. The homoerotic and queer discourse to which he was drawn inevitably spilled over into his own sculptural works.

With his varied output, Hudinilson Jr. went beyond the conventional limits of cultural life in Brazil. Sadly, when he passed away last August, he was anticipating the realization of his first solo exhibition in Brazil and the publication of a monograph. The full scope of his legacy is still being determined, but his work will surely emerge as a touchstone of Brazilian conceptual art.

Hudinilson Urbano Jr.

Tobi Maier

Tobi Maier is a curator and writer based in São Paulo.

This page:
Le Pape (The Pope), 1983

Opposite, top:
"Narcisse" Exercício
de Me Ver ("Narcissus"
Exercise of Seeing Myself),
1980

Opposite, bottom:
Detalhe do Detalhe II
(Detail of the Detail II),
1982

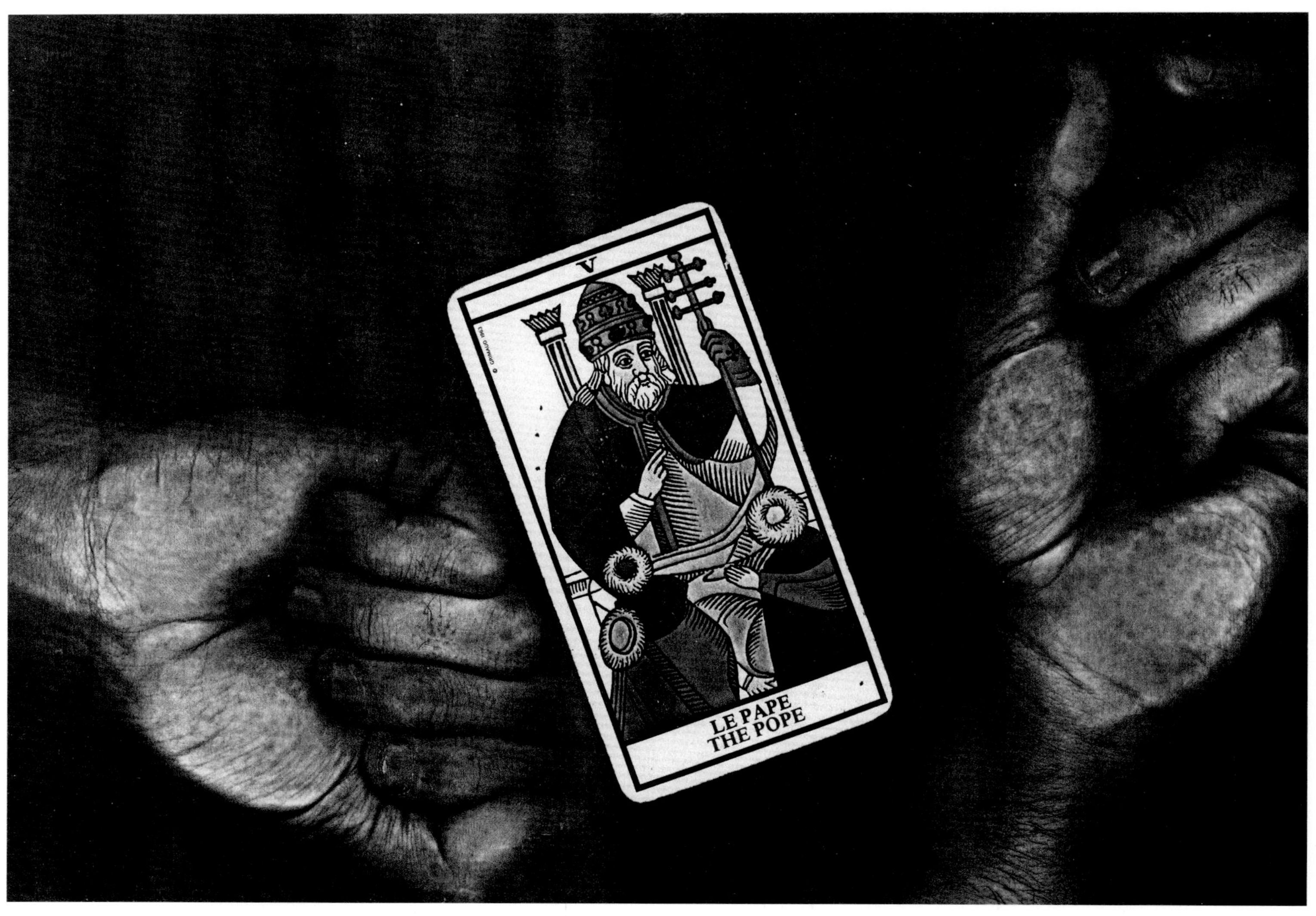

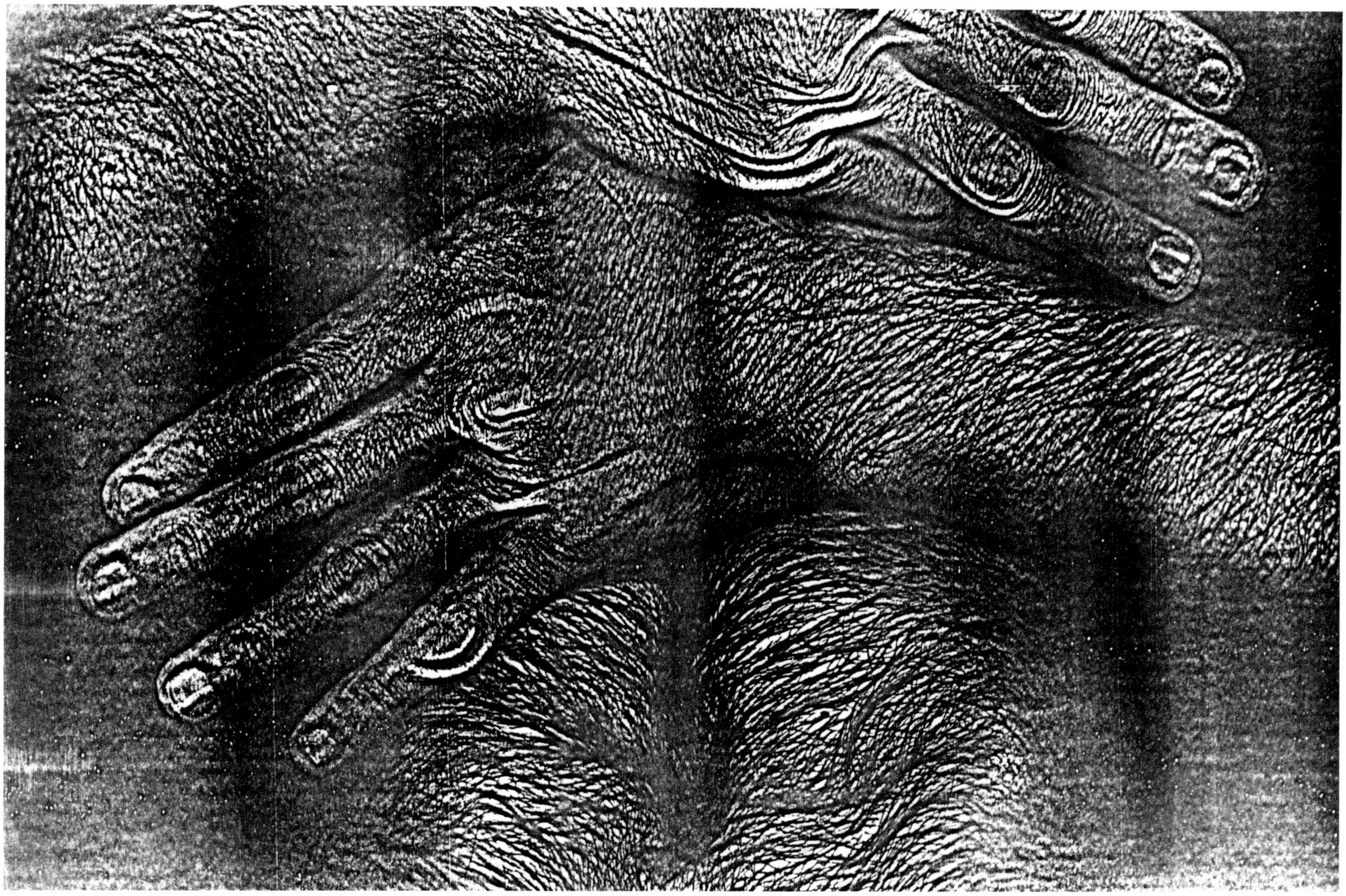

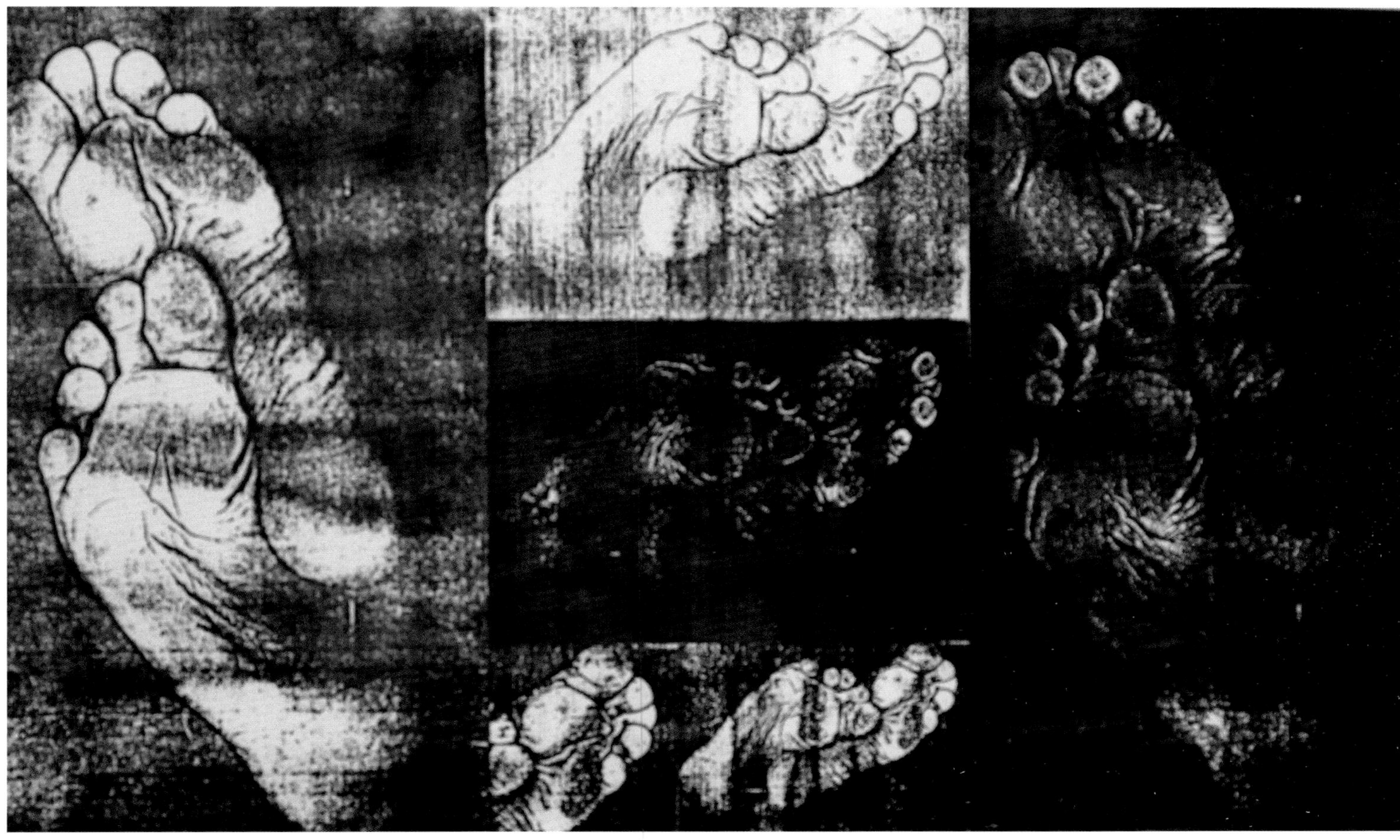

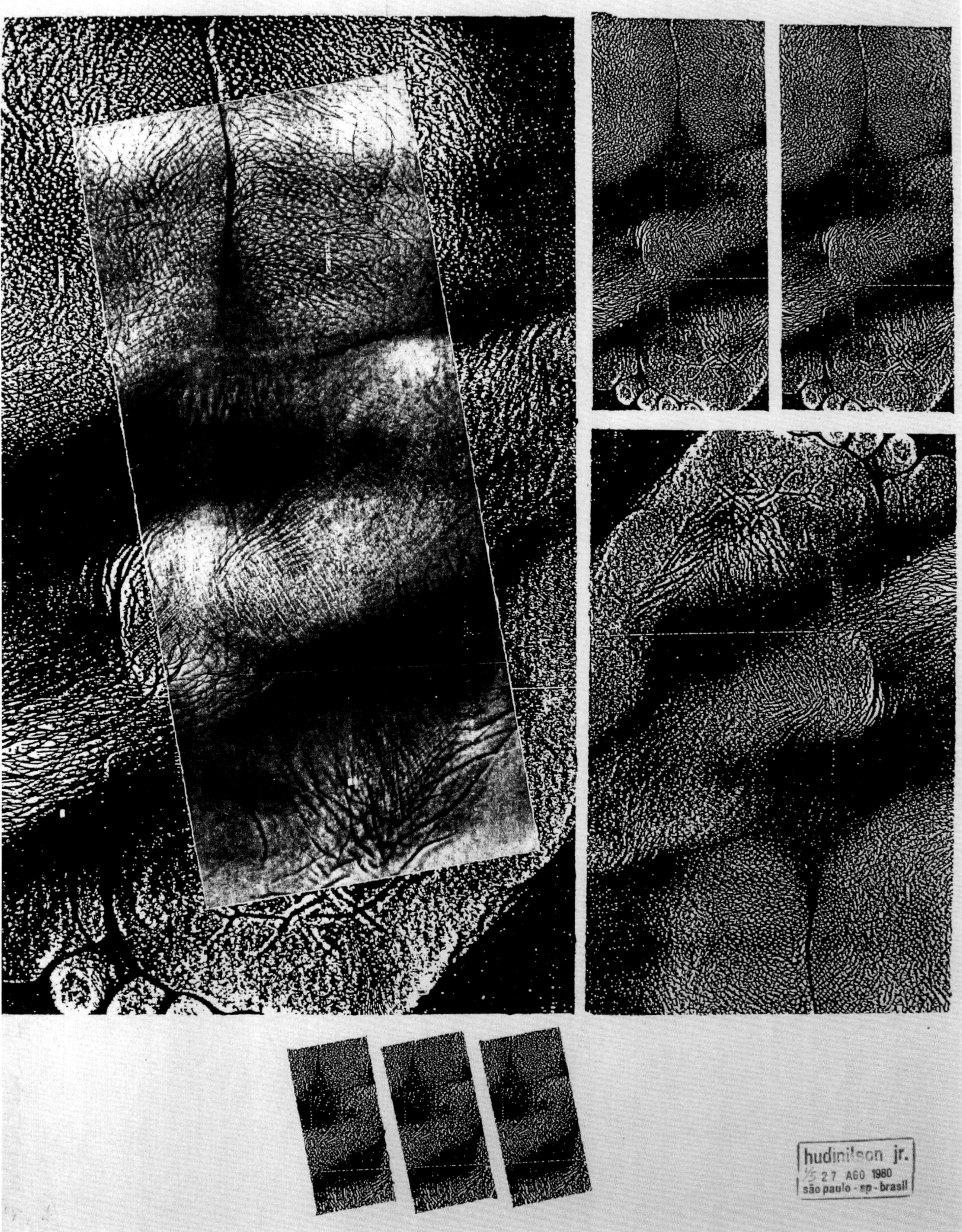

hudinilson jr.
1/5 27 AGO 1980
são paulo - sp - brasil

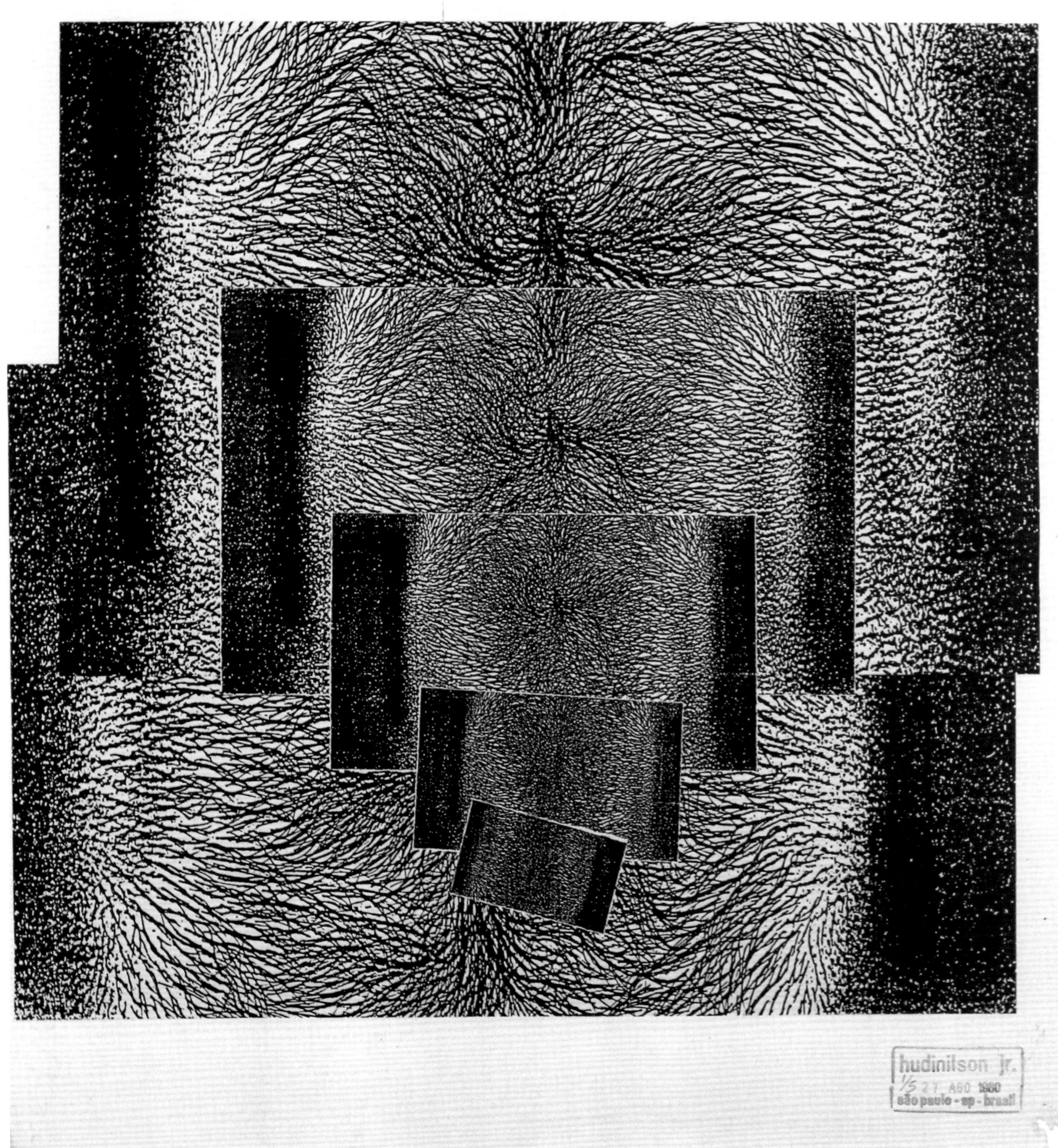

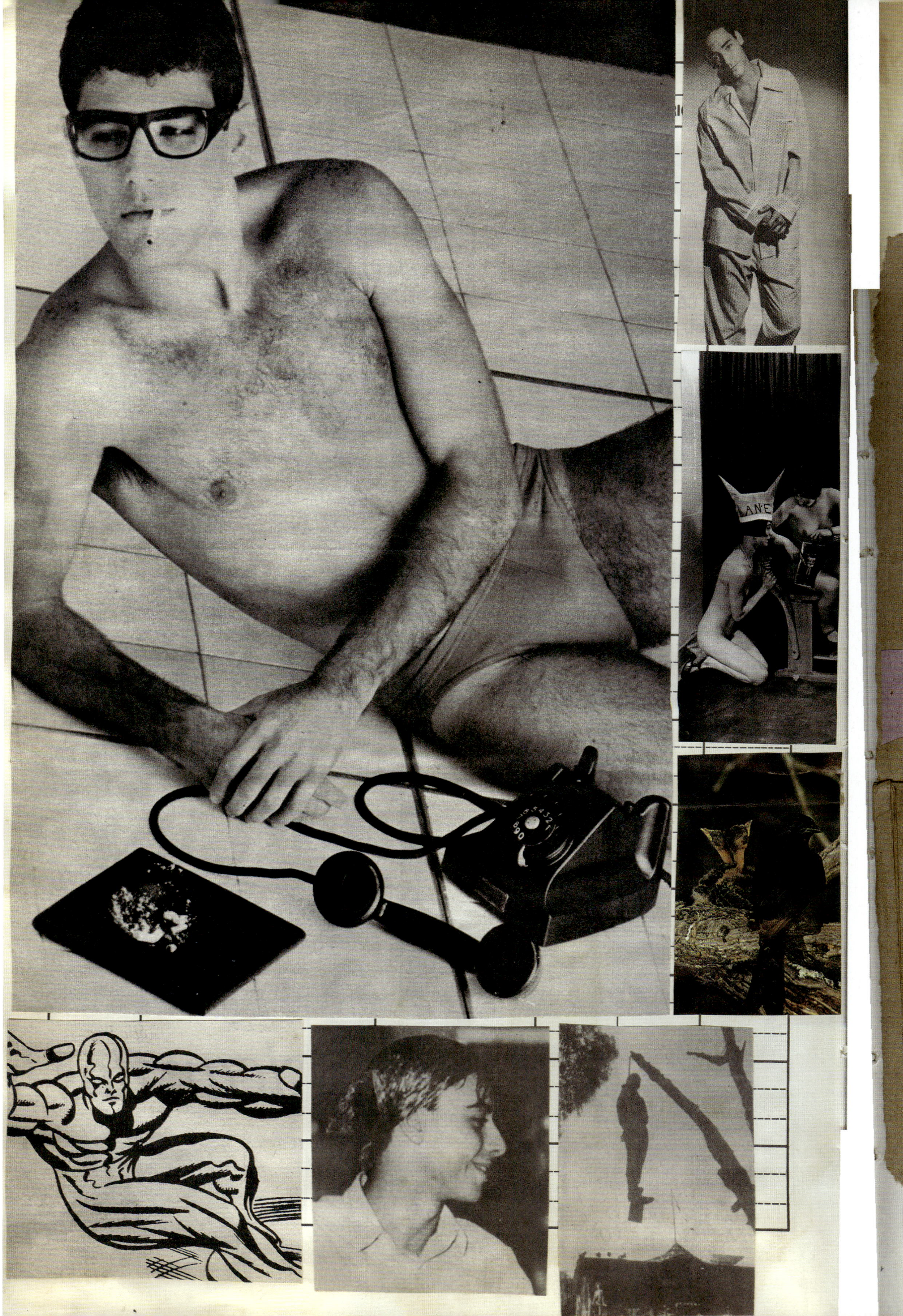

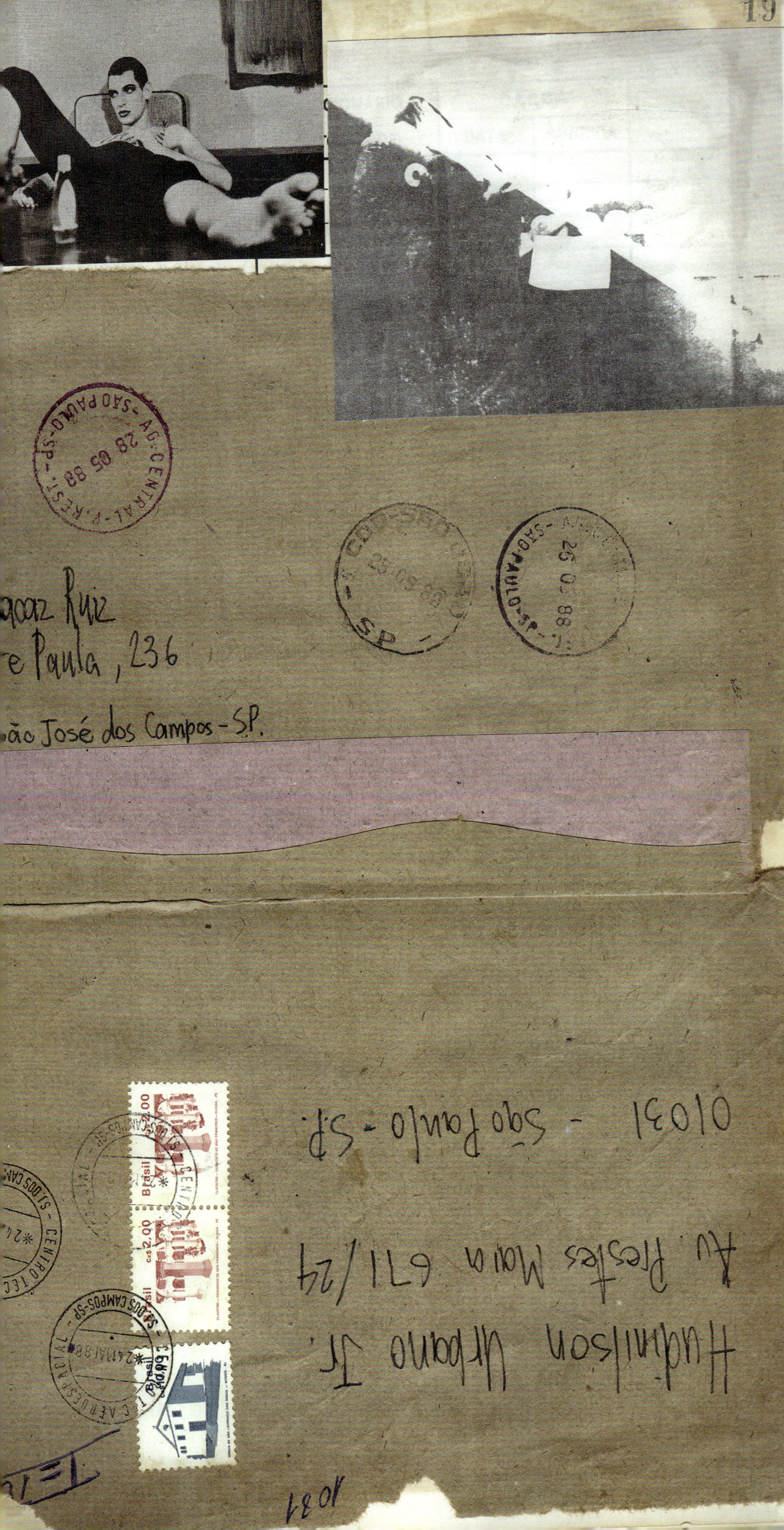

19

aqoz Ruz
e Paula, 236
ão José dos Campos - S.P.

01031 - São Paulo - S.P.
Av. Prestes Maia 671/24
Hudnilson Urbano Jr.

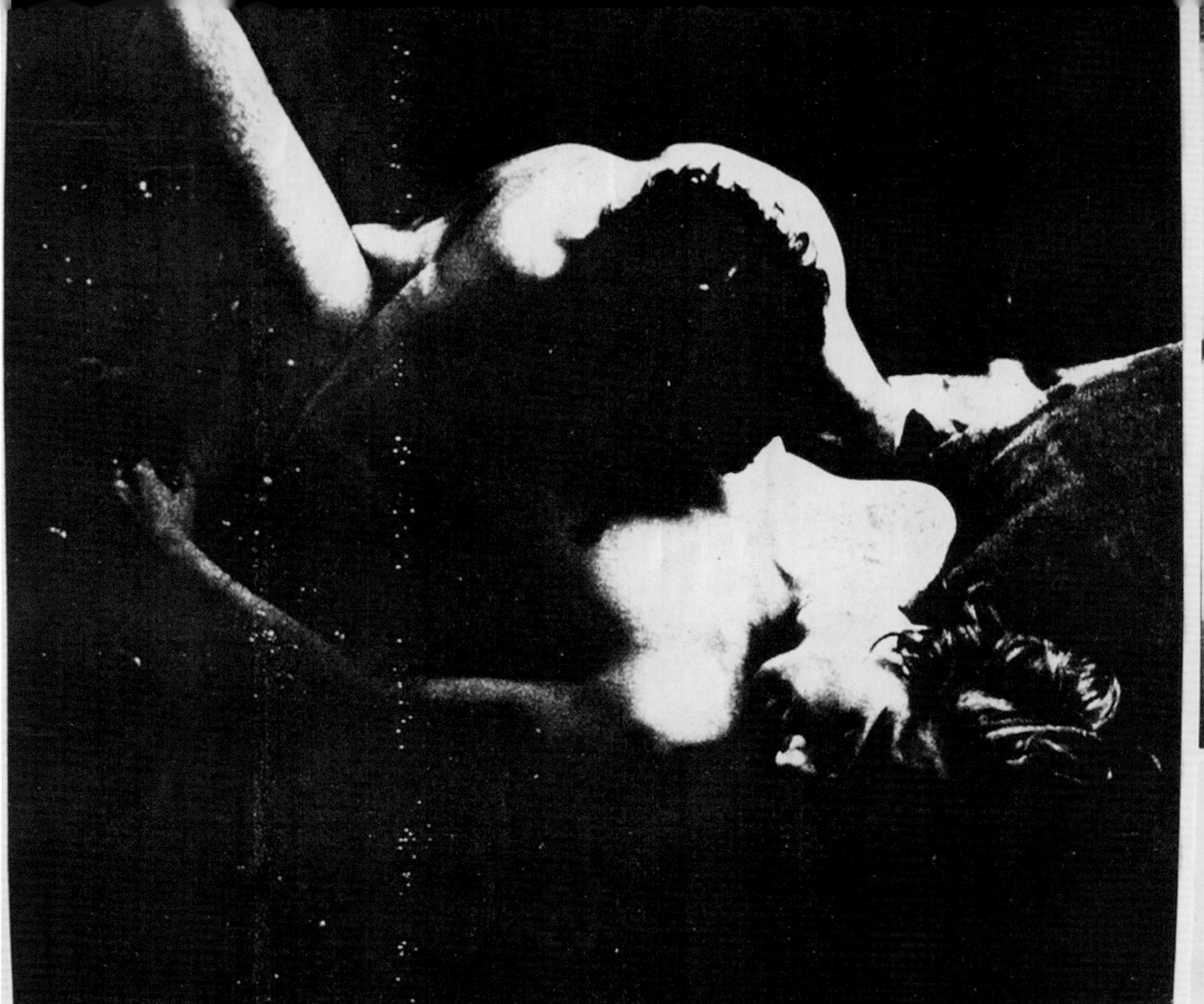

Sem título (Untitled),
1980/2009
All works courtesy Galeria
Jaqueline Martins, São Paulo

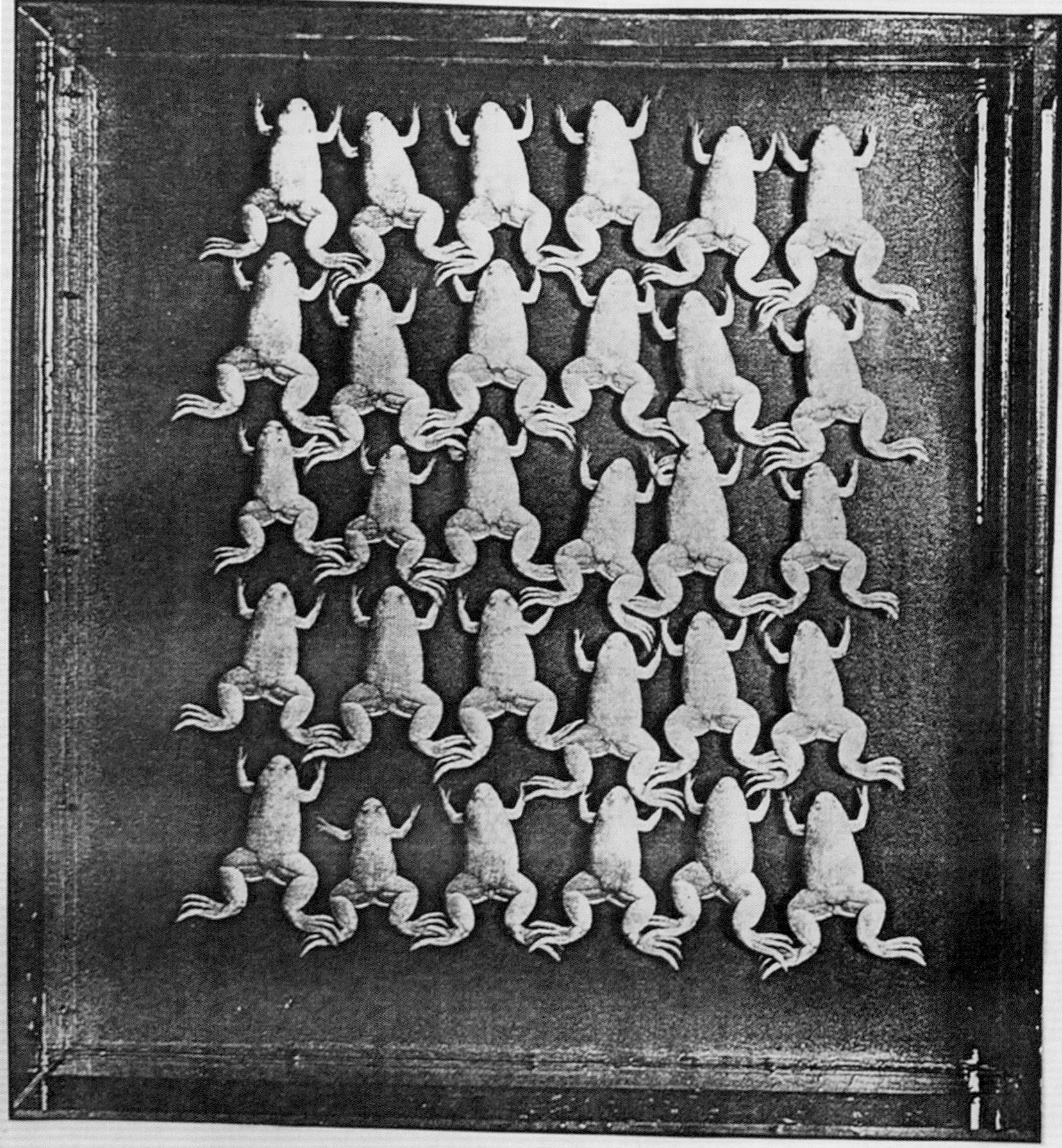

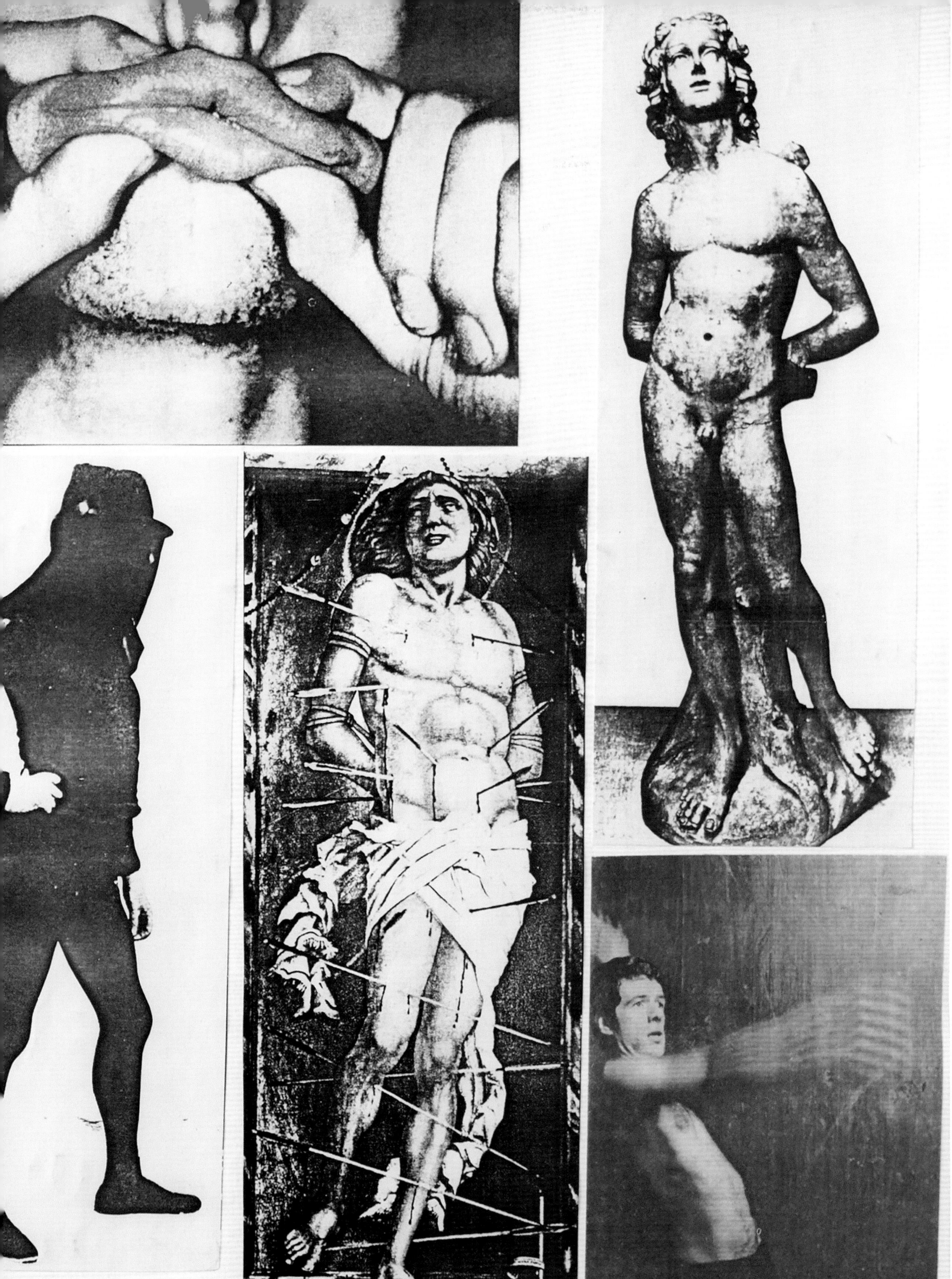

It is still unclear what Oscar Niemeyer's death, in 2012, will mean for Brazilian architecture, or, more broadly, Brazilian culture. For many, the architect—who gained fame for his exuberant work, anachronistic Communist views, and ever-controversial functionalist projects—had died some time ago. His projects were often seen as little more than a repetition of old forms, bureaucratically reassembled by assistants. According to others, his best work had been created years ago, and only diluted echoes were produced after the 1980s. One could still admire, however, his tremendous longevity and the considerable leverage he had with Brazilian authorities. Up through his final years—and he lived to be nearly 105—his office continued to dispatch projects for the major cities of the country. It will be a long time before all the municipal governments involved can bring his blueprints to fruition, and his work will therefore continue to enjoy a somewhat bizarre afterlife.

Mauro Restiffe photographed Niemeyer's funeral at the Palácio do Planalto, which is still considered one of the architect's greatest accomplishments. This building, housing the government's headquarters, was completed in 1960, along with the rest of Brasília, the country's new capital that Niemeyer helped to plan. (Previously, Rio de Janeiro was the capital.) The palace served as the focal point for the inauguration festivities held in Brasília and soon became one of the most iconic postcard images of that city. Restiffe was returning to a familiar place, since Planalto appears in many of the photographs he took of President Lula's swearing-in (evidently with ample support from Niemeyer) in 2003. The photographer knew Niemeyer from various other occasions, and he appears in Restiffe's photographs of the old Pampulha Casino (1943) and of the São Paulo Department of Transportation building (1954). Both structures were subsequently transformed into museums (in 1957 and 2012, respectively).

Restiffe's interest in modern Brazilian architecture is manifold. A generational bias could be partially blamed—artists as dissimilar as Luisa Lambri and Juan Araujo shared a critical yet reverential appreciation of Niemeyer's legacy and of what he represented for a tropical vision of modernity—along with an uncommon focus on the relationships between people and space, which can be traced back to a documentary tradition that Restiffe at least used as a point of reference. His photographs of Brasília are often associated with those that Thomaz Farkas took during the city's inauguration, given both the economy of means and the fragility of the people set against the city's looming monumentality. In the photographs of Niemeyer's funeral, a somber choreography is unleashed in the same place that once served as the venue for a great celebration, overtaking the otherwise sinuous, elegant, and organic transparencies, the ramps, columns, and reflecting pool (which was added as an afterthought). Following Brasília's inauguration, Planalto may not have enjoyed the most appropriate or photogenic use. Now that the architect has left the building, it may be liberated from his grasp.

All photographs from the series *Oscar*, 2012
Courtesy the artist and Galeria Fortes Vilaça, São Paulo

Mauro Restiffe
Niemeyer's Funeral

Rodrigo Moura

Rodrigo Moura is director of art and cultural programs at Instituto Inhotim in Minas Gerais.

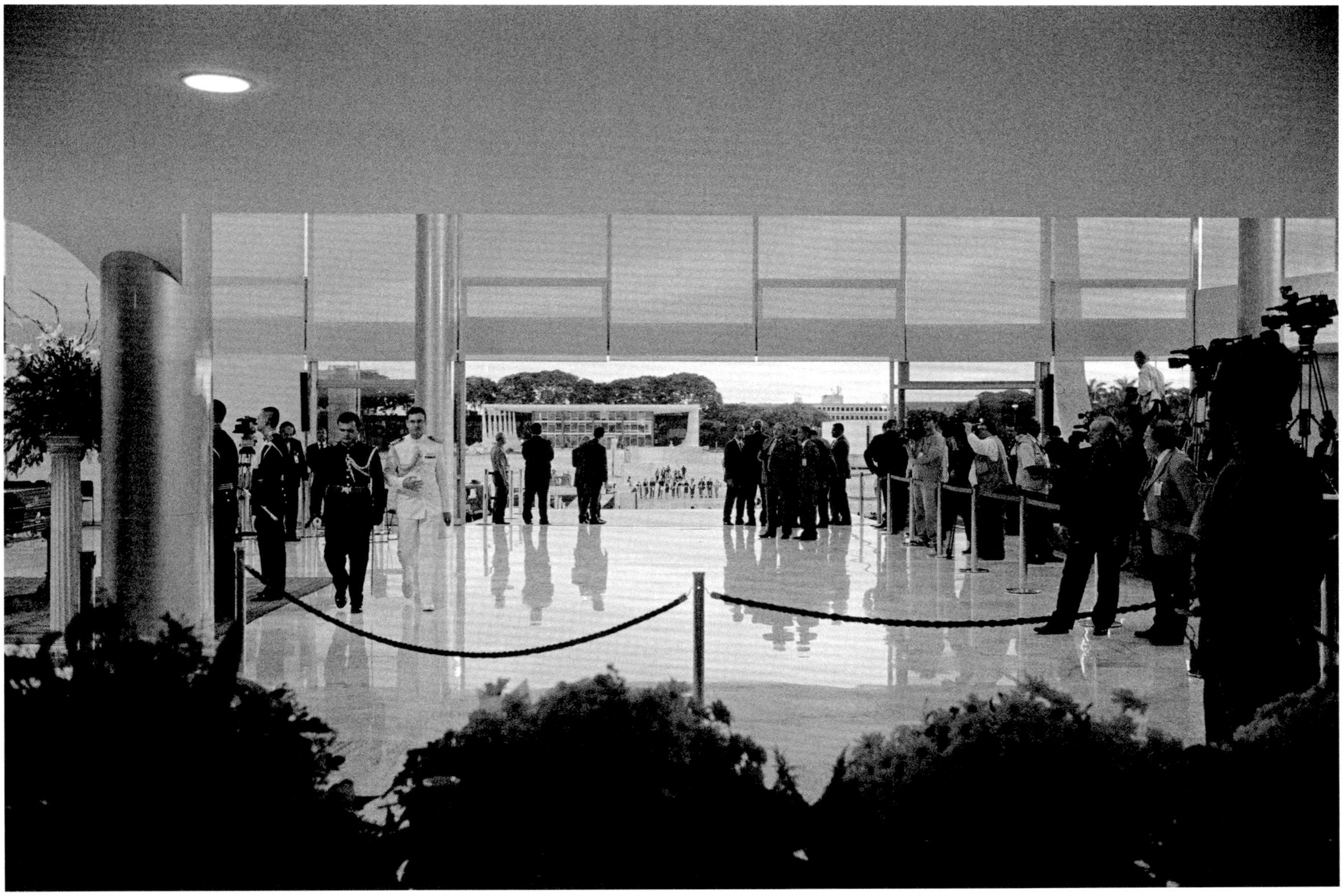

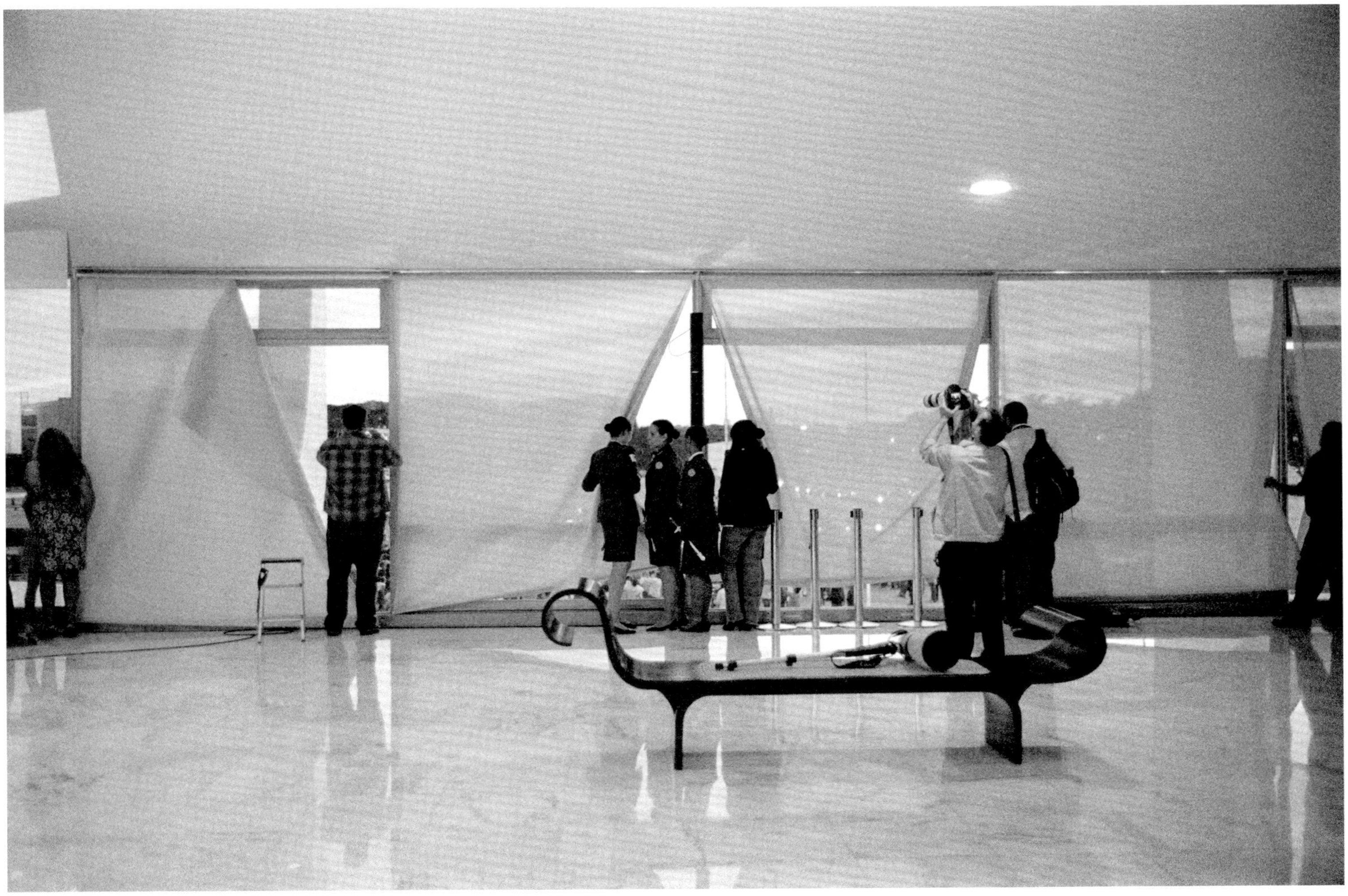

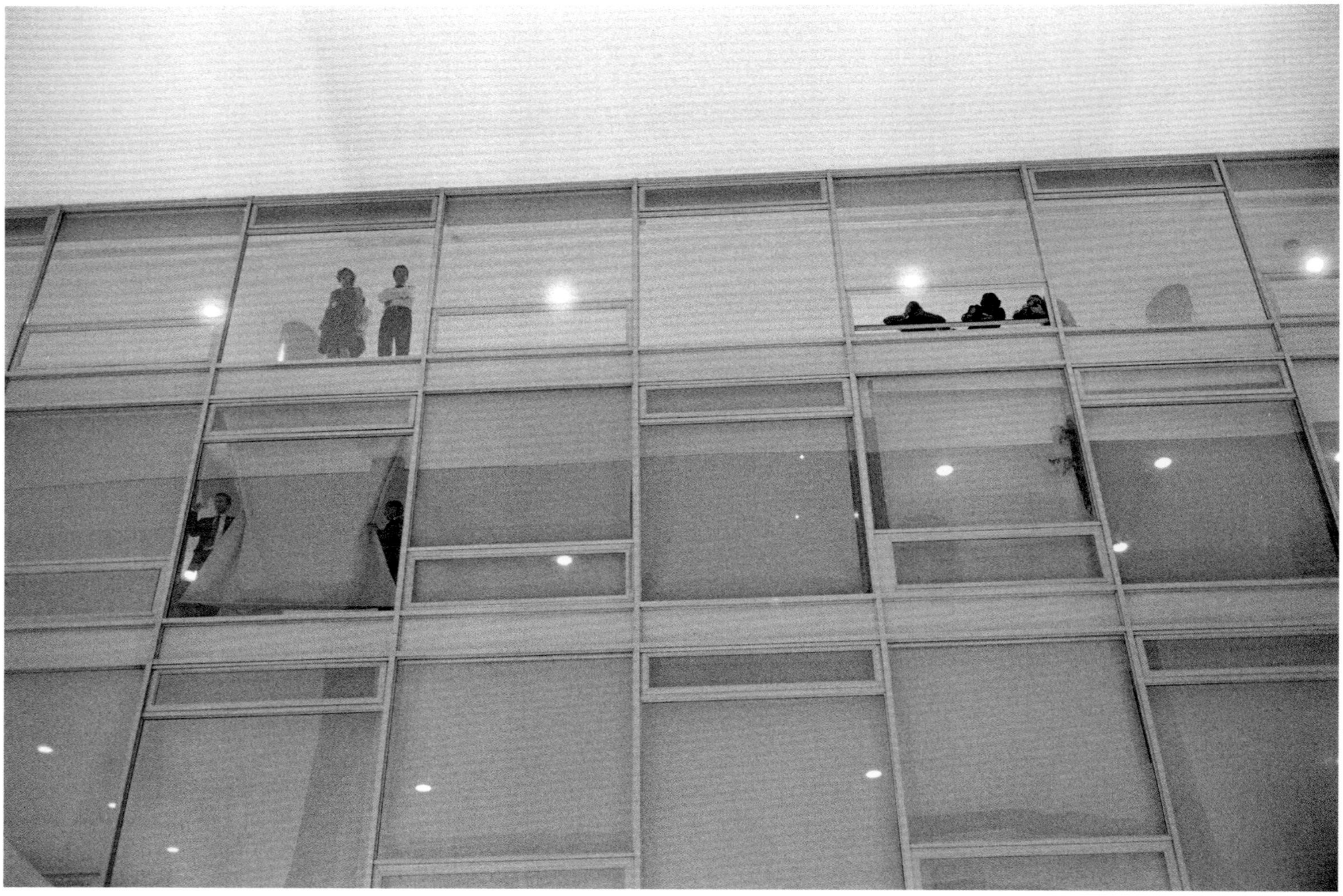

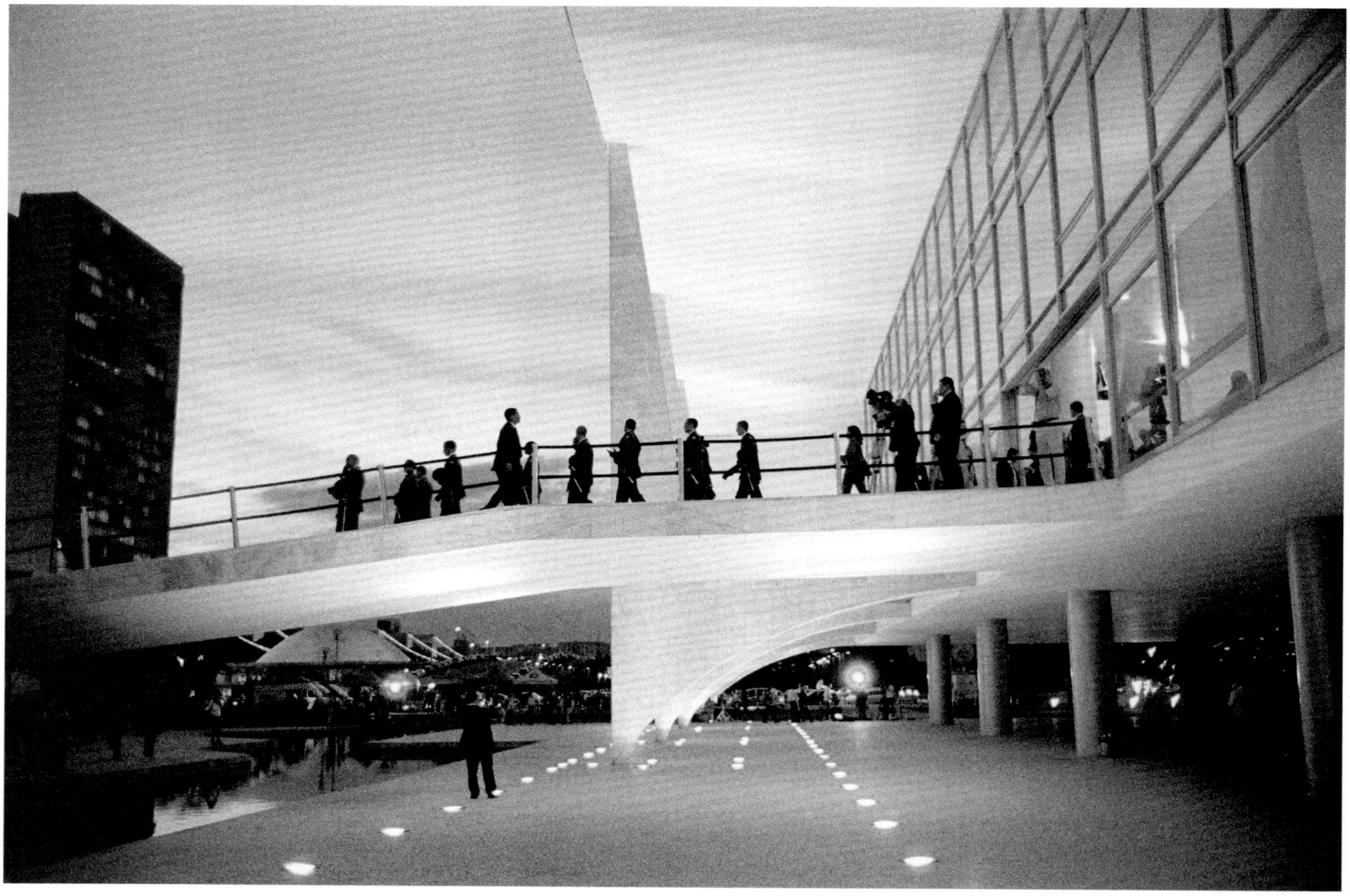

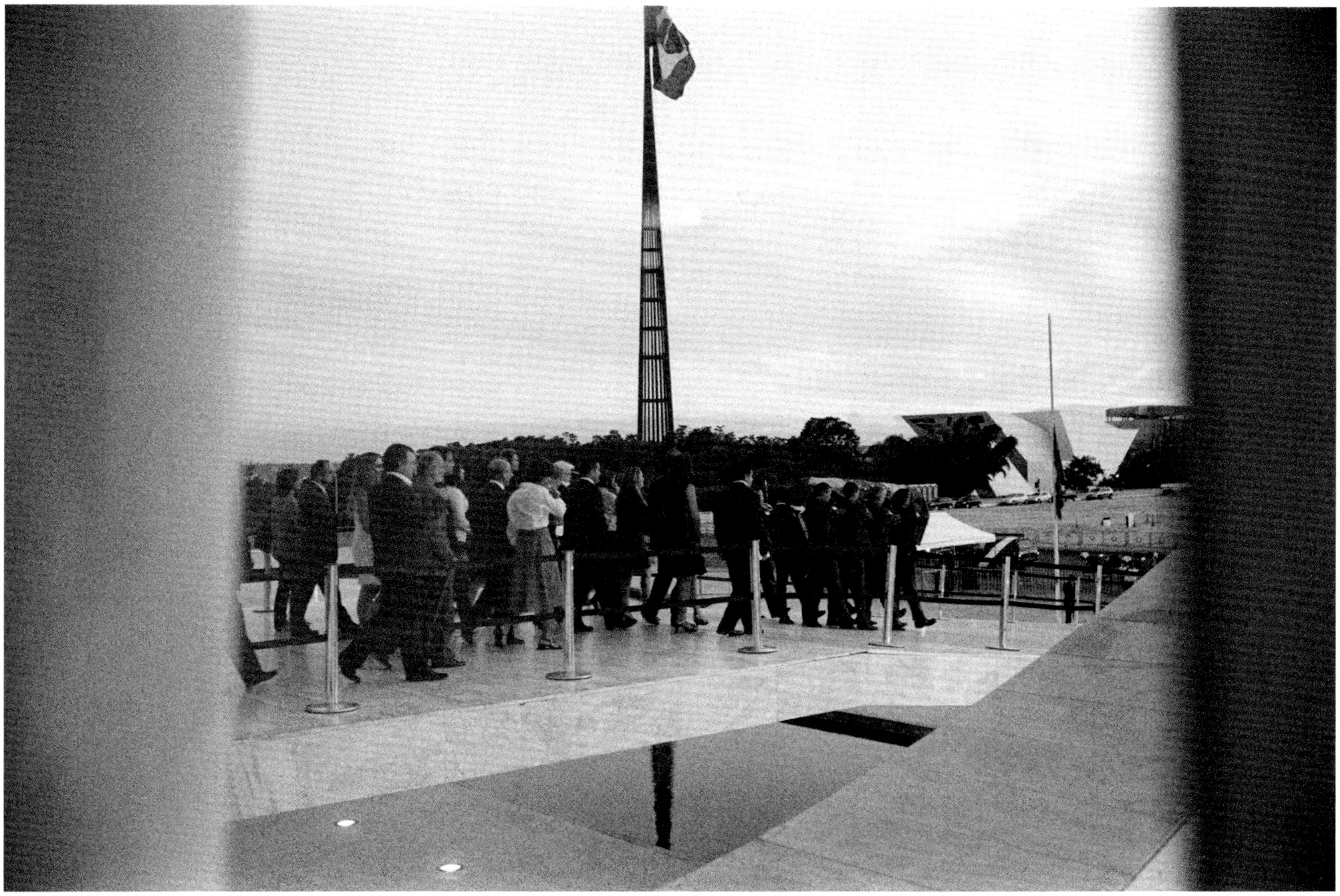

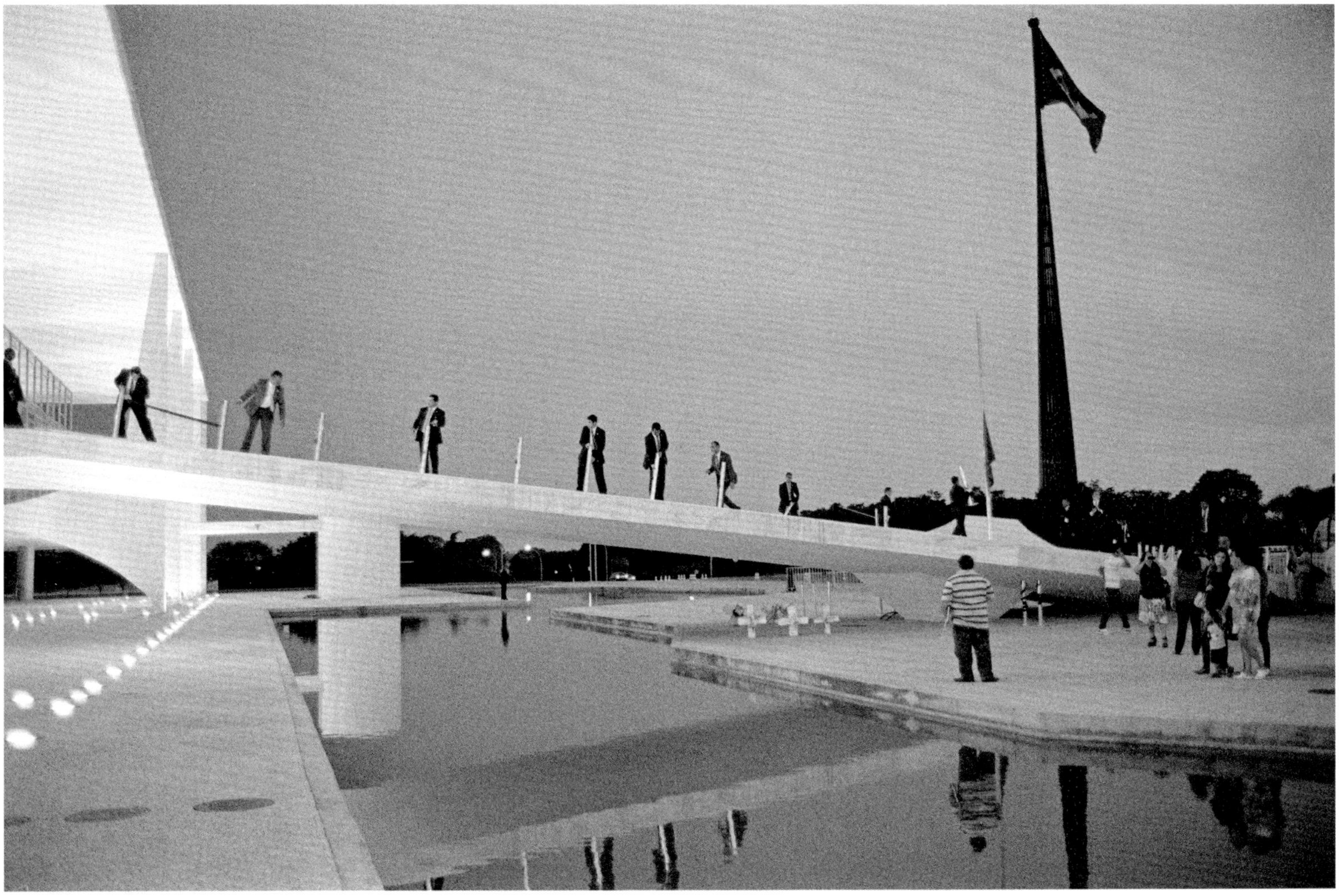

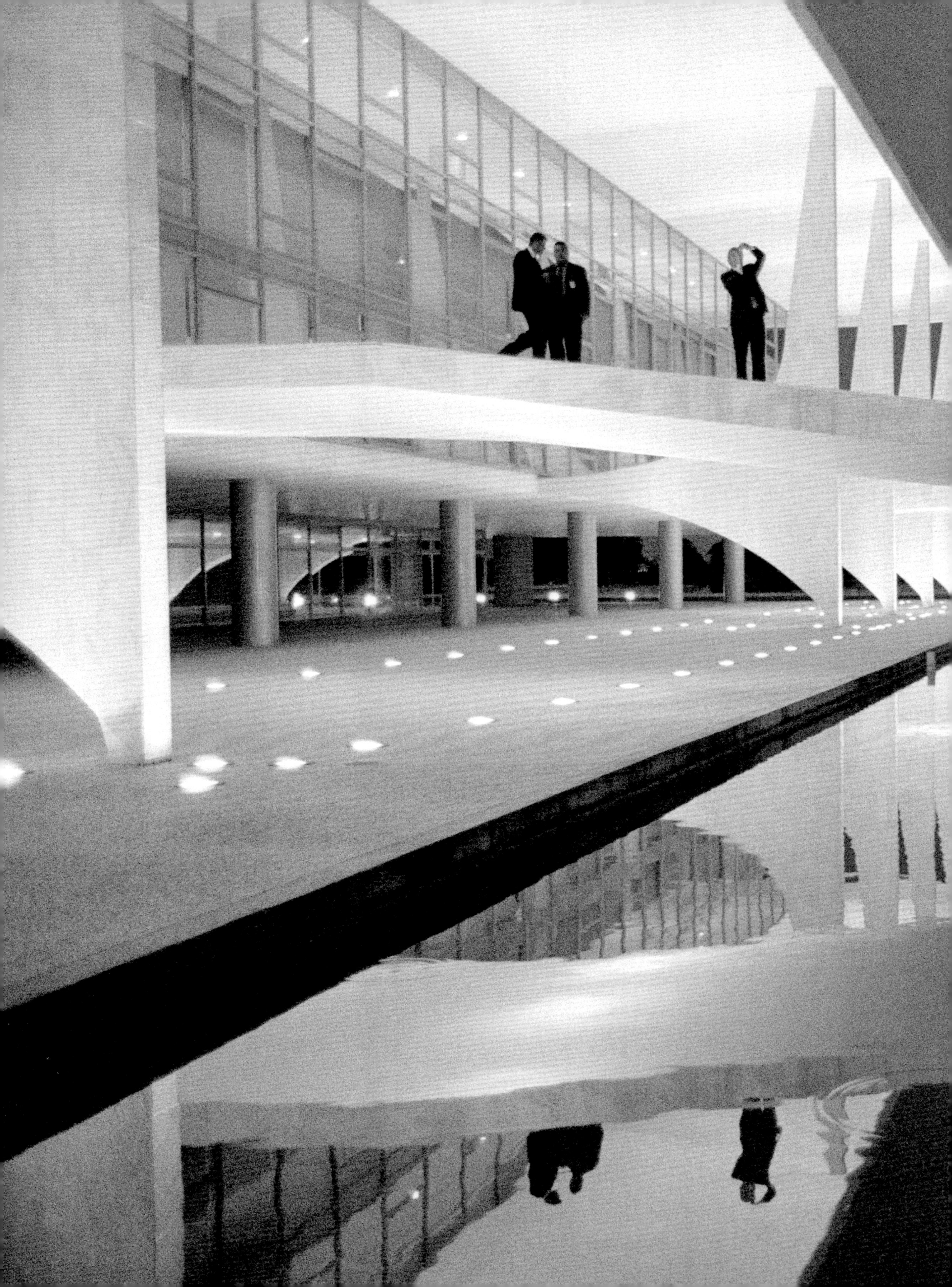

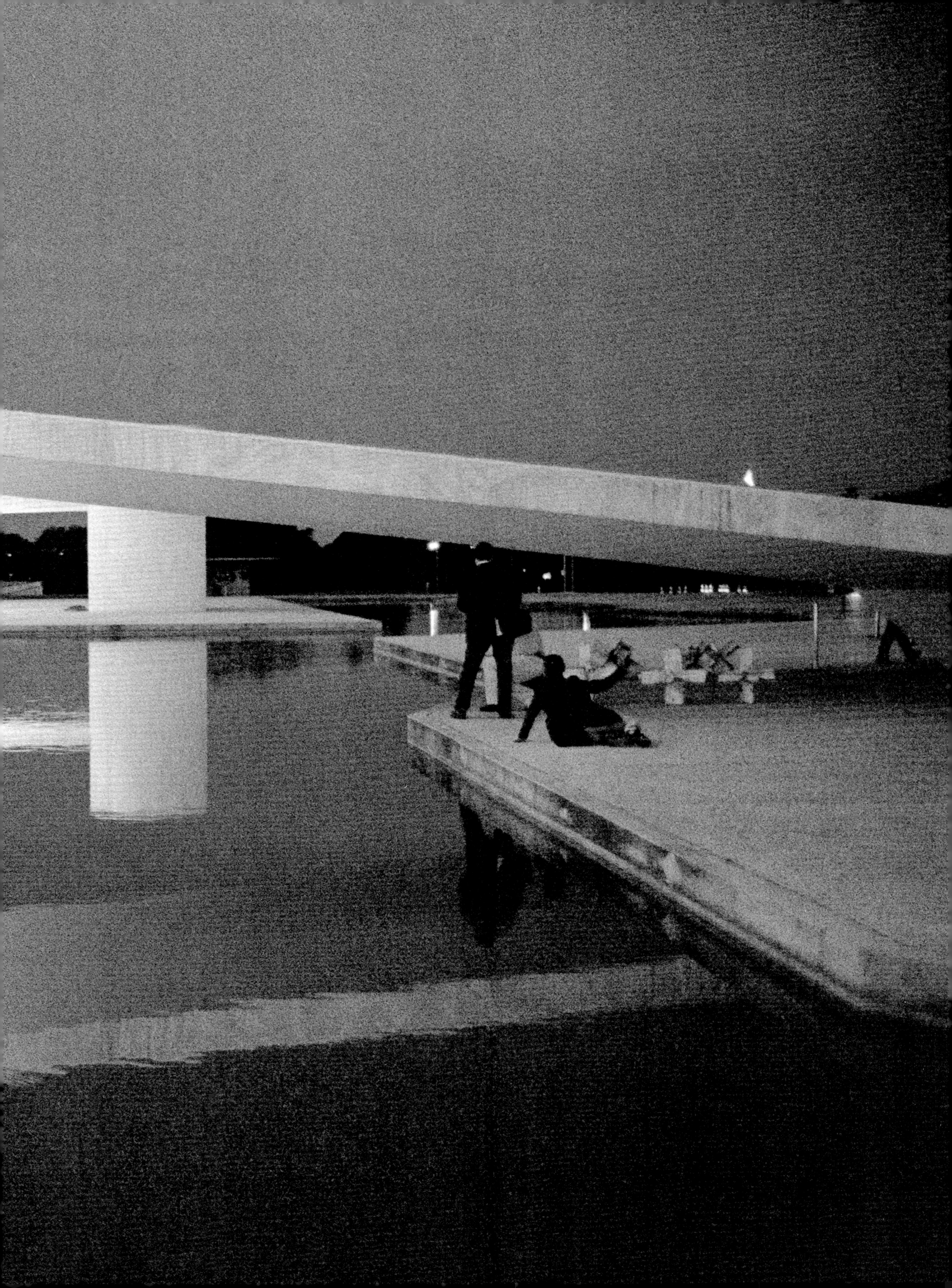

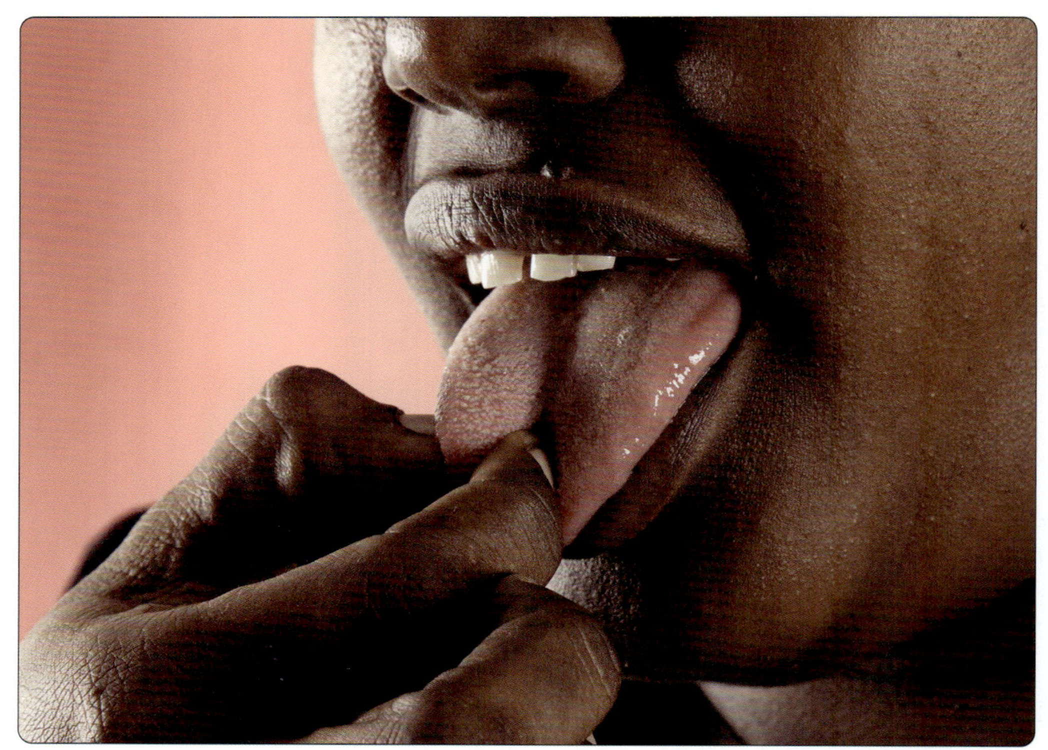

língua

tongue

Ana Maria Maia is a writer and curator living in São Paulo.

Personal and public chronologies intertwine in *Educação para adultos* (Education for adults), a collection of sixty educational posters presented as an enormous grid. Featuring a glossary of words and images, the project is the result of Jonathas de Andrade's desire to recover utopian and democratic meanings erased from Brazilian society during the years of military dictatorship between 1964 and 1985.

Before the 1964 military coup, Brazil experienced a period of optimism as a result of accelerated development and plans for structural reforms, involving education and land use, intended to redistribute wealth. Reform was urgently needed to undo a colonial mentality that had produced a system of oppressors and oppressed. In 1962, educator and philosopher Paulo Freire taught three hundred sugarcane cutters from a poor, rural area in the Northeast Region of Brazil how to read. In opposition to the official teaching handbooks that Freire viewed as instruments of control and social exclusion, his teaching method for adults was based on forty hours of meetings with his students, in which experiences were exchanged horizontally and the learning process was derived from each student's own stories and experiences. The initiative was a success and became a federal government program for teaching literacy until Freire was exiled by the military, in 1964.

In the late 1980s, during a time of political and economic possibility in the post-dictatorship period, de Andrade's mother, a teacher, used educational materials based on Freire's method. But these had been created by a large publishing company and were sold at newsstands beginning in 1971. This new set consisted of twenty posters, each representing something pertinent to the popular imagination: food, money, unions, etc. While the posters functioned as a teaching tool, they had lost their emancipatory character and now reproduced relations of power, since the words and images were chosen not by students but by a major publisher. Born in 1982, de Andrade belongs to a generation that did not live through the dictatorship but is nonetheless marked by the collective trauma left in its wake. For this generation, the reopening of historical archives is a way of facing a difficult past and of searching for ways to reflect on the present in light of projects and utopias that were never attained.

In 2010, after finding the educational posters in his mother's home, de Andrade became interested in Freire's legacy and worked with a group of illiterate seamstresses to create a new set of posters based on Freire's unique method. The participants suggested words for which de Andrade produced the corresponding images. His new posters were designed according to the collection his mother had used, and in his installation of the project he mixed twenty of the posters from the past with his new set, creating a series of temporal and semantic ambiguities. In the grid's horizontal and vertical lines, associations of analogous terms generate commentary on Brazilian realities, as when the word *Brasil (*Brazil) is followed by *colônia* (which means both "cologne" and "colony"), or when the same image is used to illustrate both *união* (united) and *saque* (looting). Ultimately, this sequence of word-image combinations connects the years 1962, 1964, 1971, and 2010, undoing any sense of strict chronology, allowing different historical moments to shade one another.

Jonathas de Andrade
Education for Adults

Ana Maria Maia

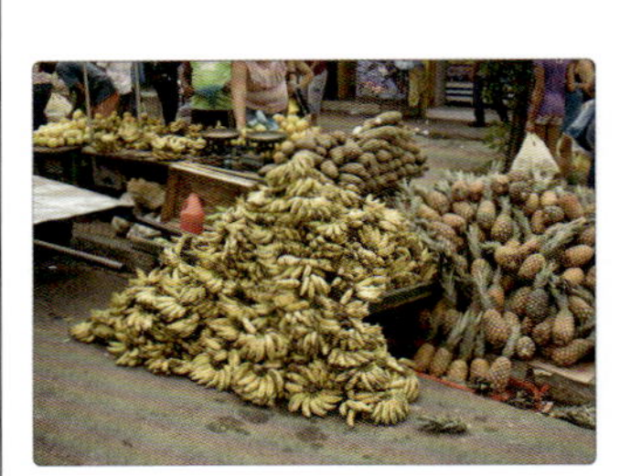

banana

banana

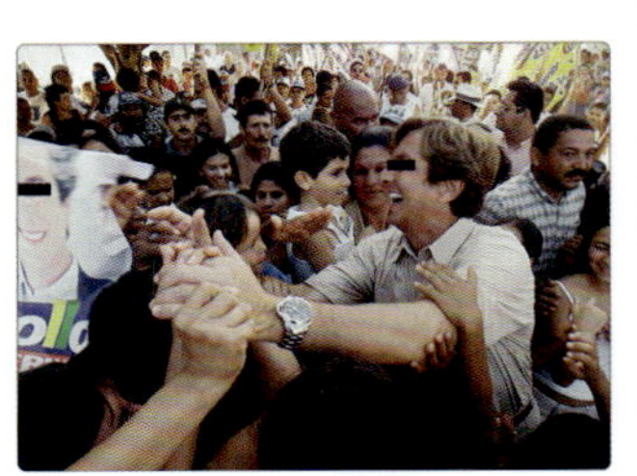

candidato

candidate

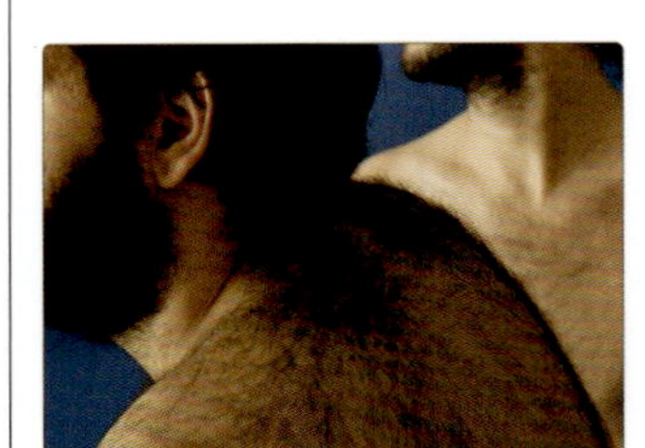

cabelo

hair

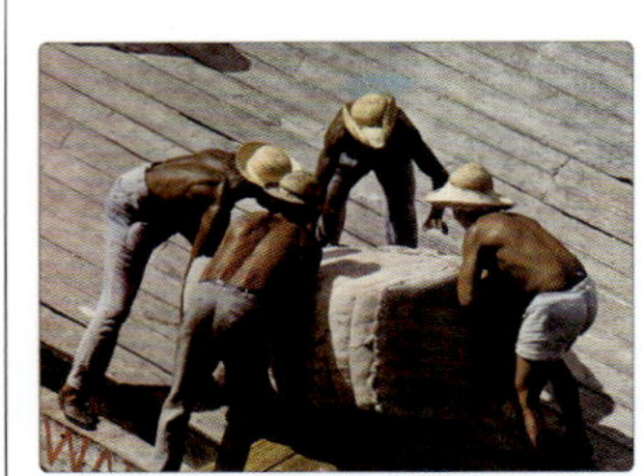

união

united

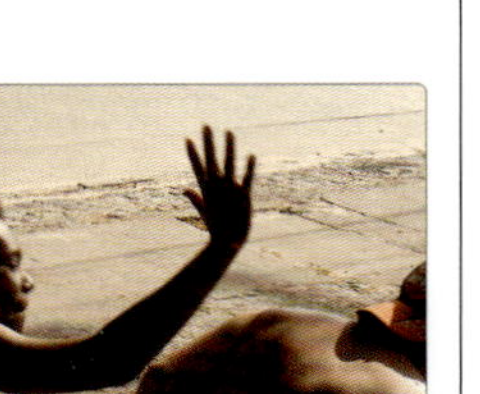

tapa

slap

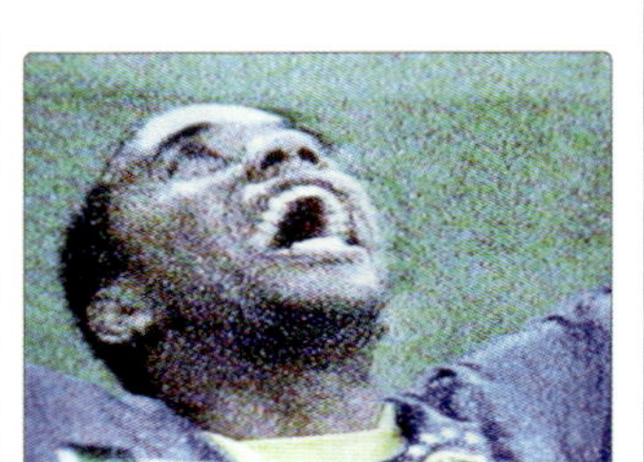

feliz

happy

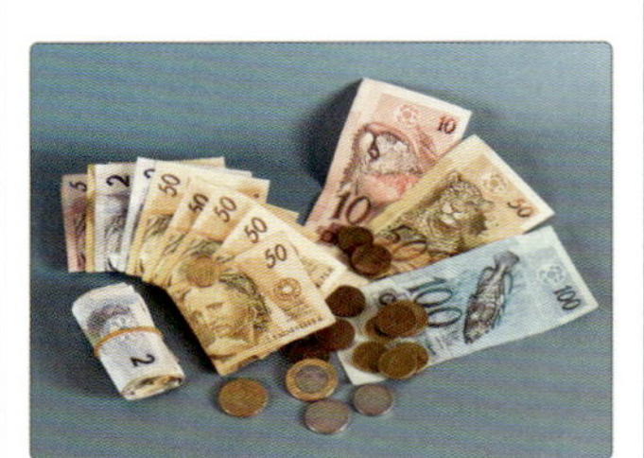

dinheiro

money

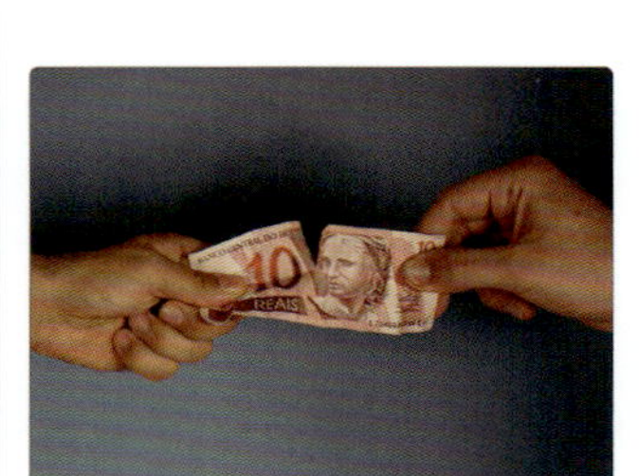

rasgar

ripping

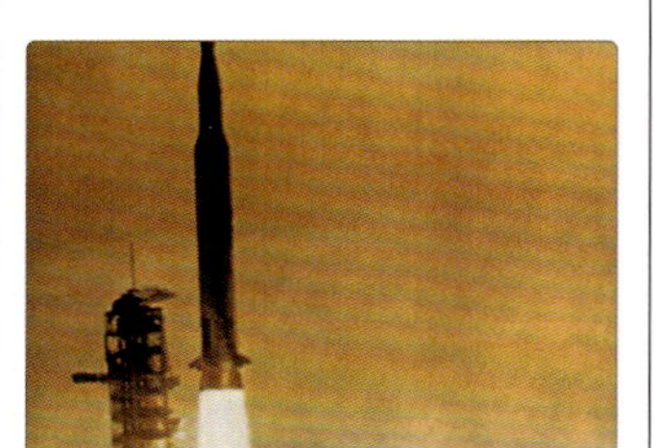

foguete

rocket

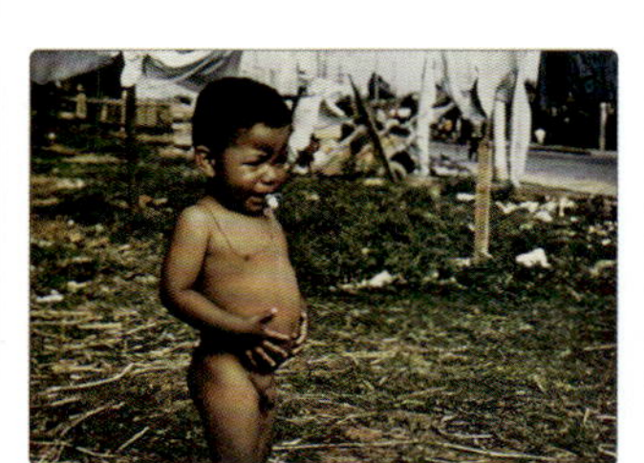

barriga

belly

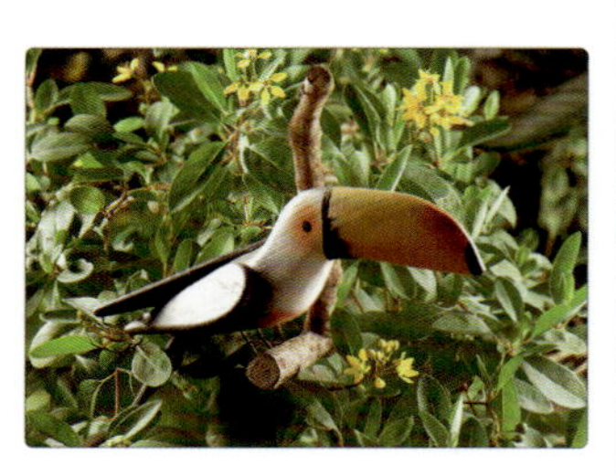

tucano

toucan

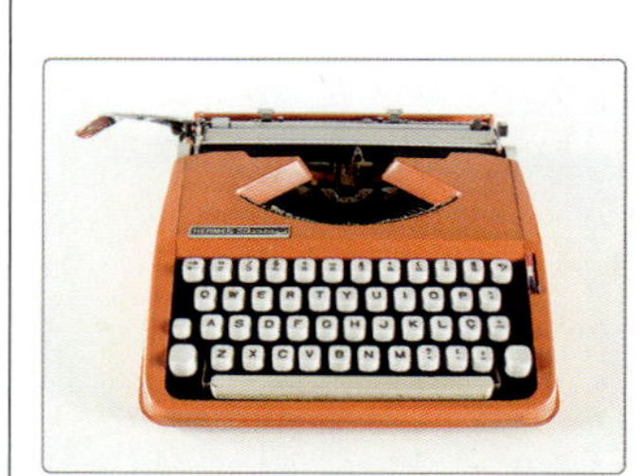

máquina

machine

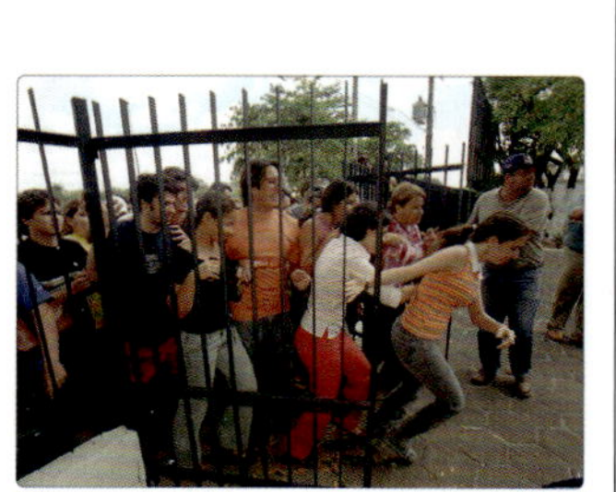

concurso

contest

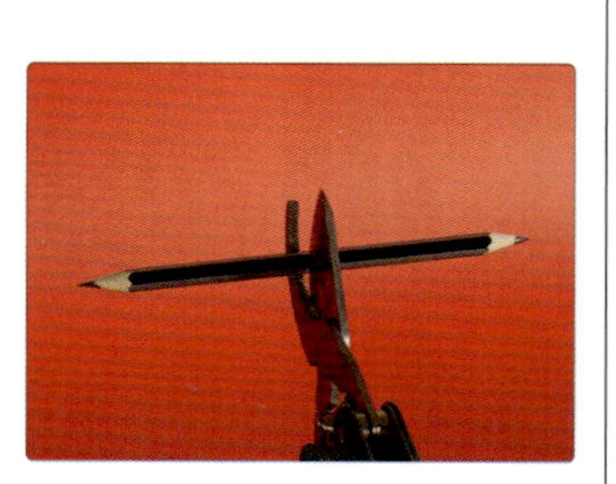

dividir

sharing

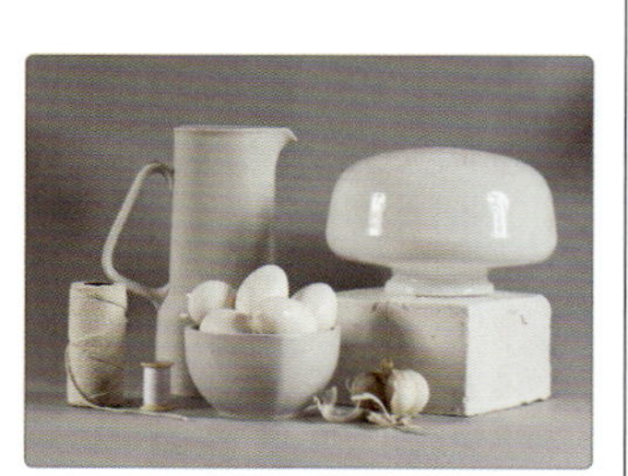

branco

white

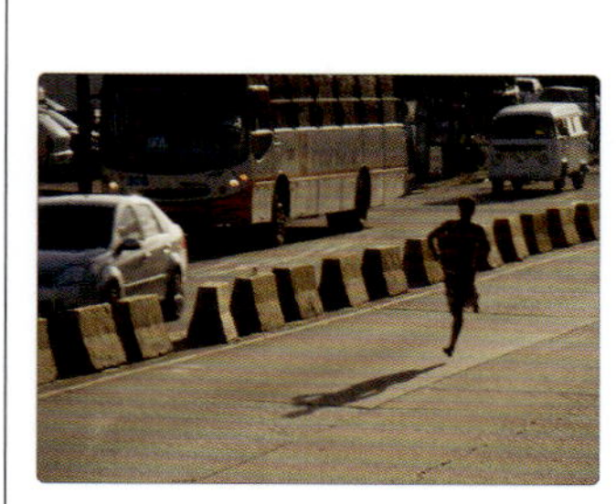

arriscar

risking

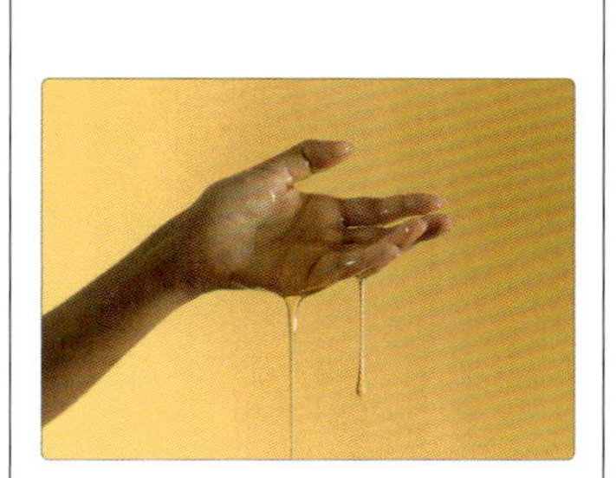

mel

honey

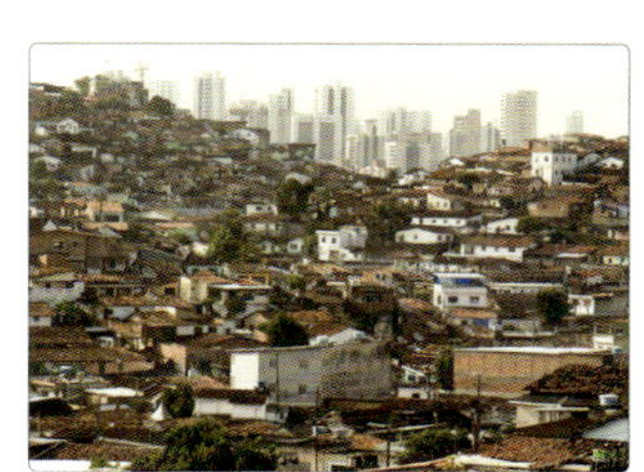

excesso

excess

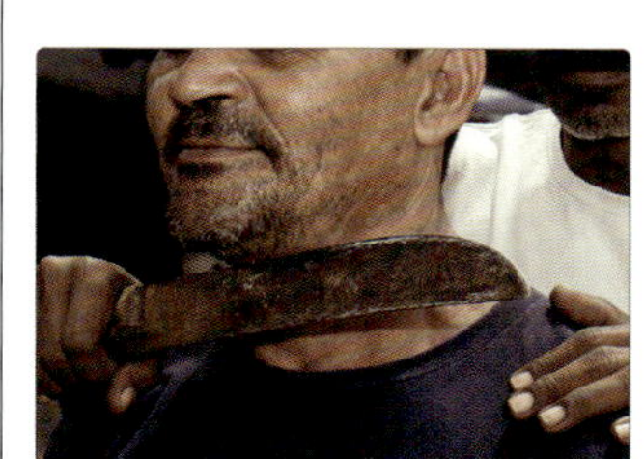

faca

knife

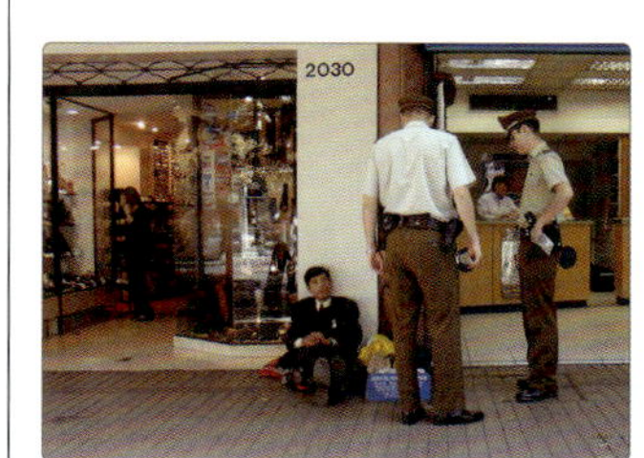

razão

reason

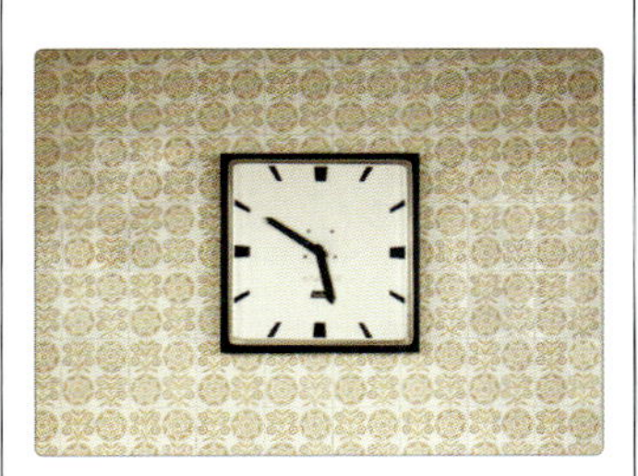

atrasado

late

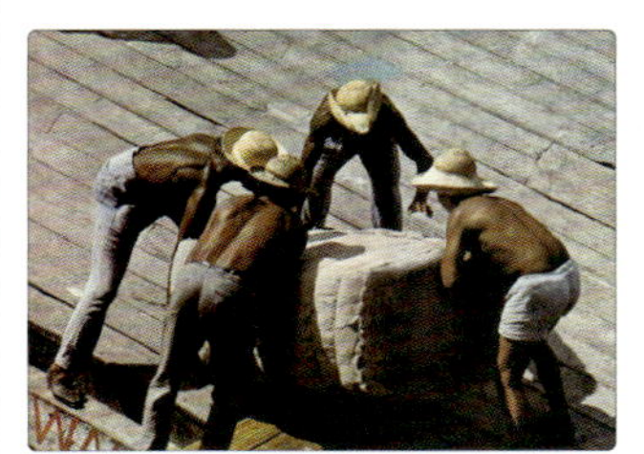

saque

looting

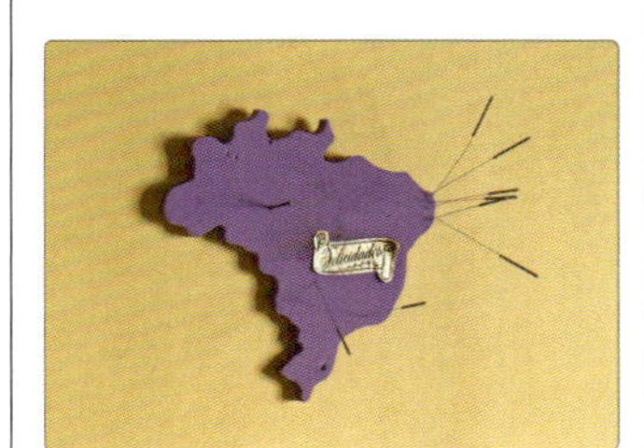

brasil

brazil

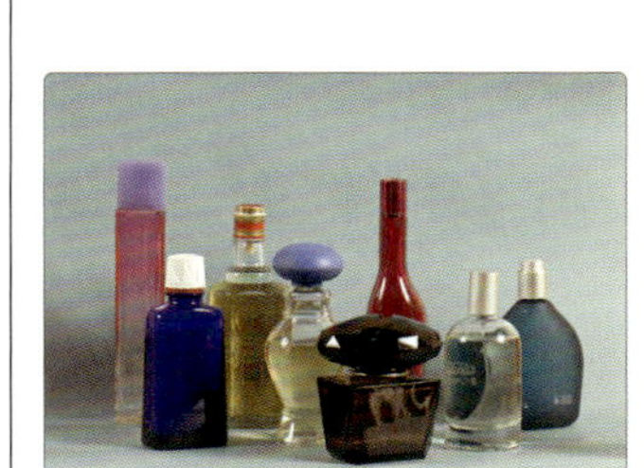

colônia

cologne

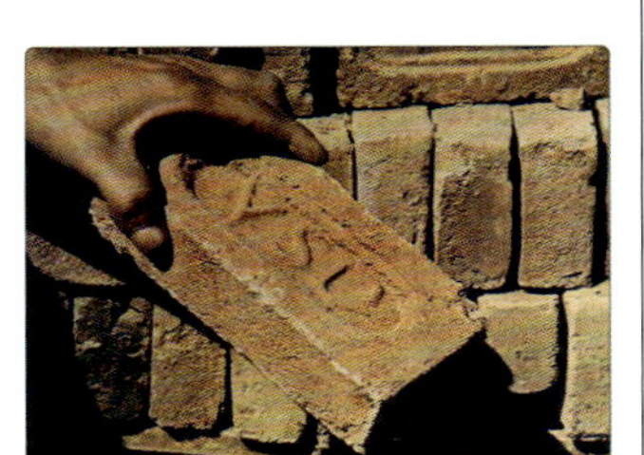

tijolo

brick

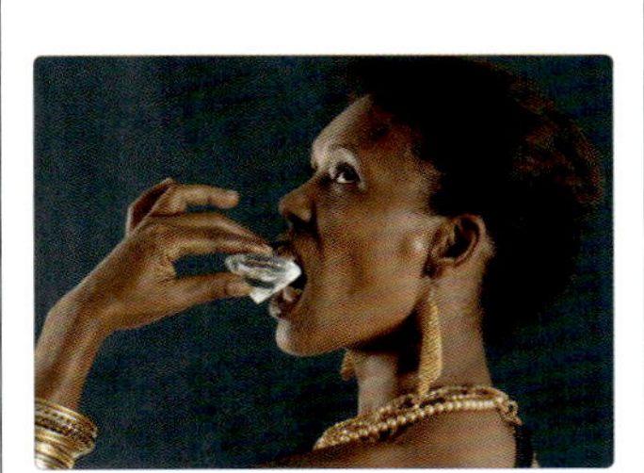

riqueza

wealth

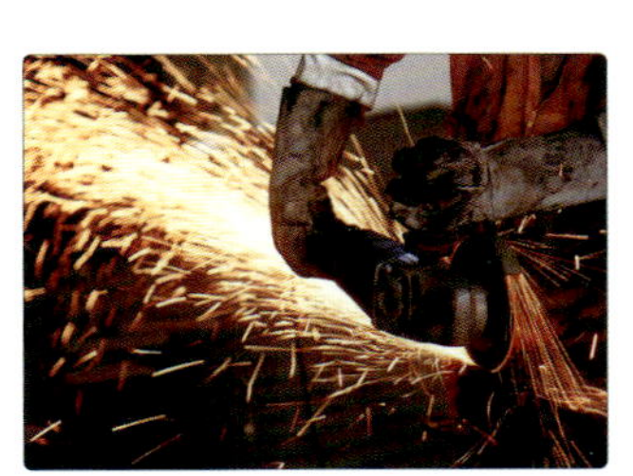

faísca

sparks

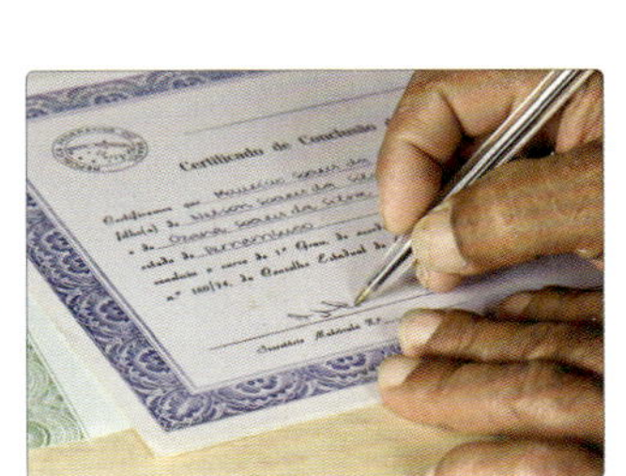

assinatura

signature

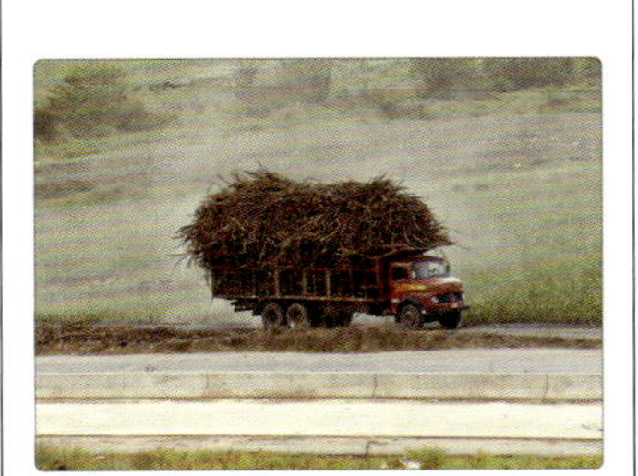

pai

father

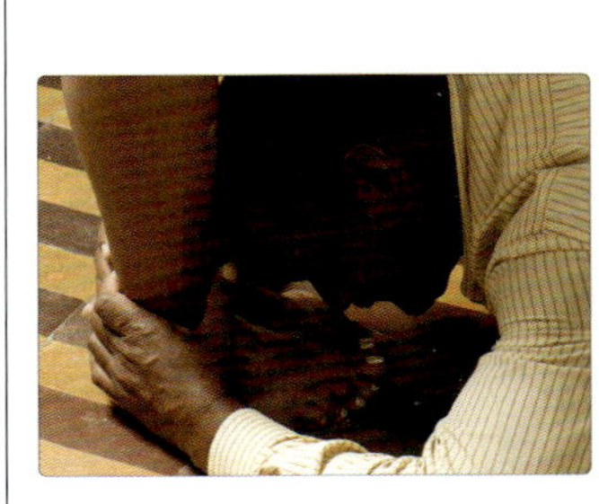

safra

crop

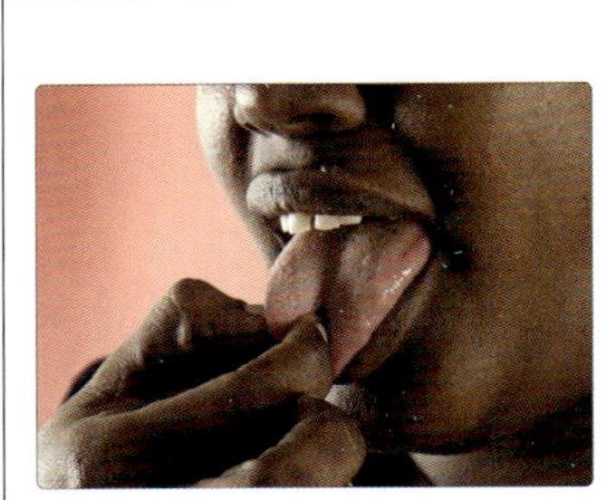

devoção

devotion

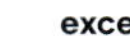

língua

tongue

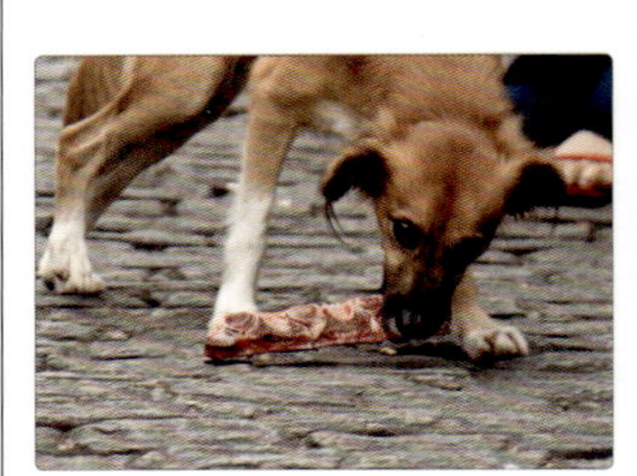

ossinho

bone

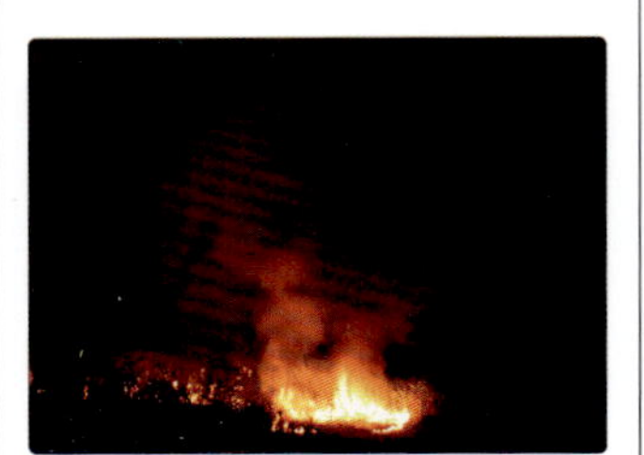

fogo

fire

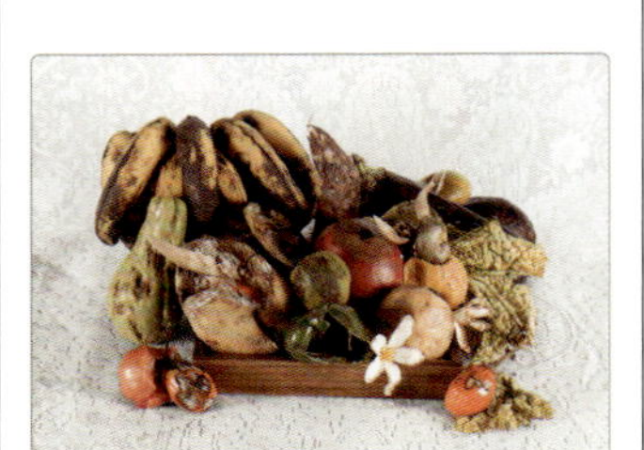

perdido

lost

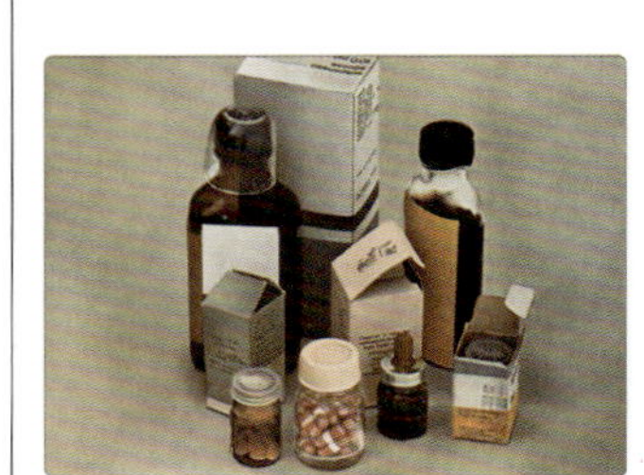

remédio

medicine

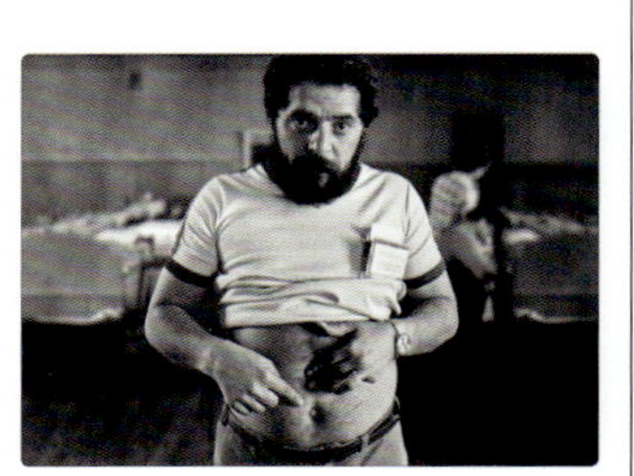

nordeste

northeast

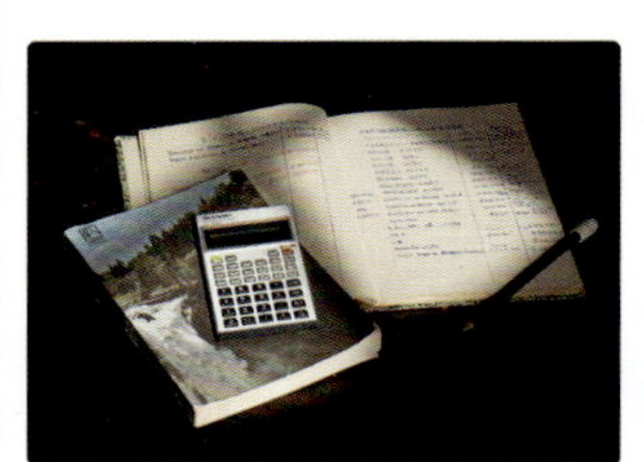

conta

bill

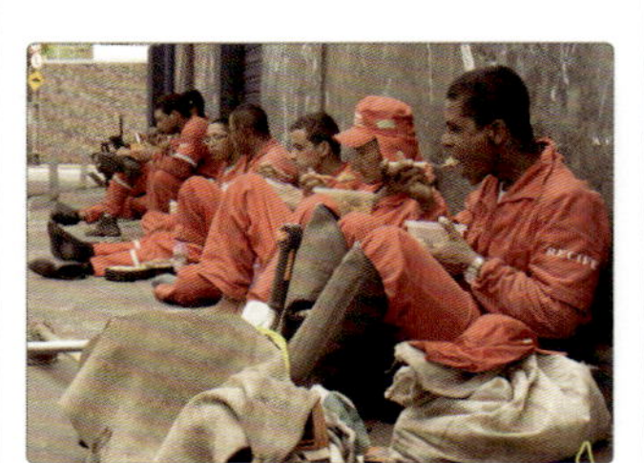

calçada

pavement

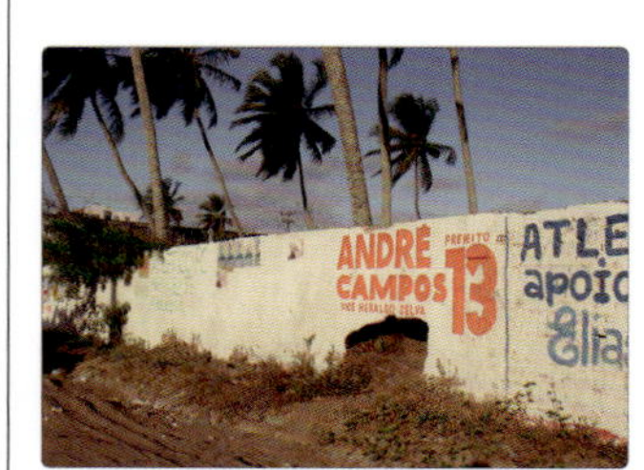

acesso

access

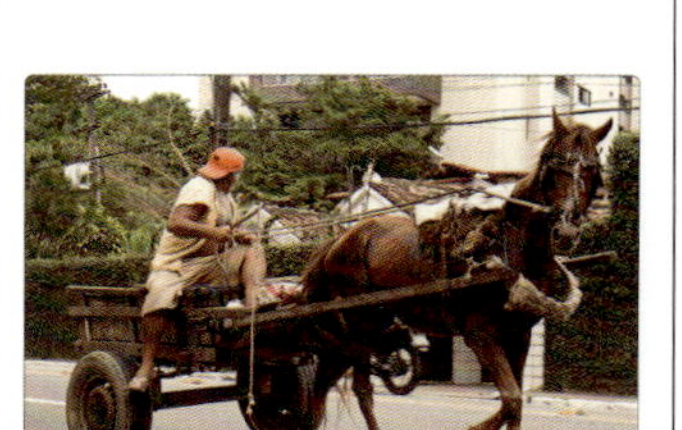

carroça

cart

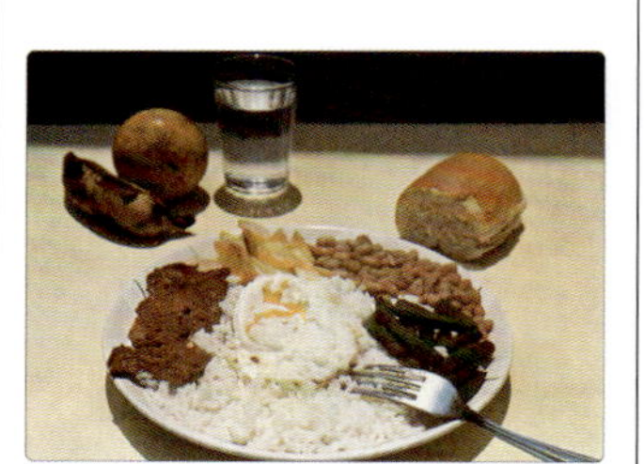

comida

food

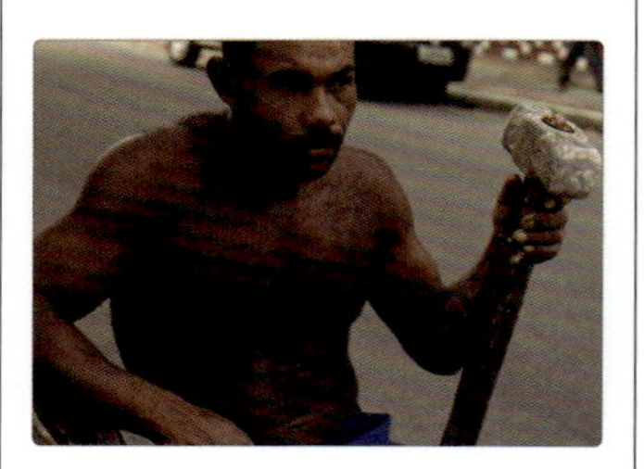

homem

man

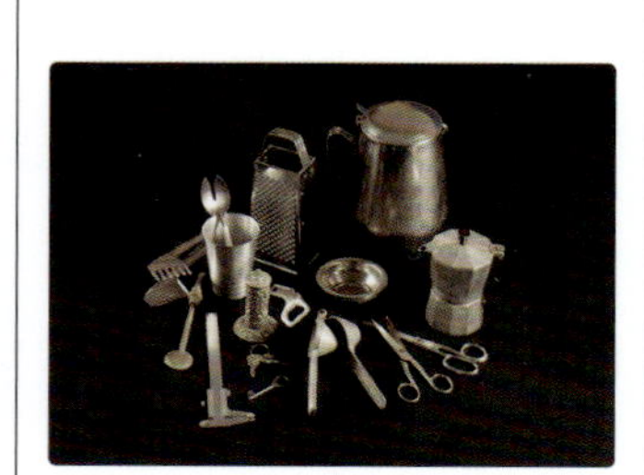

metal

metal

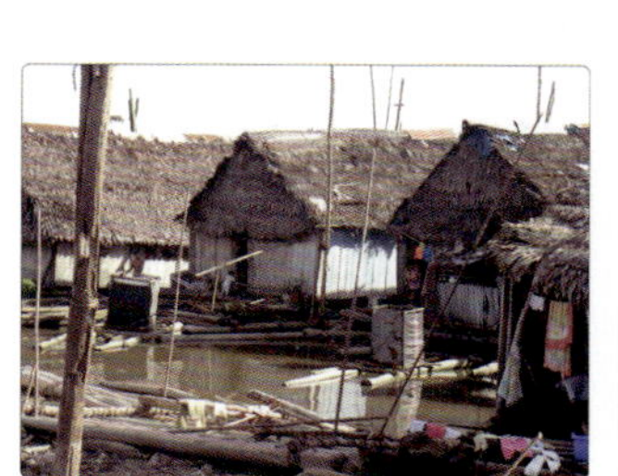

moradia

housing

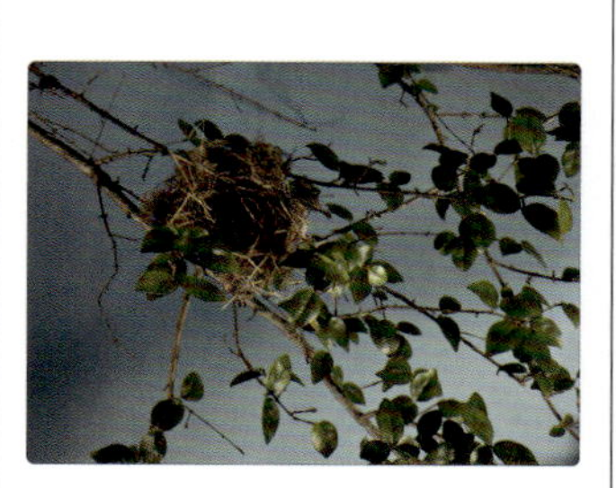

ninho

nest

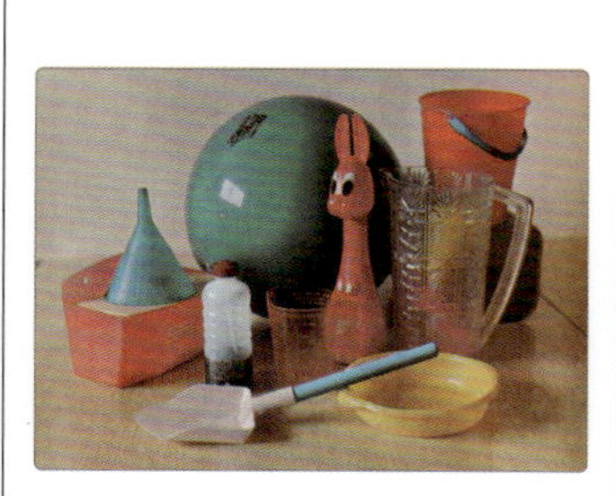

plástico

plastic

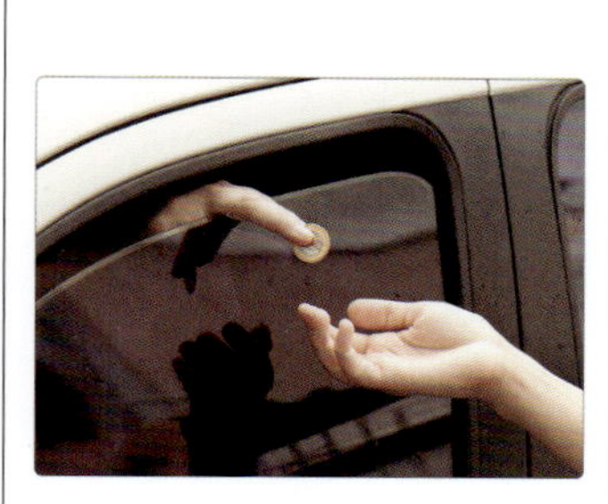

preço

price

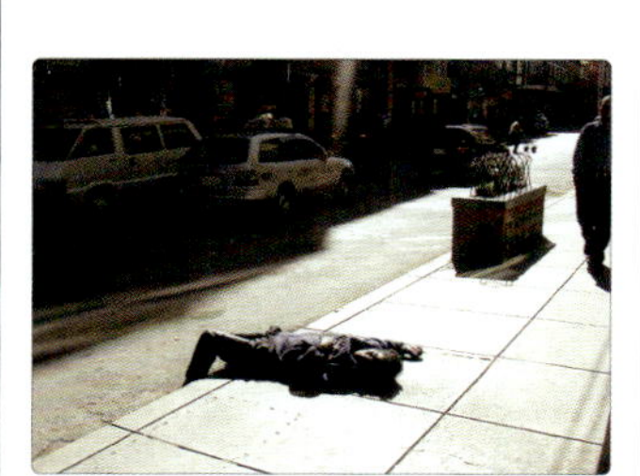

preguiça

laziness

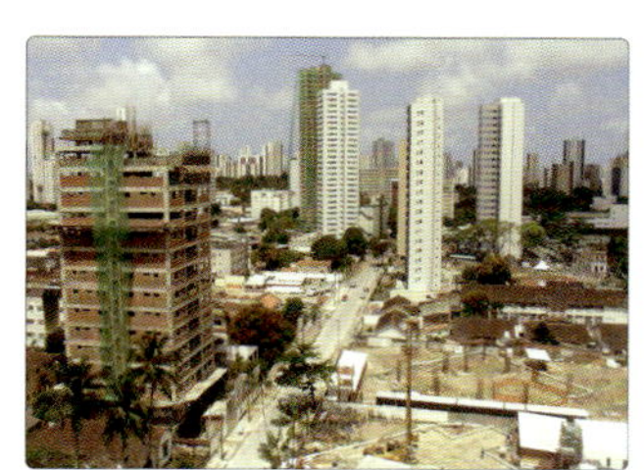

progresso

progress

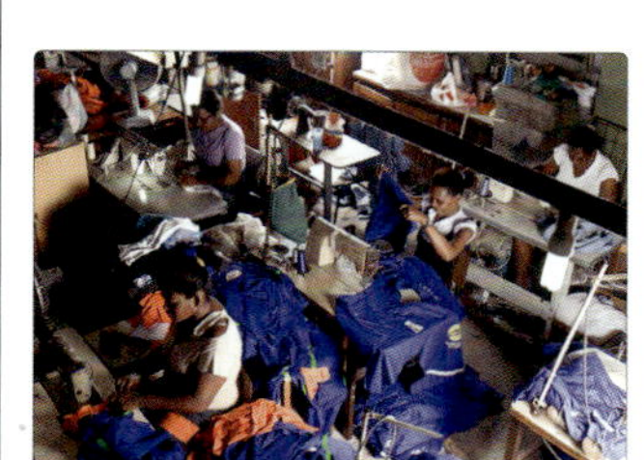

roupa

clothing

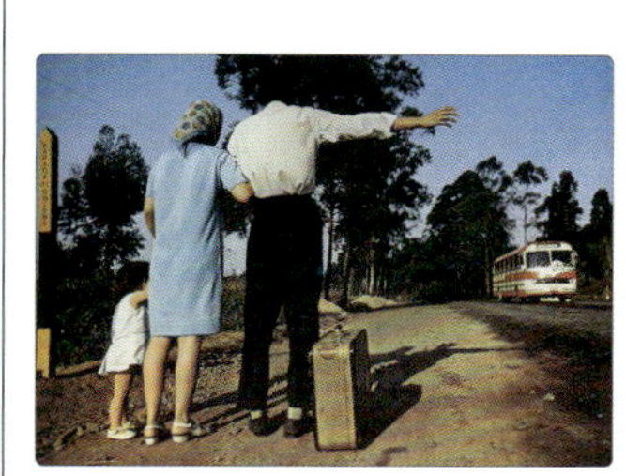

viagem

travel

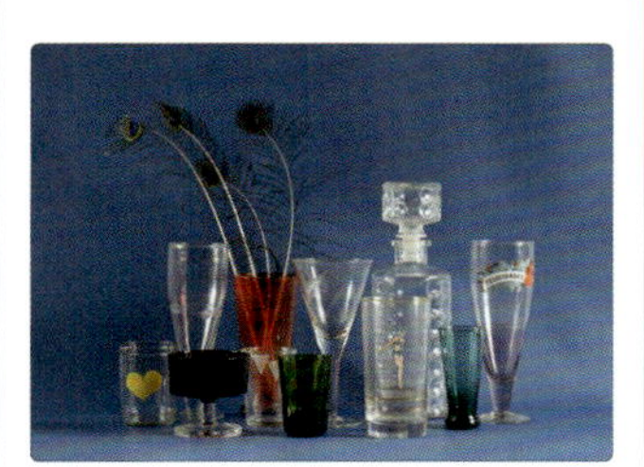

vidro

glass

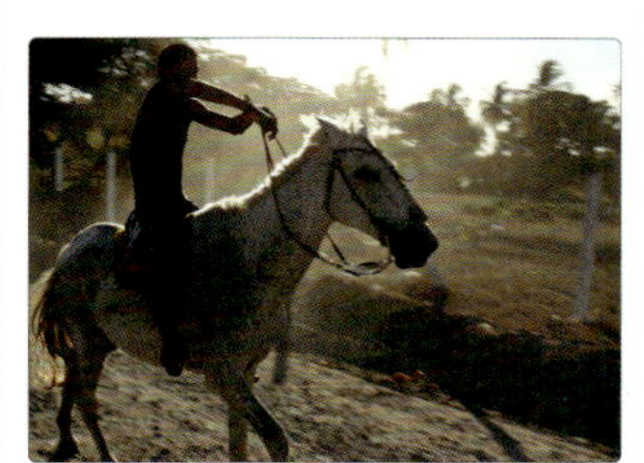

agora

now

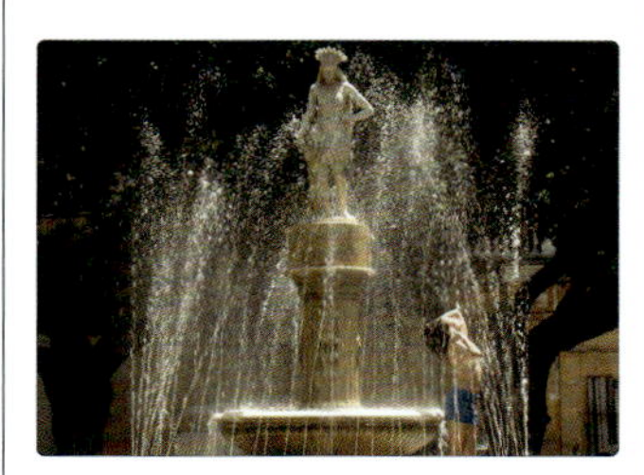

banho

bath

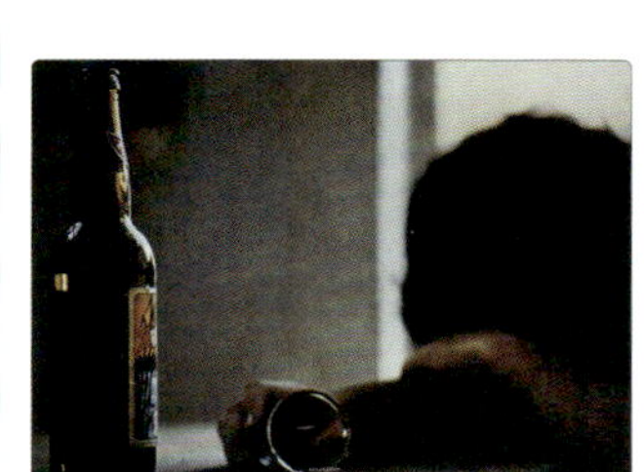

cachaça

cachaça

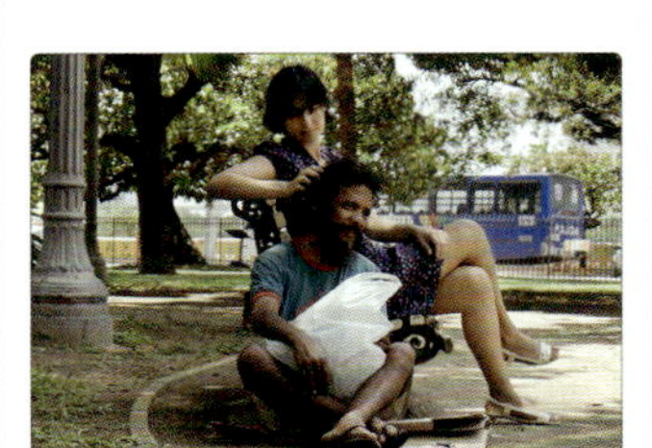

carinho

caress

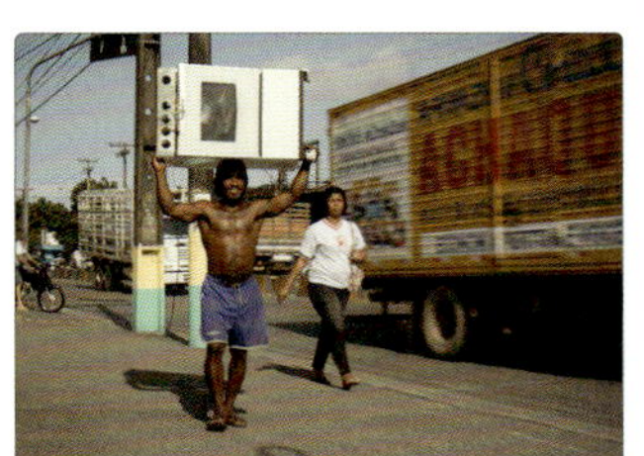

carregar

carrying

enxada

hoe

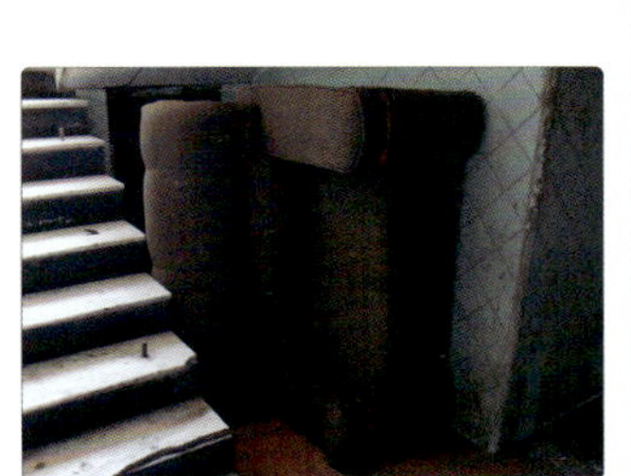

encaixe

fit

Jonathas de Andrade,
Educação para Adultos
(Education for Adults),
2010
Courtesy the artist and
Galeria Vermelho, São Paulo

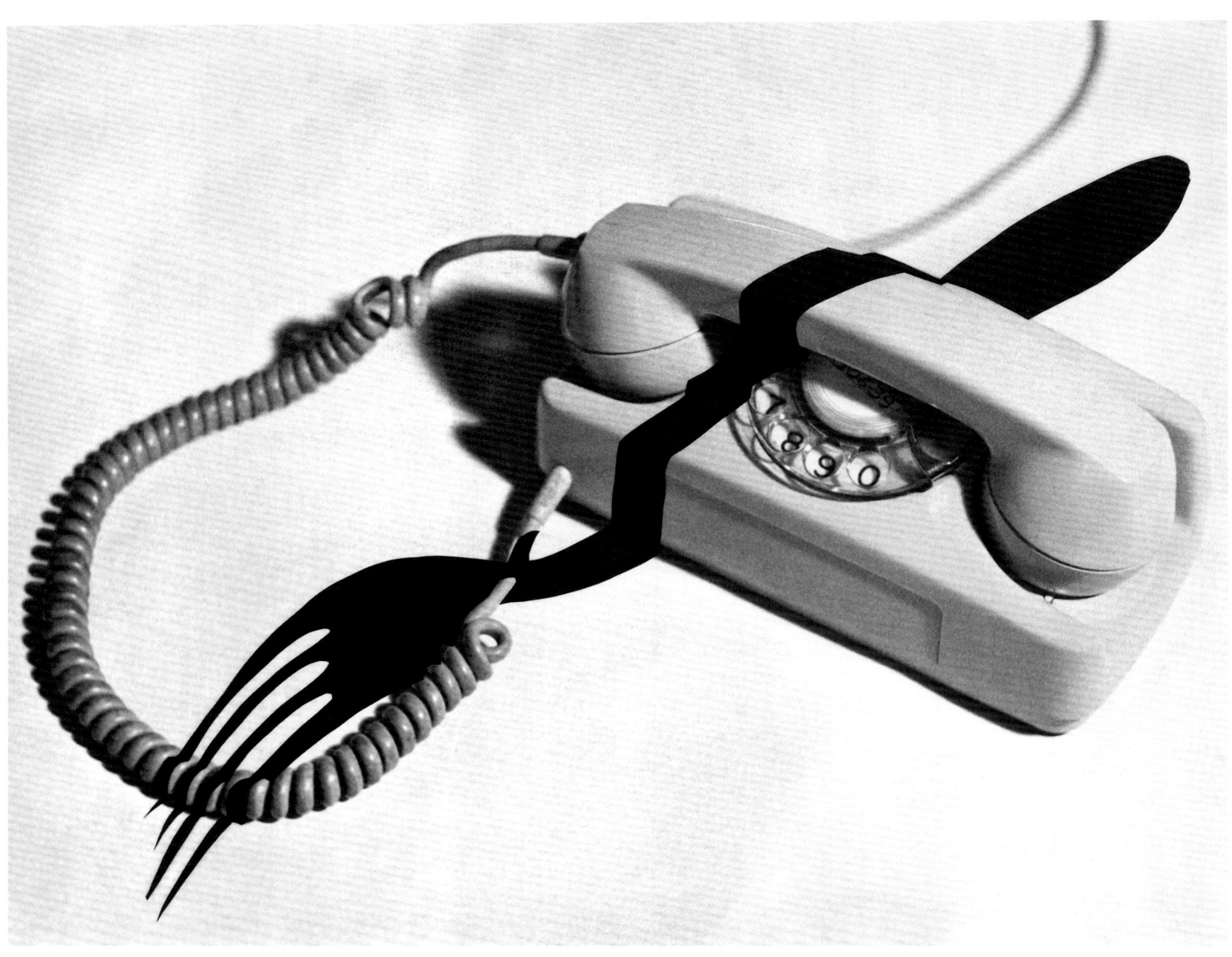

Enigma 1, 1981

Regina Silveira
Enigmas

Sarah Hermanson Meister

Sarah Hermanson
Meister is a curator
in the department of
photography at the
Museum of Modern Art,
New York.

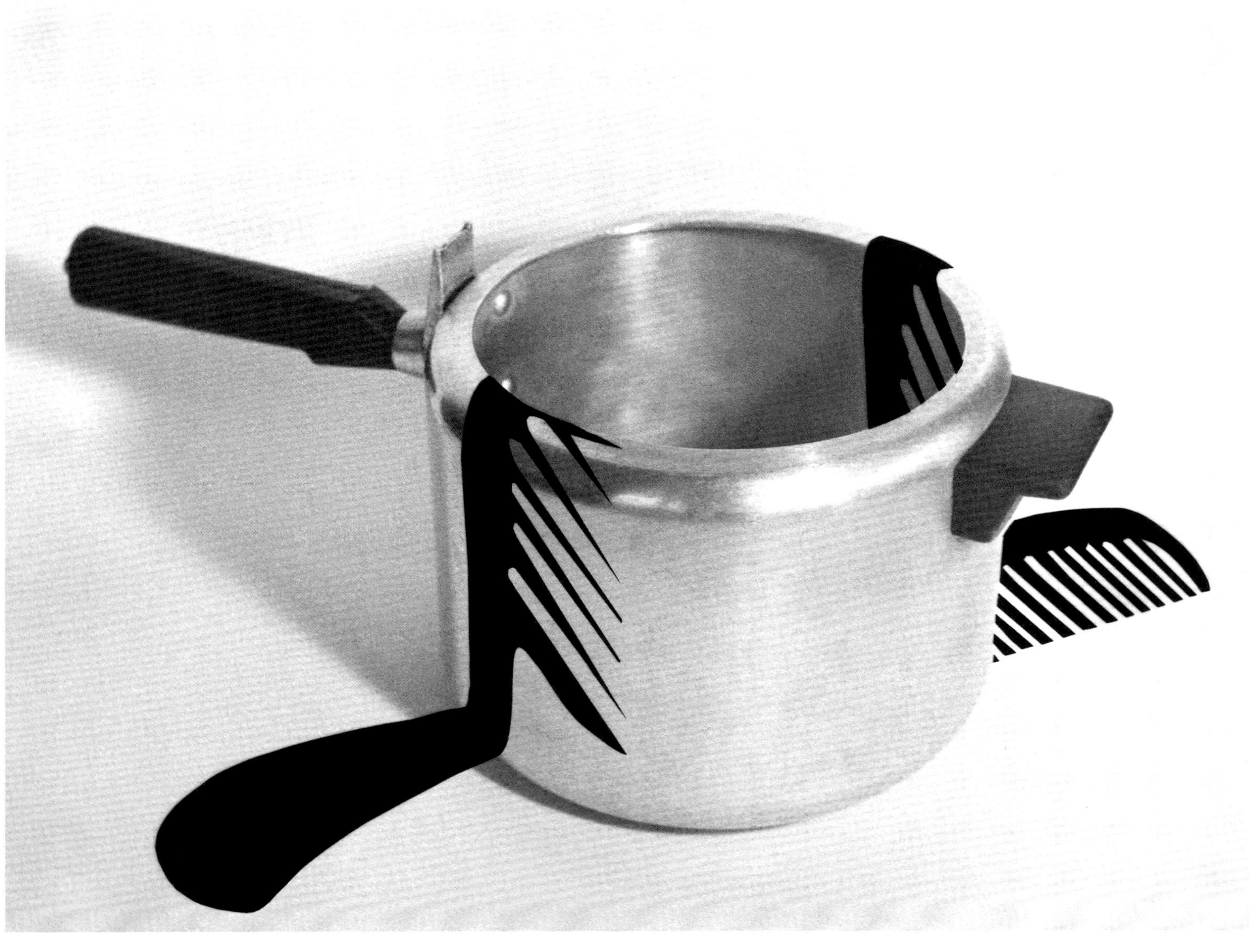

Enigma 2, 1981

In the shadow of the Brazilian military dictatorship, Regina Silveira pursued an elusive art, by necessity and by design. Absence and isolation, illusion and distortion were not only promising artistic strategies but also richly meaningful metaphors in an era of severe political repression. Trained as a painter and printmaker in her native Porto Alegre, Silveira studied with the expressionist painter Iberê Camargo. By the early 1970s she was experimenting with photographic imagery (mostly found), and became an active participant in the mail-art circuits then proliferating throughout Latin America.

These unique photograms named *Enigmas* date from 1981, and were made using an opaque mask (drawn by the artist to simulate a cast shadow) in perfect registration over a traditionally enlarged photographic image during the exposure process. Around this time, shadow (and its corollaries absence, trace, and afterimage) became an essential subject for Silveira, as she sought new alternatives to the rigid authority of a singular perspective. The incongruous pairings of mundane household objects with shapes that are more difficult to classify (and that are alternately menacing and harmless) hint at Silveira's fascination with Marcel Duchamp's *Readymades*. This exploration became public in 1983 with her heralded installation *In Absentia M.D.* at the São Paulo Biennial, where she filled the space with painted shadows of absent, imaginary representations of Duchamp's iconic *Bottle Rack* and *Bicycle Wheel*, shadows apparently cast from pedestals that were patently empty. This representation of traces left by imagined events is a hallmark of her more recent monumentally scaled installations. Silveira's *Enigmas* deftly synthesize her fascination with the ancient art of skiagraphia (shadow painting) and anamorphosis (the distortion of a singular perspective captured from oblique angles) that would become central to her practice.

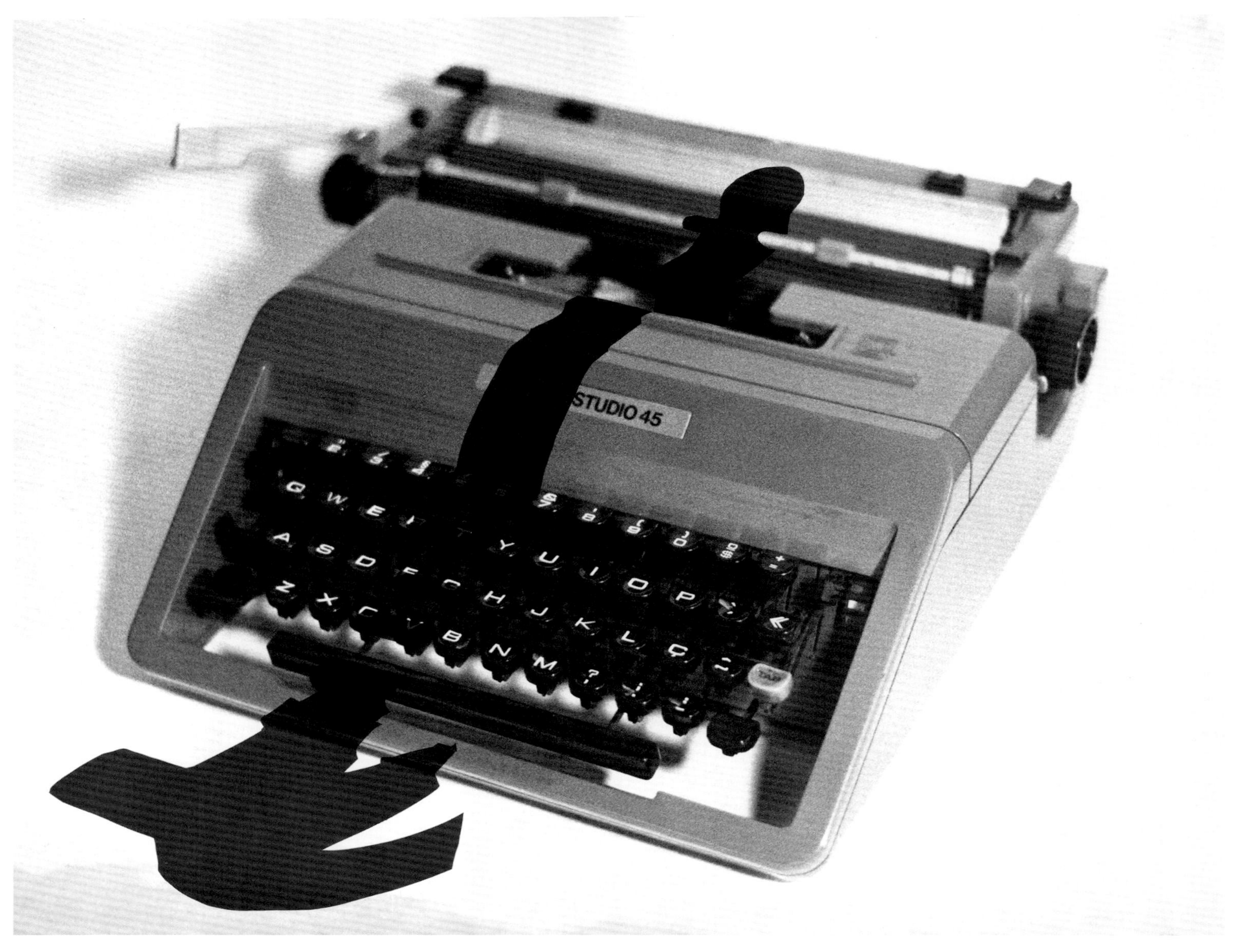

Enigma 3, 1981

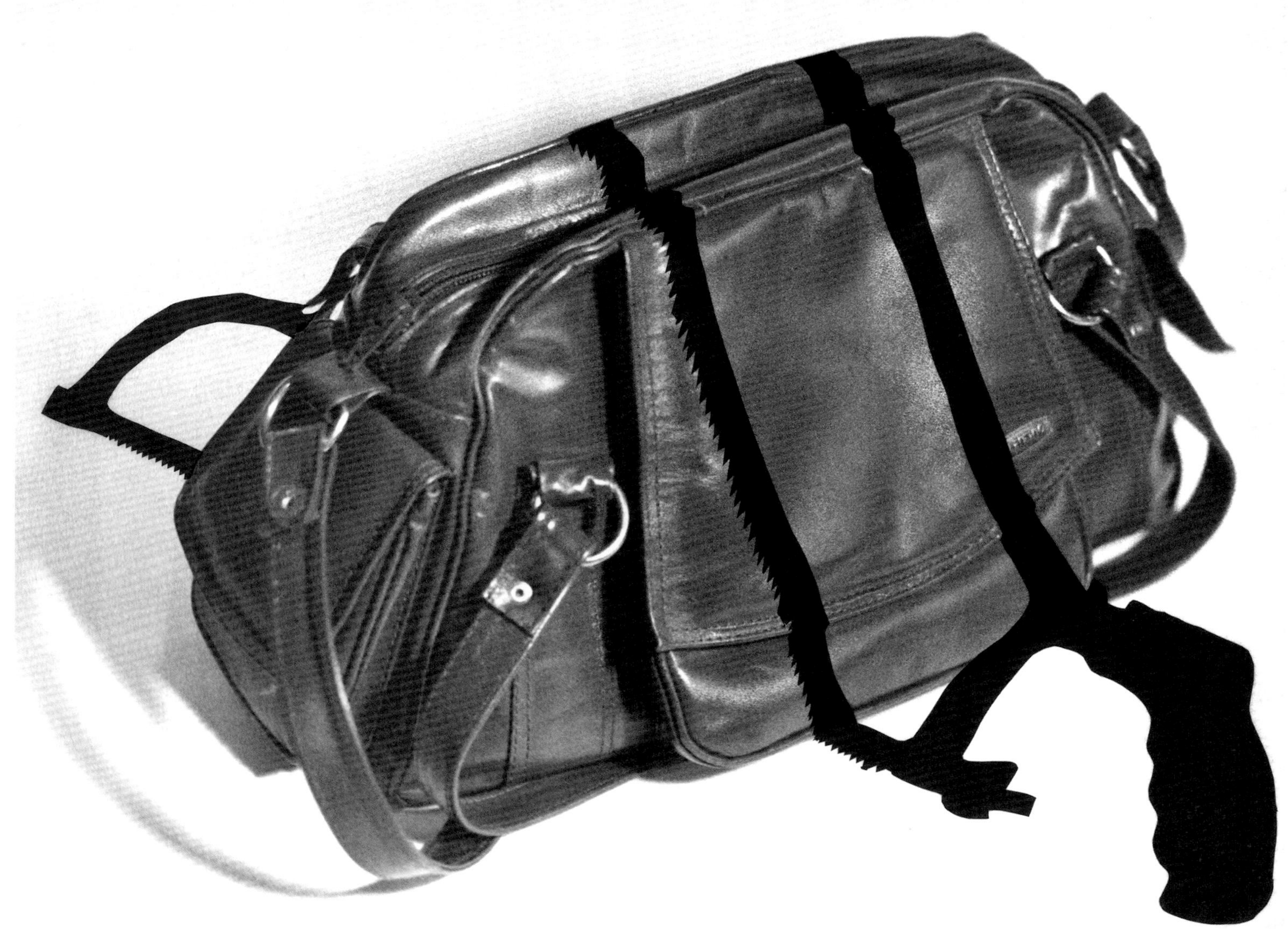

Enigma 4, **1981**
All photographs courtesy
the artist

"My work is not constituted by series but exposed sets," Sofia Borges commented in a recent interview. Borges freely mixes her incongruous image sets—from those taken inside natural history museums in São Paulo and Paris to those from the domestic sphere, including a portrait of her sister—to explore the mechanics of image types.

As the pictures in the following pages, culled from a few exhibitions (or sets)—*Pre-História* (Pre-history), *Les Artifices* (The Artifices), and *Estudo para Ausência* (Study for Absence)—underscore, Borges is interested less in photography as a window onto the world and more in how cropping creates ambiguous abstractions and juxtapositions, opening the possibility for myriad associations. Borges oversees and designs each presentation of her work, as at the 30th São Paulo Biennial, in 2012, where in one room she exhibited nine large-scale photographs related to varied subjects. But specific subject matter is less significant than a particular effect the São Paulo–based photographer is after. "I'm interested in understanding a photograph's ability to forbid meaning," she says. The result is David Lynchian, as if the contents of a detective's case file were scattered on a tabletop—an anatomical diagram once illustrating the musculature of a horse's head is absent any useful information; an animal ventures into the brush on the side of the road; two Japanese girls (in a rephotographed image) crouch in front of an illustrated backdrop; curiosities rest on a table— these clues don't add up to a narrative, but the pleasure here is in the layering of artifice and suggestion. —The Editors

Pre-History
Sofia Borges

Opposite:
Minha Irmã 20 Anos Atrás
(My sister 20 years ago),
2010

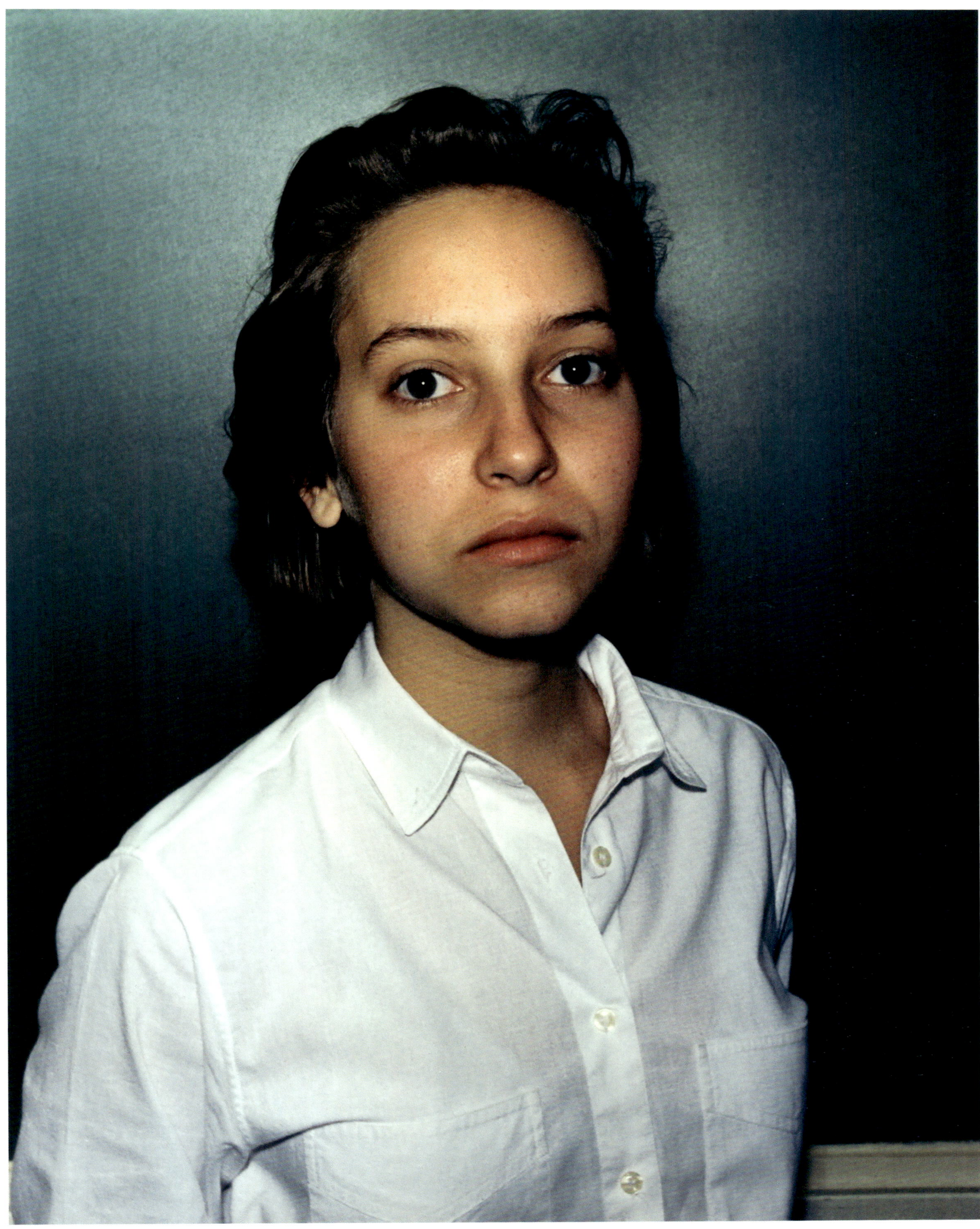

Left to right:
Camelo (Camel), 2010

Pre-história (Pre-history),
2011

Artifício (Artifice), 2013

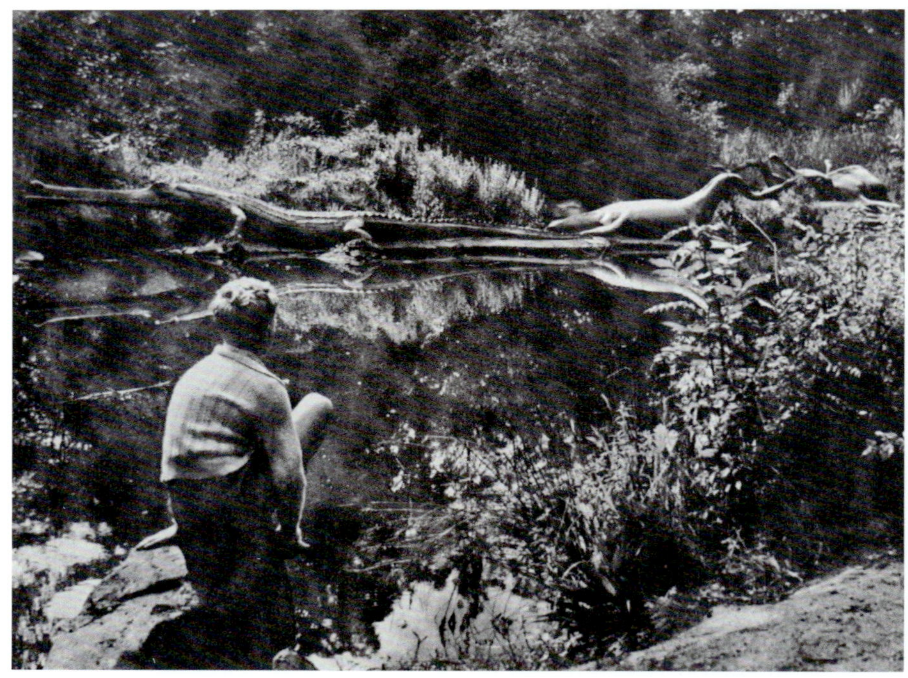

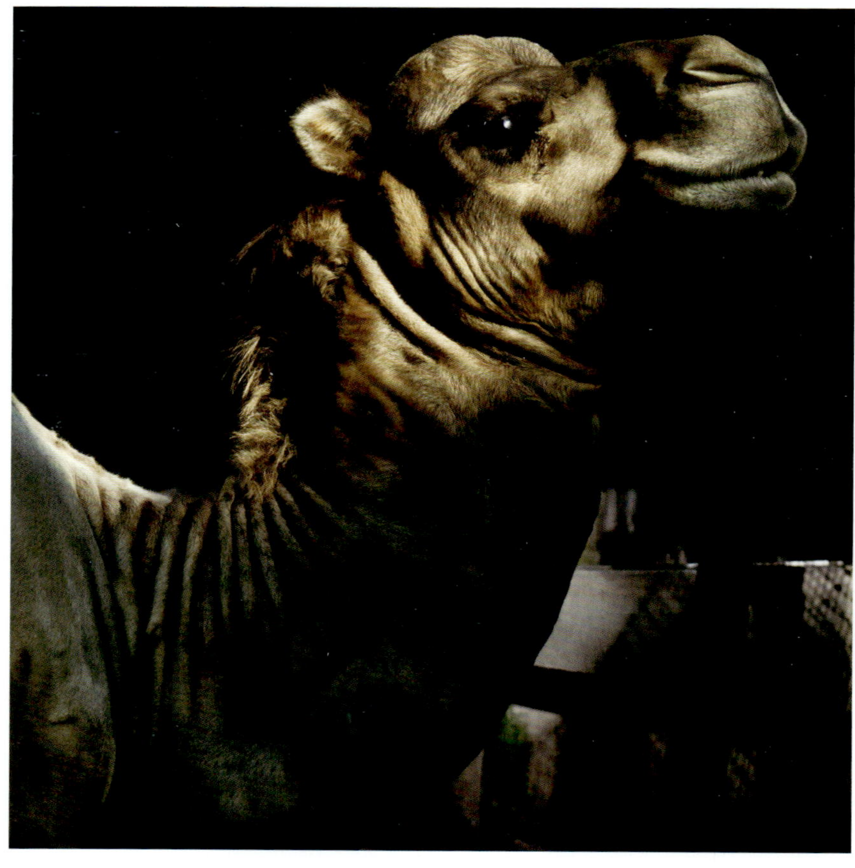

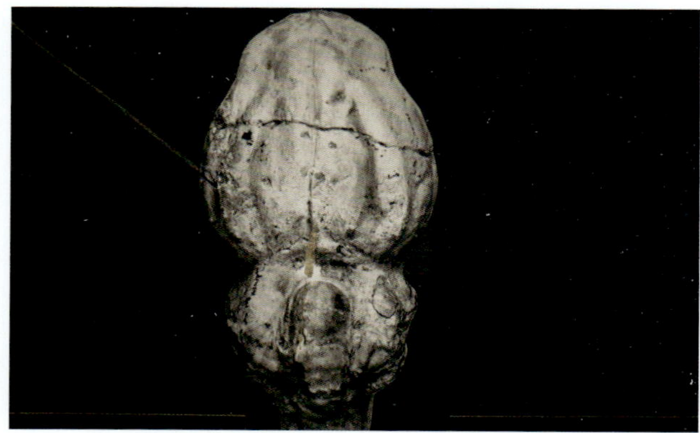

Clockwise from top left:
Xavier, 2009

Coruja (Owl), 2012/2013

*Oitenta Milhões de Anos
(Eighty Million Years)*, 2012

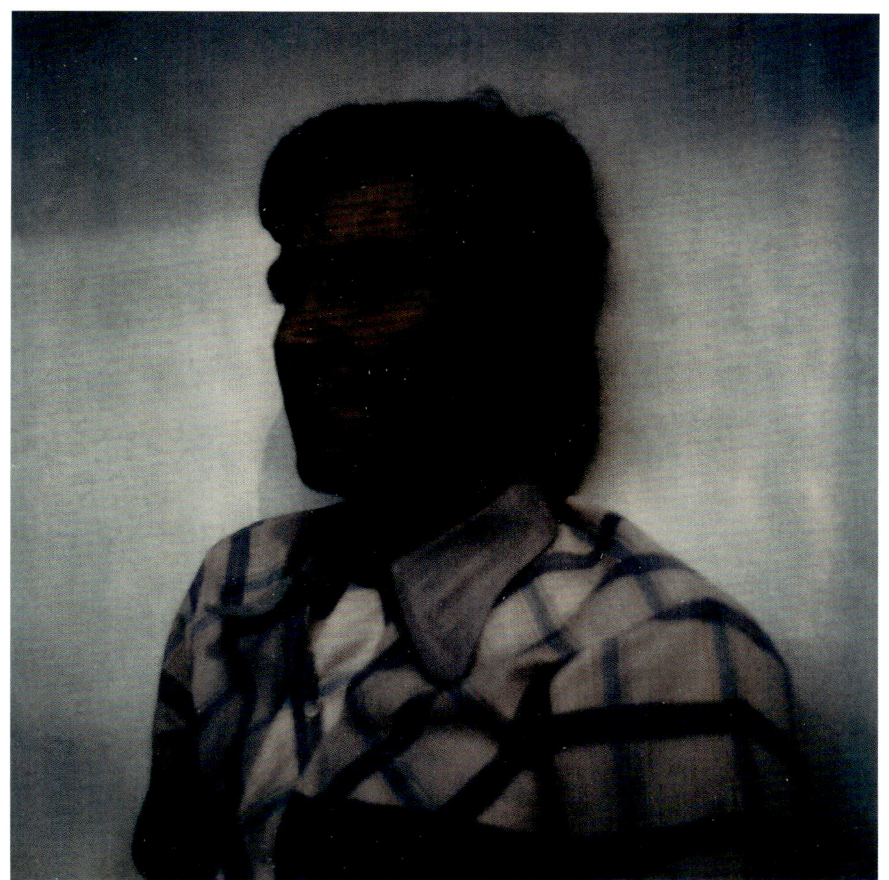

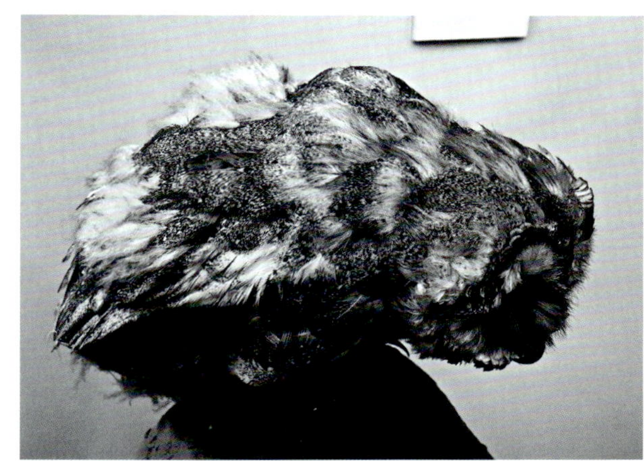

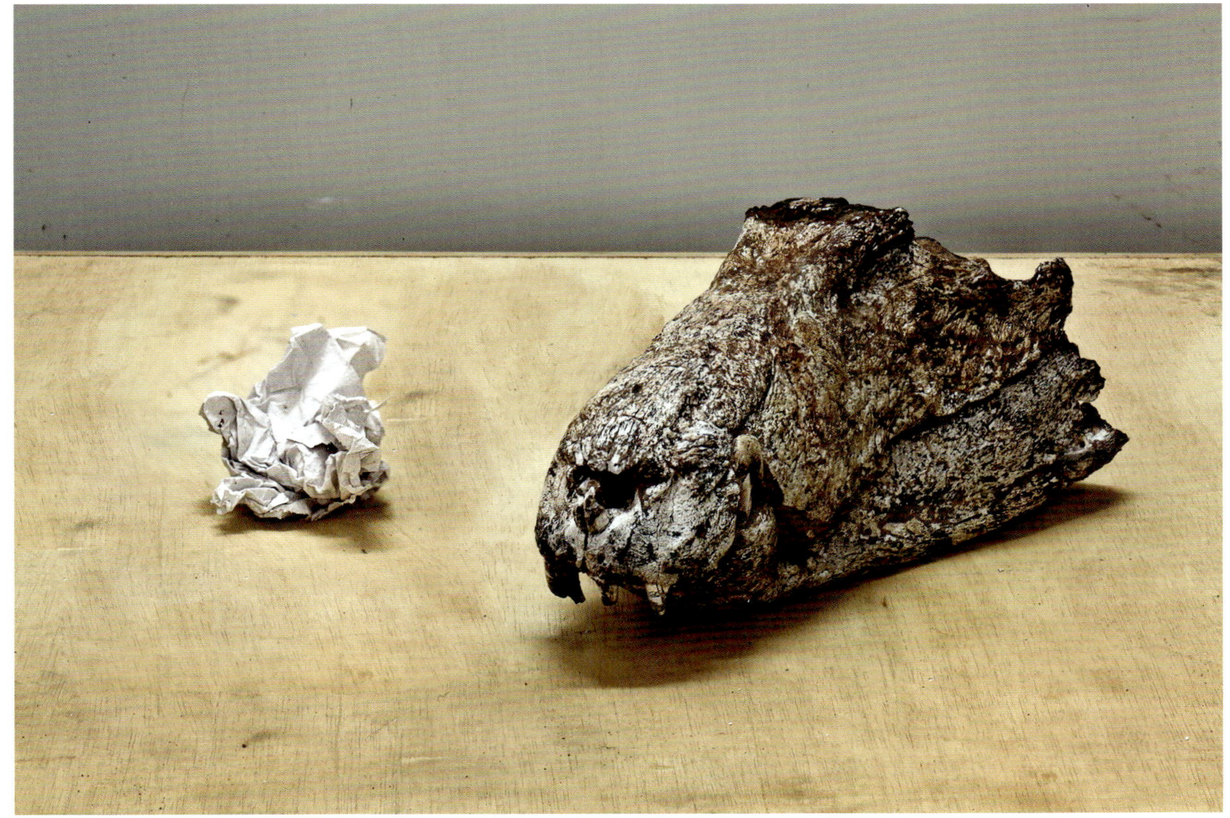

Clockwise from top:
Mapa (Map), 2012

Cavalo no Mato
(Horse in the forest), 2010

Japonêsas (Japanese
women), 2010

Opposite:
La Tête du Cheval
(The horse's head),
2012/2013
© Sofia Borges and
courtesy Galeria Millan,
São Paulo

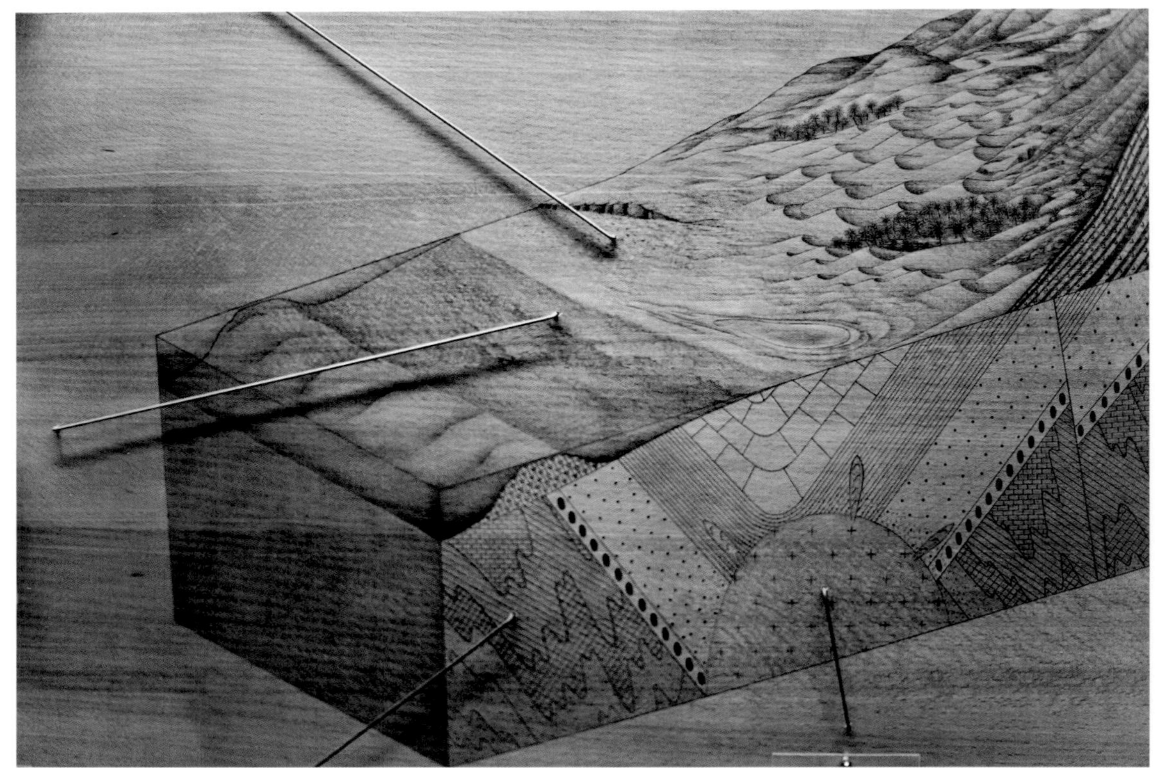

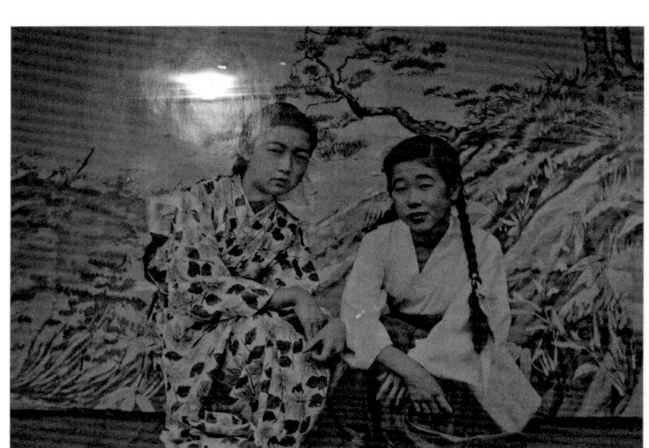

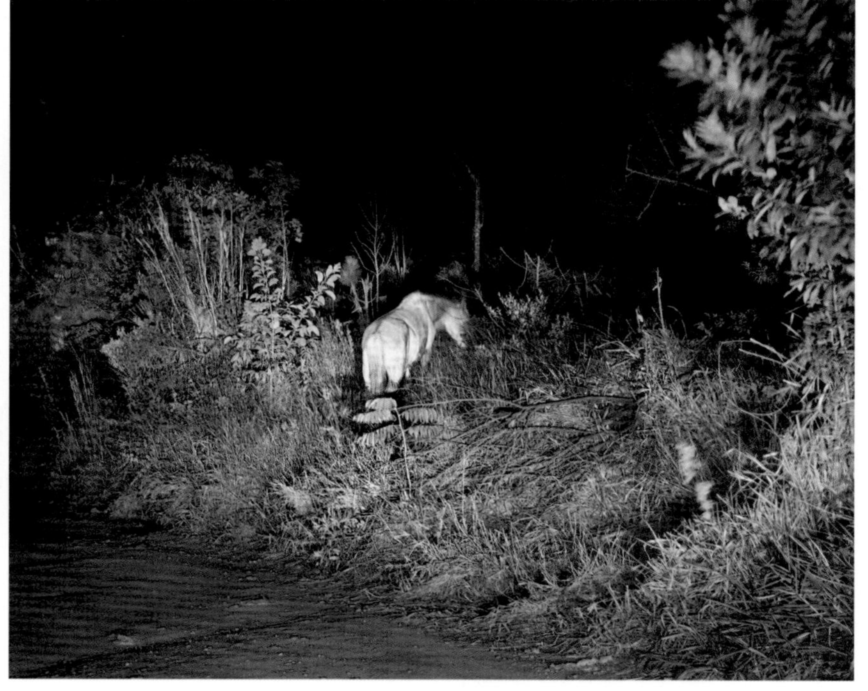

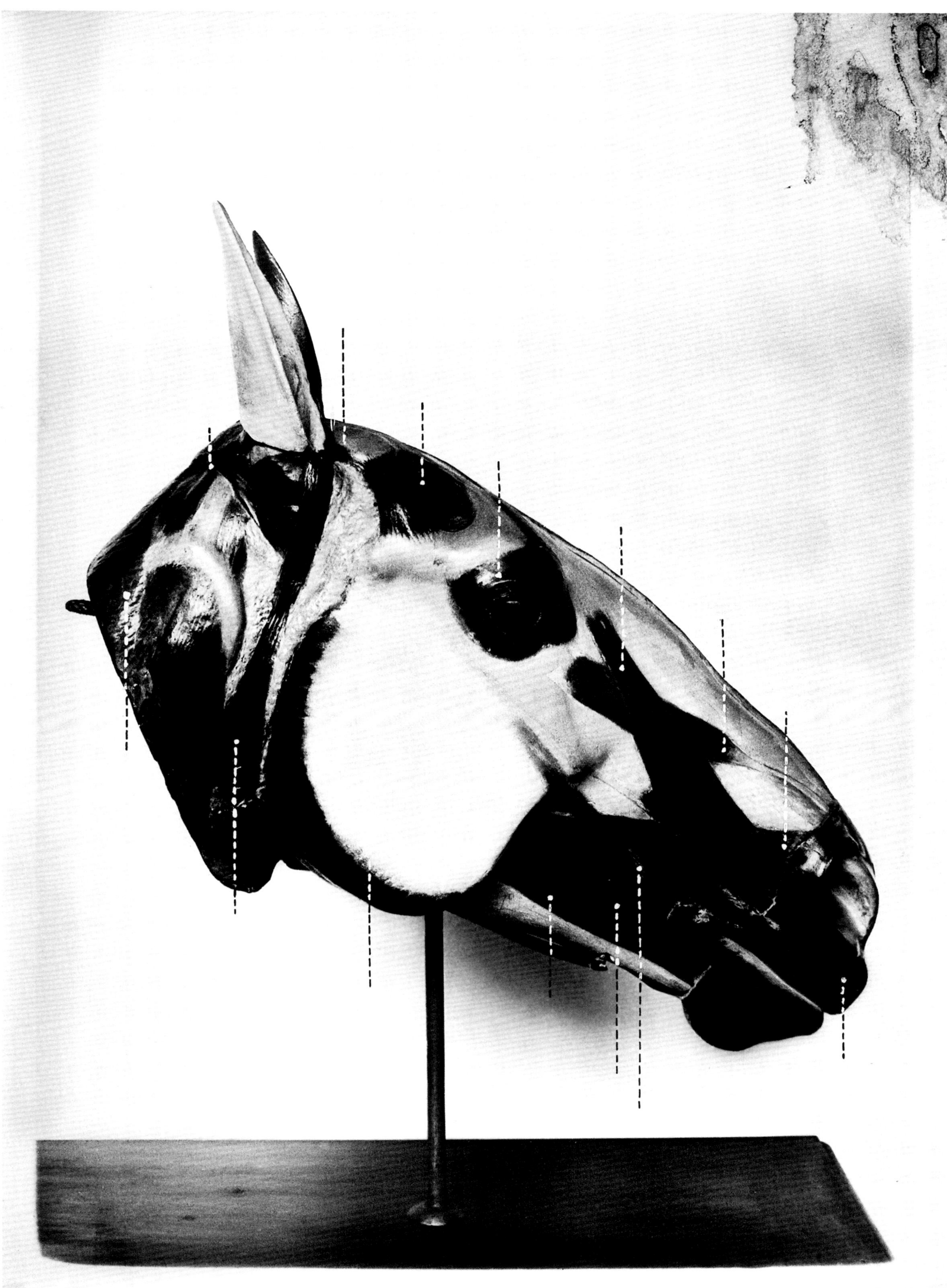

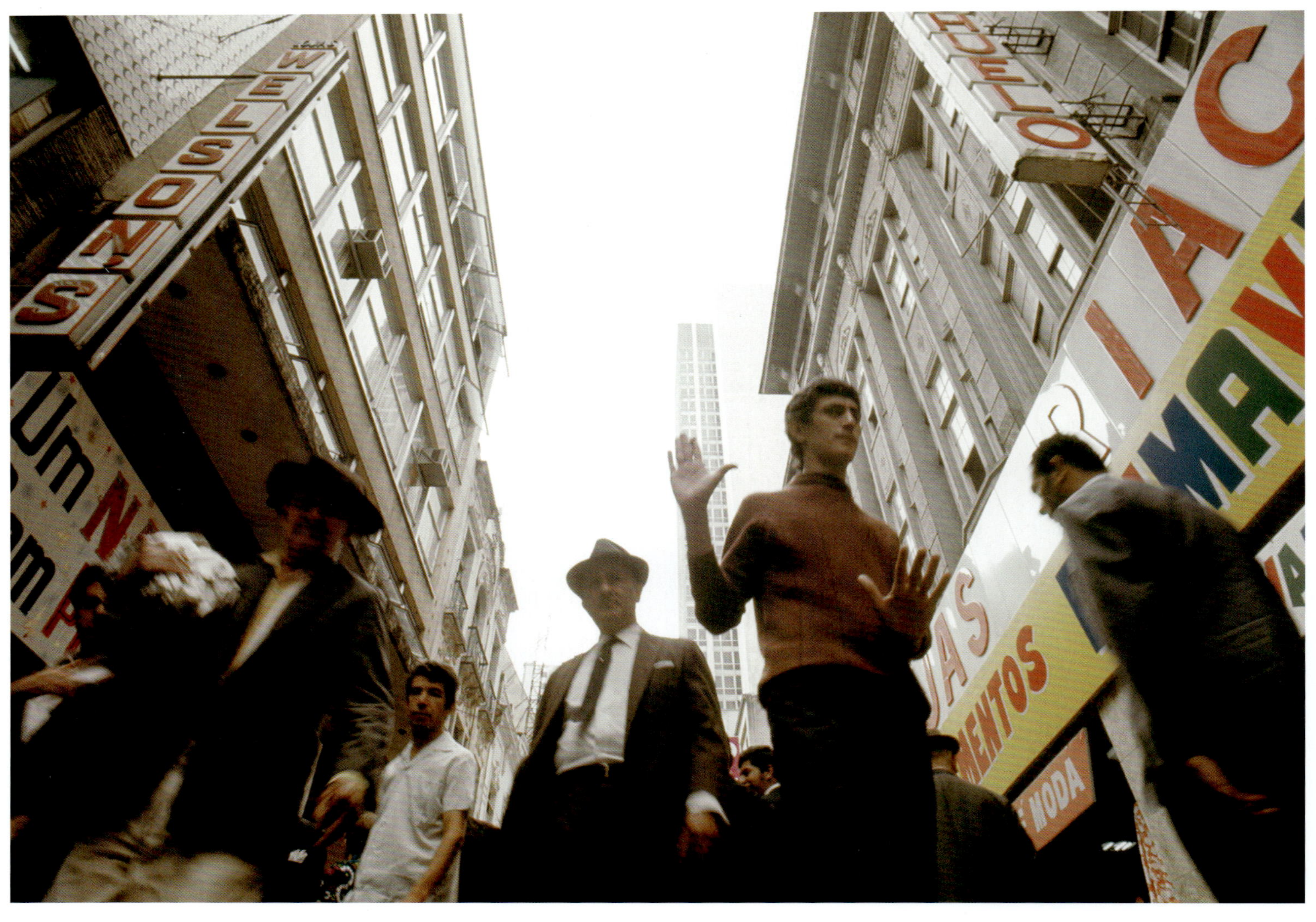

Claudia Andujar

in conversation with Thyago Nogueira

This page and opposite:
Rua Direita (Direita Street),
São Paulo, ca. 1970

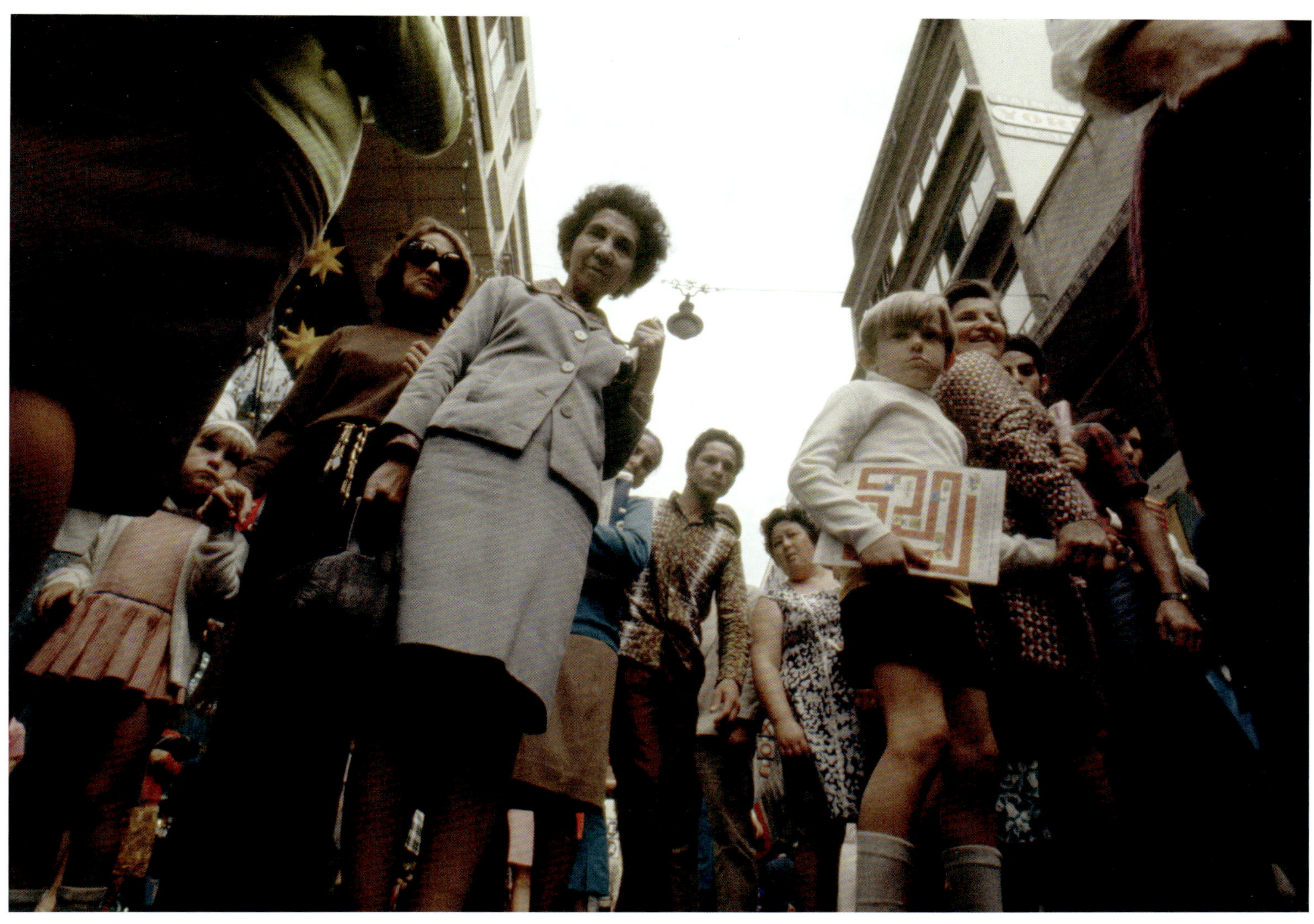

Thyago Nogueira is editor of *Revista ZUM*, a Brazilian photography magazine, and the head of the contemporary photography department at Instituto Moreira Salles, São Paulo.

On one of the hottest days of the Brazilian summer last February, I sat with Claudia Andujar in her apartment to talk about her remarkable life and career in photography. Claudia, now eighty-three, has lived in São Paulo since the mid-1950s, but the story of how she came to live in Brazil parallels some of the tragedies of the twentieth century. Born in Switzerland, Claudia spent her early years in Hungary, before fleeing during World War II. She lived in New York, where she finished high school, attended Hunter College, and embarked on a career as a painter. After a brief marriage, Claudia rejoined her mother who was living in São Paulo, in 1955, and left painting for photography. During the 1960s, Claudia returned regularly to New York, maintaining ties to the city's artistic community, including figures like Edward Steichen and documentarian W. Eugene Smith, who would profoundly influence her humanist vision. Her photographs were published in *Life* magazine and in *Aperture*, in 1971, then edited by Minor White. In 1960, her work was included in an exhibition at the Museum of Modern Art.

In Brazil, Claudia worked as a photojournalist for magazines such as *Realidade*, until the early seventies, when she quit everything to focus on a personal project about the struggles of an indigenous group in the Amazon region called the Yanomami. This would become her life's work. She photographed the Yanomami extensively, in hopes of preserving and understanding their culture, and fought politically for the respect of their traditions and land. Today, Claudia has not slowed down. In September, Inhotim, a contemporary art museum in the state of Minas Gerais, north of São Paulo, will inaugurate a permanent pavilion dedicated to her work on the Yanomami. I am currently organizing an exhibition, opening at the Instituto Moreira Salles in Rio de Janeiro in 2015, focused on Claudia's career, which includes her years in photojournalism and her experiments with color and infrared film. The images shown in these pages relate to my research for this exhibition.

—T.N.

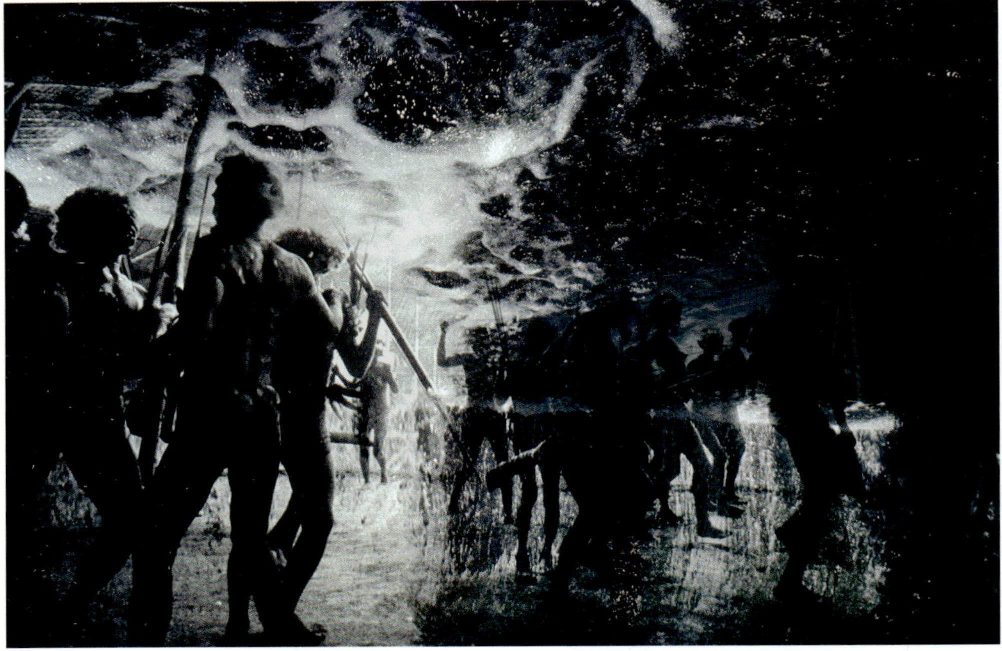

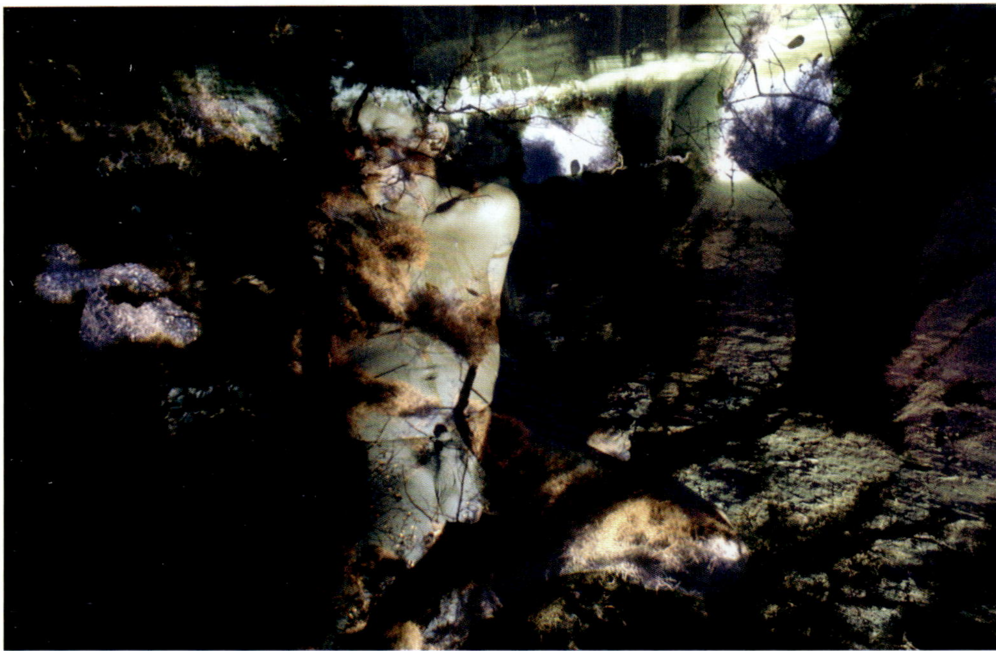

Sem título — Sonhos Yanomami (Untitled — Yanomami Dreams), 1974

closing in, so my mother decided to go to Switzerland. The rail trip took weeks because of all the broken bridges on the way. We also had to stop in Vienna, because my mother became ill. In the city, which was under German rule, my mother stayed at a hospital and I was interrogated daily. They wanted to know why we had fled. I had to hide the fact that my father was Jewish or they would have taken me. They never discovered my story. I stayed in Switzerland for two years, until one of my father's brothers found out that I was there and asked me if I wanted to come to the United States. I went as a refugee to New York in 1947 to live with my aunt and uncle.

TN: **How was your time in New York? Why did you leave for Brazil?**

CA: I didn't really get along with my aunt and uncle. They accused my mother of leaving my father. It's a complicated story .... I decided to rent a room and go to work. I worked at the United Nations and I painted. At night I studied at the university. After a while I felt abandoned and married a Spanish refugee; that's why I have the name Andujar. But he became a soldier in the Army and had to go to Korea. I was really unhappy. At that time my mother was living in Brazil, where she had gone to marry a Romanian who ran away from the Russian occupation. After two years, my husband returned from Korea and we separated. I then decided to visit my mother. That's how I came to Brazil, in 1955.

TN: **When did you take up photography?**

CA: I abandoned my painting career when I arrived in Brazil. But I needed a language to communicate—for me, this was photographing people I met. I wanted to get to know Brazil because I felt at home there. So I picked up a camera, and when I could, I photographed. I'm self-taught. I would go to the north coast of São Paulo a lot, and I began to travel to the islands of the fishermen and became friends with the families. What interested me were the origins of Brazil, the native population. I wasn't interested in the middle or upper classes.

TN: **Did you ever feel unsafe as a European woman traveling alone?**

CA: No, traveling was easy. In the crowd I was mixing with, this wasn't a problem at all. I was adopted by the families of these people. I think that the connection through photography, showing the work to the people I was photographing, helped me identify with people and learn Portuguese.

Thyago Nogueira: **How did someone who was born in Switzerland and grew up in Hungary end up living in São Paulo?**

Claudia Andujar: It's a long story. My mother was Swiss and my father was Hungarian. They lived in Transylvania, a place that was sometimes Romania and sometimes Hungary. For some reason—I should have asked why—she wanted me to be born in Neuchâtel, Switzerland, and so she went there for my birth.

We then came back to our city, which is called Oradea in Romanian (in Hungarian it's called Nagyvárad). We lived there until World War II. In 1944, all the Jews were deported. My father was Jewish. He and his whole family were deported; they died in a concentration camp. I was living with my mother, who was divorced from my father. After he was deported, the Russians began

At that time, I met the famous anthropologist Darcy Ribeiro, and he suggested that I go visit an indigenous village. I embraced the suggestion and went to meet the Karajá Indians. Later, I tried to show my work to the Brazilian magazines *O Cruzeiro* and *Manchete*. But they weren't interested.

TN: **Why?**

CA: I was a foreigner, a woman who was messing with things she shouldn't. I stayed with the Karajá twice, two months each time. Then I decided to go back to the States to show my photography and was well-received. I went to *Life* magazine, to the museums. I had tried in Brazil, but nothing had panned out. In New York, I knew the world of photography. But I didn't want to stay in the States; I wanted to go back to Brazil.

TN: **When you came back, you worked for the magazine *Realidade* (1966–1976), which was critical to the history of Brazilian photojournalism. The majority of their photographers were immigrants like you. What was it like there?**

CA: The story of *Realidade* is special. The magazine's journalists were against the military government that took power in 1964; they looked for stories that spoke of the difficulties in Brazil. I did well there because the places I went were always places with people who were in some way oppressed by the political situation.

TN: **You photographed stories on the erotic theaters in downtown São Paulo, childbirths, prostitutes in the countryside. What moved you?**

CA: I was the person the magazine could always send to shoot in difficult places. I always sought out people on the margins. I wanted to get into people's souls. Later I got interested in the spiritualist medium Chico Xavier. There are things that to this day I don't understand. I would almost say that he had a connection with shamanism. But it isn't shamanism. He had a very strong spiritual life. The way he managed to do certain things—I can't explain it. Once I photographed someone being cured of cataracts. He hypnotized the person, gained some power over her, and stuck a knife into her eye. A knife! A regular knife, to cure her. And he cured her, but I don't know how this person kept quiet, leaning against the wall, and letting him do that. If I hadn't seen it, I wouldn't have believed it.

TN: **You were also exploring the city.**

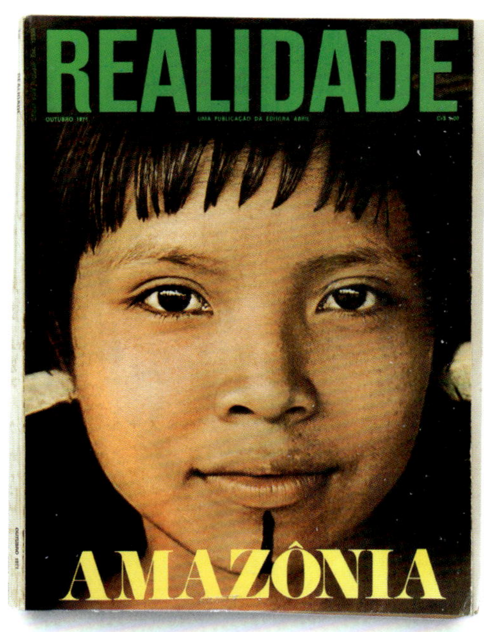

Cover and inside views of *Realidade* magazine, featuring Andujar's photographs. This 1971 edition was dedicated entirely to the Amazon and the strife of Yanomami indigenous groups. It was one of the most costly editions the magazine ever made, by a team of forty journalists and photographers that included Claudia Andujar, George Leary Love, and Maureen Bisilliat, among many others.

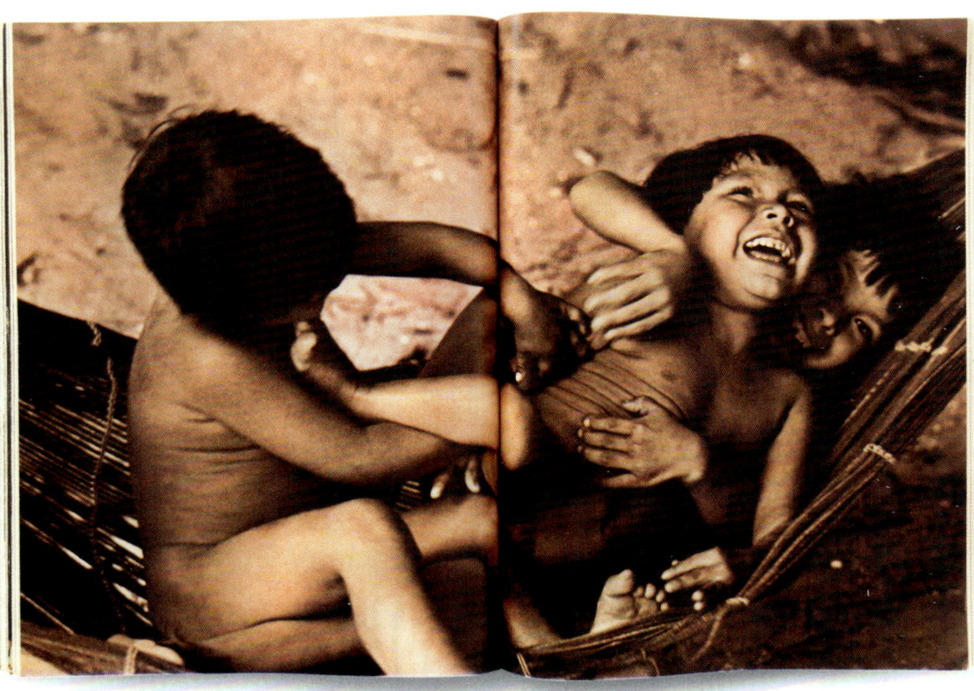

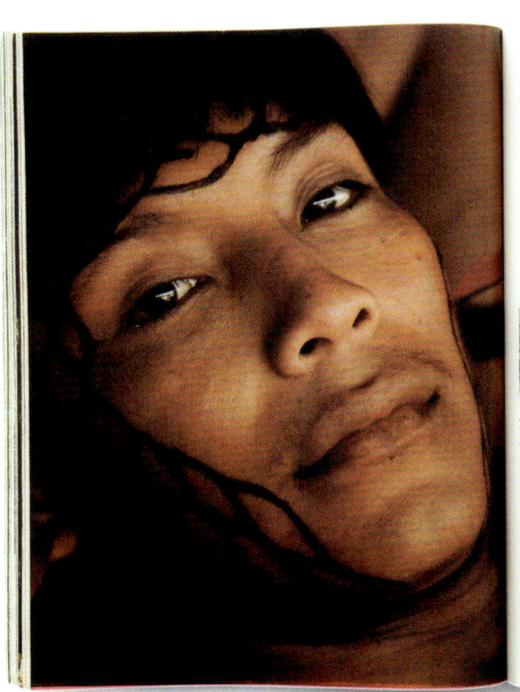

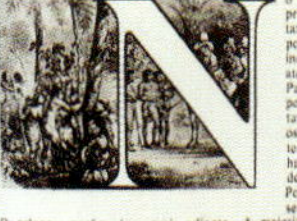

CA: Yes, my photos of Direita Street and those made with infrared film are from that time, but those weren't for *Realidade*. I did those for myself. Before *Realidade*, I didn't photograph in color.

TN: You squatted on the ground to make the Direita Street photos. Did people find that strange?

CA: Well, they didn't find it very common; they thought it was a little curious, but nobody messed with me. They got a kick out of my attitude, that's for sure.

TN: Your 1970s work has a visual freedom that's rare for someone who worked for the press—the infrared film, the dislocated point of view, or even when you rephotographed slides, like in the photos of Sônia. Where did that experimentation come from?

CA: I would say that it was my contact with George Love, my second husband. He was interested in new angles, new ways of photographing. But even with these new techniques, I still maintained a humanist vision, don't you think?

TN: You once took a model and magazine crew to do a fashion shoot in an indigenous village. How did that come about?

CA: In the 1970s there was a fashion magazine called *Setenta*, for which I did various jobs. I suggested a fashion piece with the Xicrin Indians, which *Setenta* published.

TN: You were criticized severely for this piece, weren't you?

CA: I was—an anthropologist said I had gone to the Xicrin to show that they were inferior. For me it was nothing like that. I wanted to show that the Xicrin had their own style, their own inventiveness, that they were creative. But everyone has their own interpretation.

TN: In 1971, *Realidade* did a special edition on the Amazon. Why were they interested in the region?

CA: The Trans-Amazonian Highway was being built; an American had bought all this land there. When I went to photograph, there was so much deforestation going on. It was a disaster, but the Brazilian government allowed it to happen. They said that the Amazon was an empty space that had to be developed. The magazine was interested in showing what the Amazon was like at that time.

TN: Was it then that you made your first contact with the Yanomami?

CA: Yes. When I went to photograph in the Amazon, they asked me not to photograph the indigenous people because the Brazilian government was mistreating them. It was a type of government repression. But after I had been there for some time, I found out that a priest had died suddenly, and nobody knew how. I asked the magazine if they would be interested in this story. They said yes. So I went to the Yanomami. I never found out why the priest died, but I photographed the Yanomami. I liked them a lot, and in the end the magazine published many pages and put one Yanomami on the cover. The Yanomami hadn't received any Western influences yet; they were first-contact people. The magazine accepted the story … and we all forgot about the priest.

TN: *Realidade* had a short life span, did it not?

CA: After the special edition on the Amazon, they started letting people go. The whole office was fired for political reasons, because all of us were leftists. I decided to leave and no longer work in photojournalism. I decided to go deeper into the question of the Yanomami.

TN: So you went on to photograph them regularly, as an ongoing project?

CA: I tried to penetrate the Yanomami culture. I wanted to understand their beliefs, social practices, shamanism. I began this work in 1971. Later, in 1974, the government began the construction of the Northern Perimeter Highway, the second longest roadway in the Amazon. I was there when it began. And it changed me profoundly. I saw hundreds and hundreds of people dying. These people had no immunity to the diseases that were suddenly brought there. And, because of that, I decided to dedicate my life to their lives and culture.

I tried to show the shamanism, which is essential to their culture. And I explored the contact [with the outside world] and the harm this brought to these people, which was sickness and death. I used color a lot, and double exposures. I thought that I had found a kind of visual expression that referred to the culture.

TN: Therein lies the beauty of the work. You are always experimenting with visual language to deal with cultural questions.

CA: That's right.

TN: What was your routine in the village like? Did you take special precautions?

CA: In the beginning, they didn't know what photography was. When they first saw it, they didn't recognize themselves. With time I believe they will refer to the images I took of them as a reference to their past, their cultural heritage. But I think that to this day, it still isn't totally clear to them. I never photographed anything they didn't want me to. The death rituals, for example. They thought that through photography something of the person was stolen. In their funeral rites, they destroyed and burned everything that linked the person to his life, to free his soul so he could live for eternity. That included burning the photographs.

TN: You received many grants to continue the work, including two from the Guggenheim, but in 1977, together with foreign anthropologists and researchers, you were taken by force from Yanomami lands. What happened there?

CA: I was ousted by the Brazilian government. They didn't understand what I was doing there. They thought I was trying to show how the government was mistreating the Indians. That I did this to show to people abroad, that I was some sort of spy.

TN: You've said you are not convinced your work in photography has been the most important thing you've done to date. What do you mean?

CA: Photography is an eternal search for myself—a language. But the work of trying to understand the life and the culture of a people is much more than photography. Photography is part of that, but not everything. One day we asked the Indians what art was for them. And they said we make our categories, and one of them is art, but for them it is not the same. Photography has brought me many things, but the survival of the world, of humanity, is something we struggle for constantly.

TN: Do you see a parallel between your story and that of the Yanomami?

CA: Yes, I do, of course. I lost my whole family and I always think my relatives were marked to die. I've learned so much from the Yanomami. We are destroying nature, destroying life. The Indians consider themselves part of this totality of nature, the human being as part of the whole. If you destroy any part of the whole, you destroy the world. That's why I did the photo of the end of the world in the series *Sonhos Yanomami* (Yanomami Dreams).

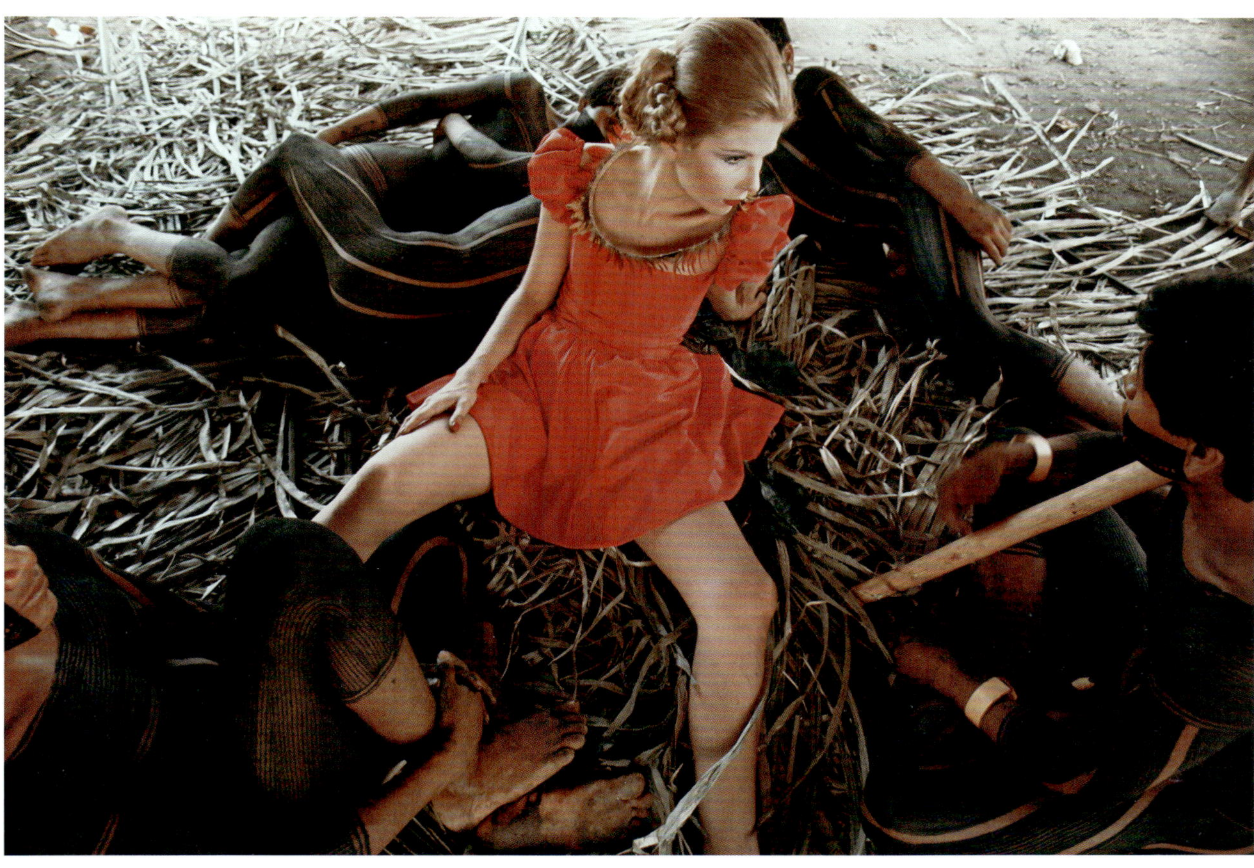

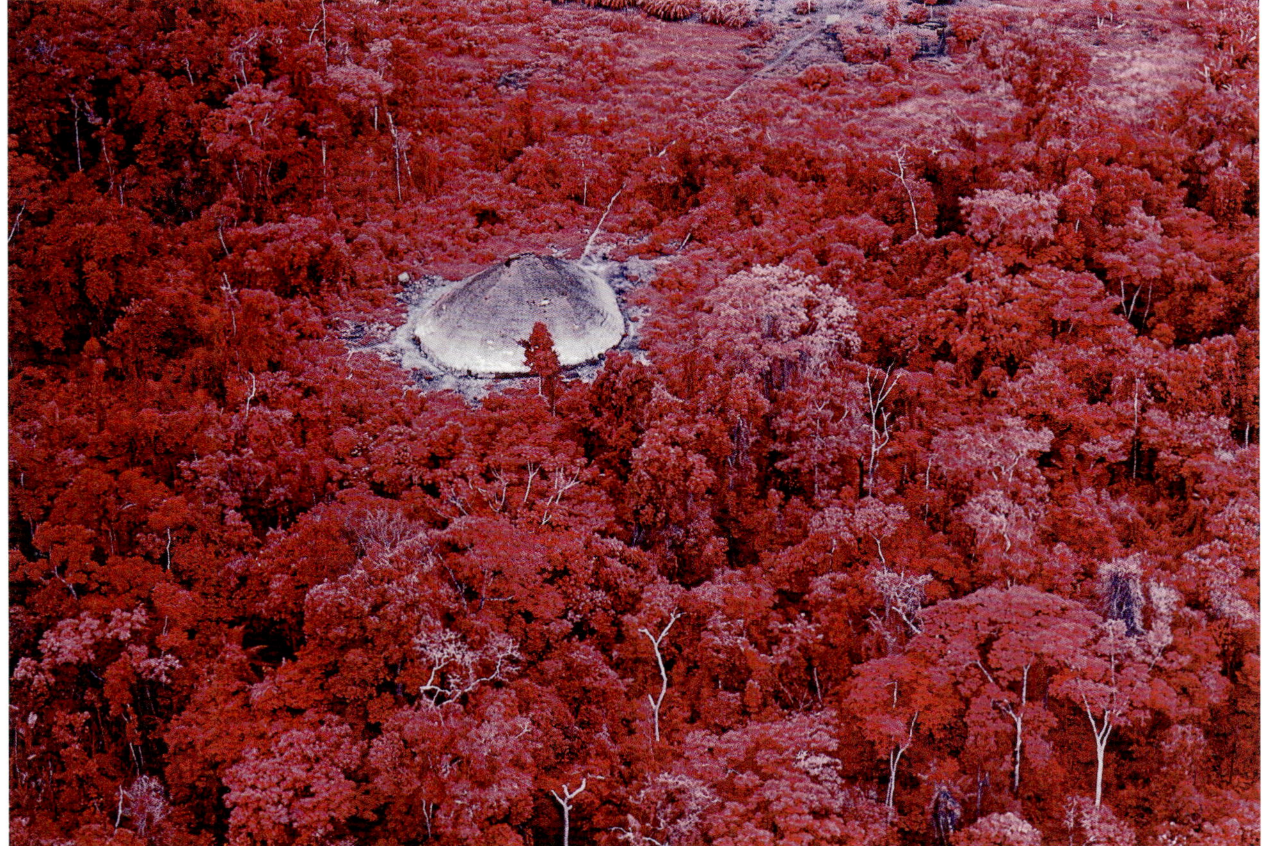

Following spreads:
Metrópole (Metropolis), 1974

From *Exercises with Sônia*, early 1970s (superposition of infrared photographs)

View of São Paulo, 1974 (yellow-infrared photograph)

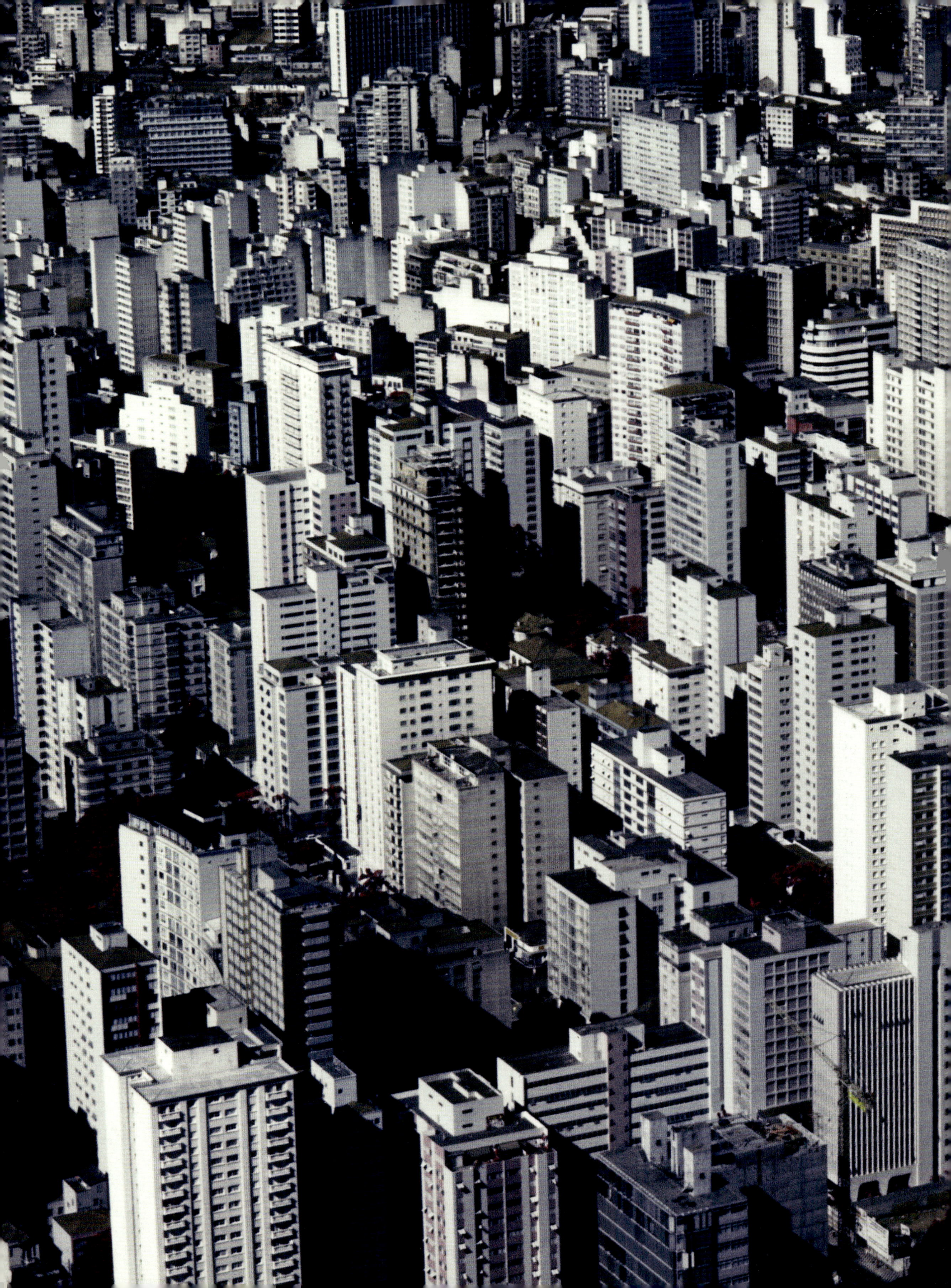

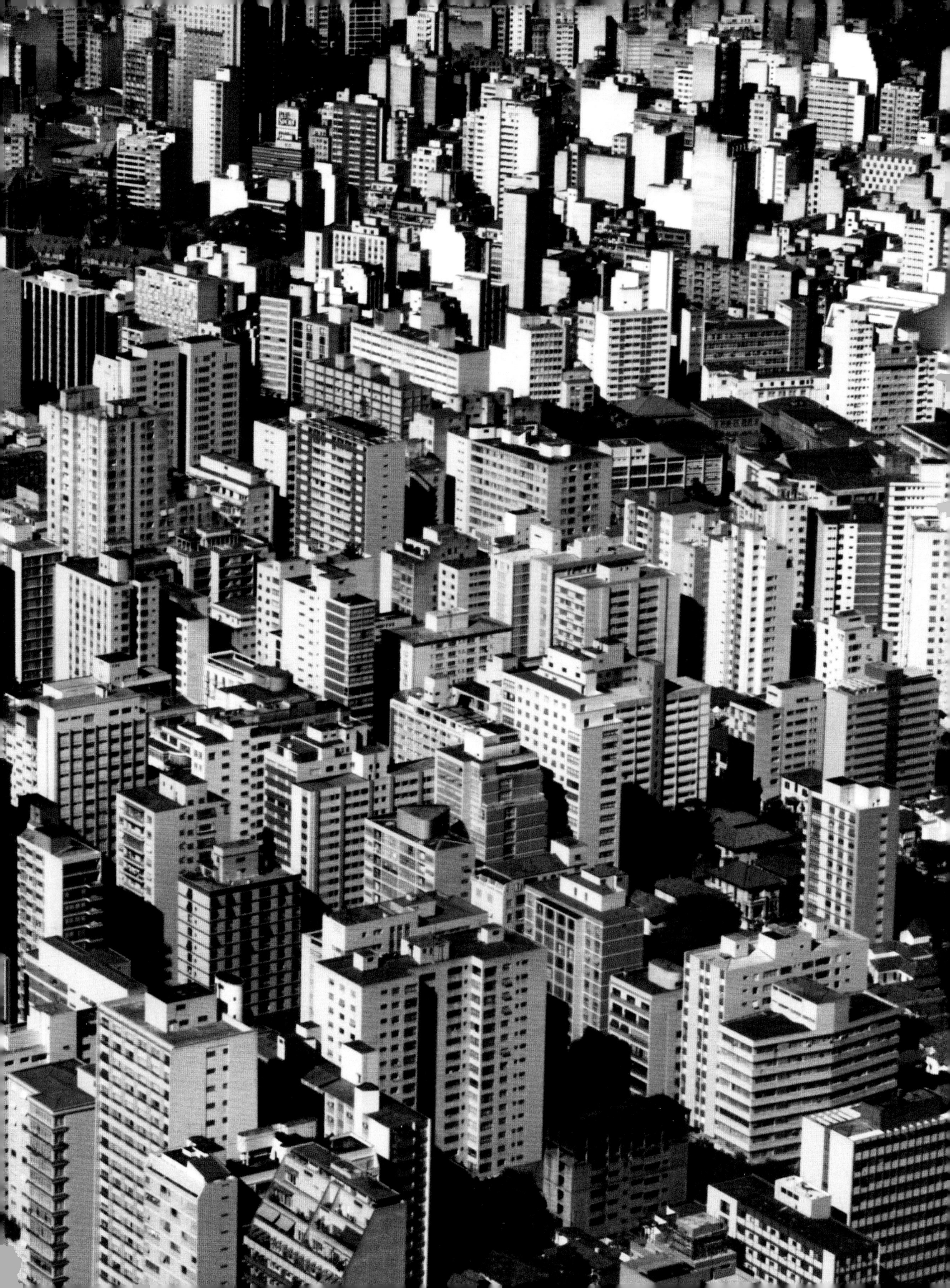

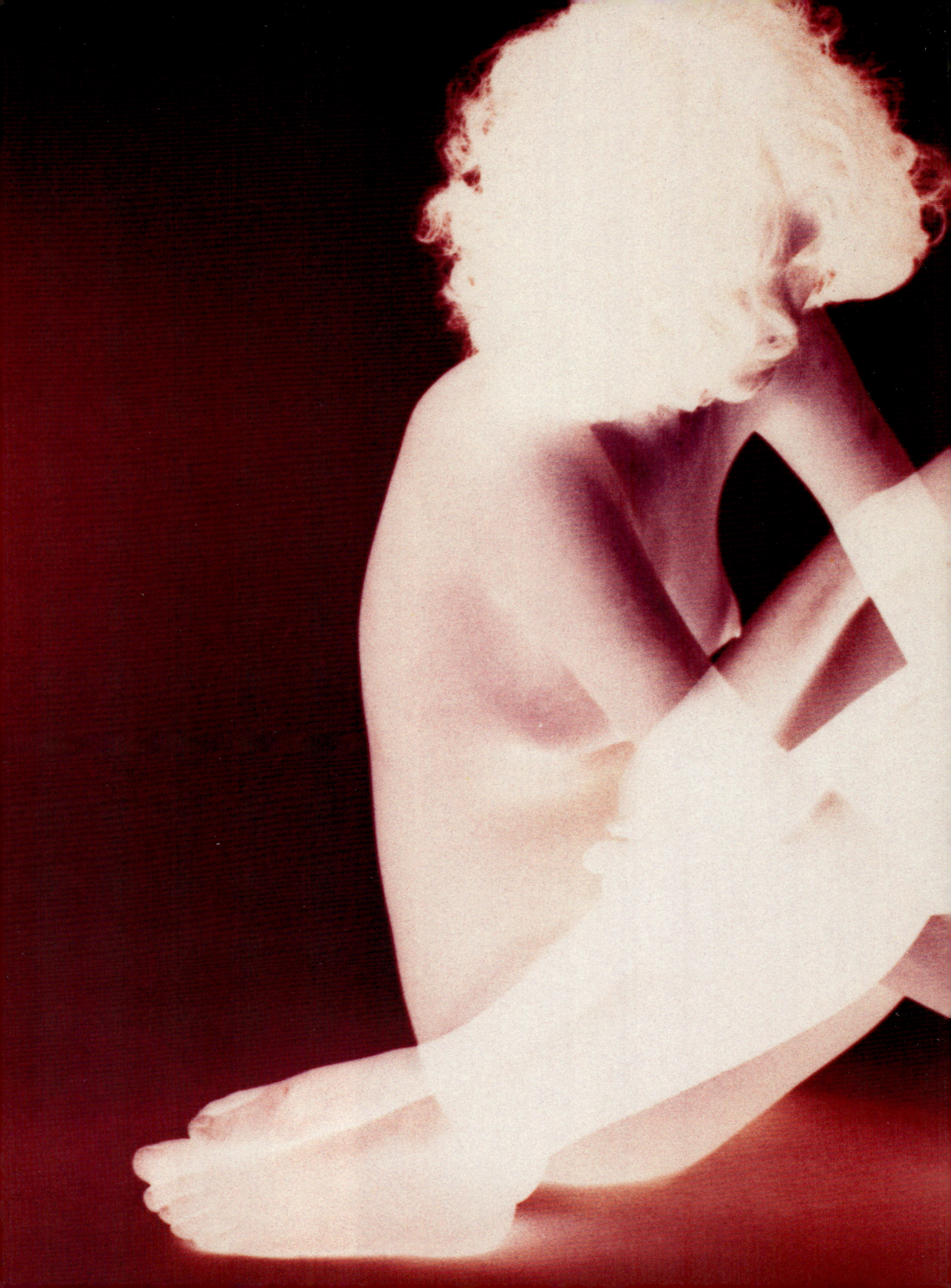

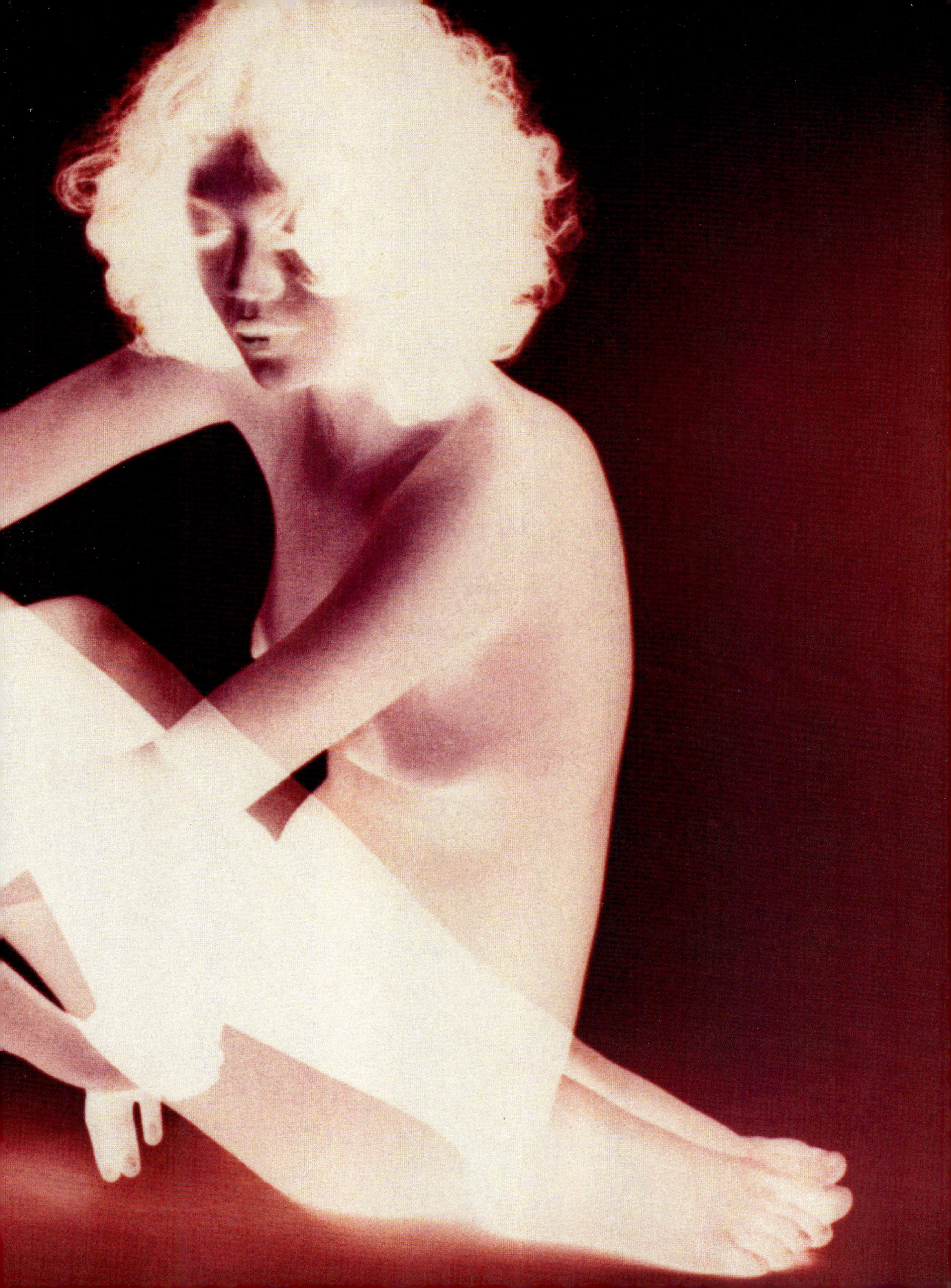

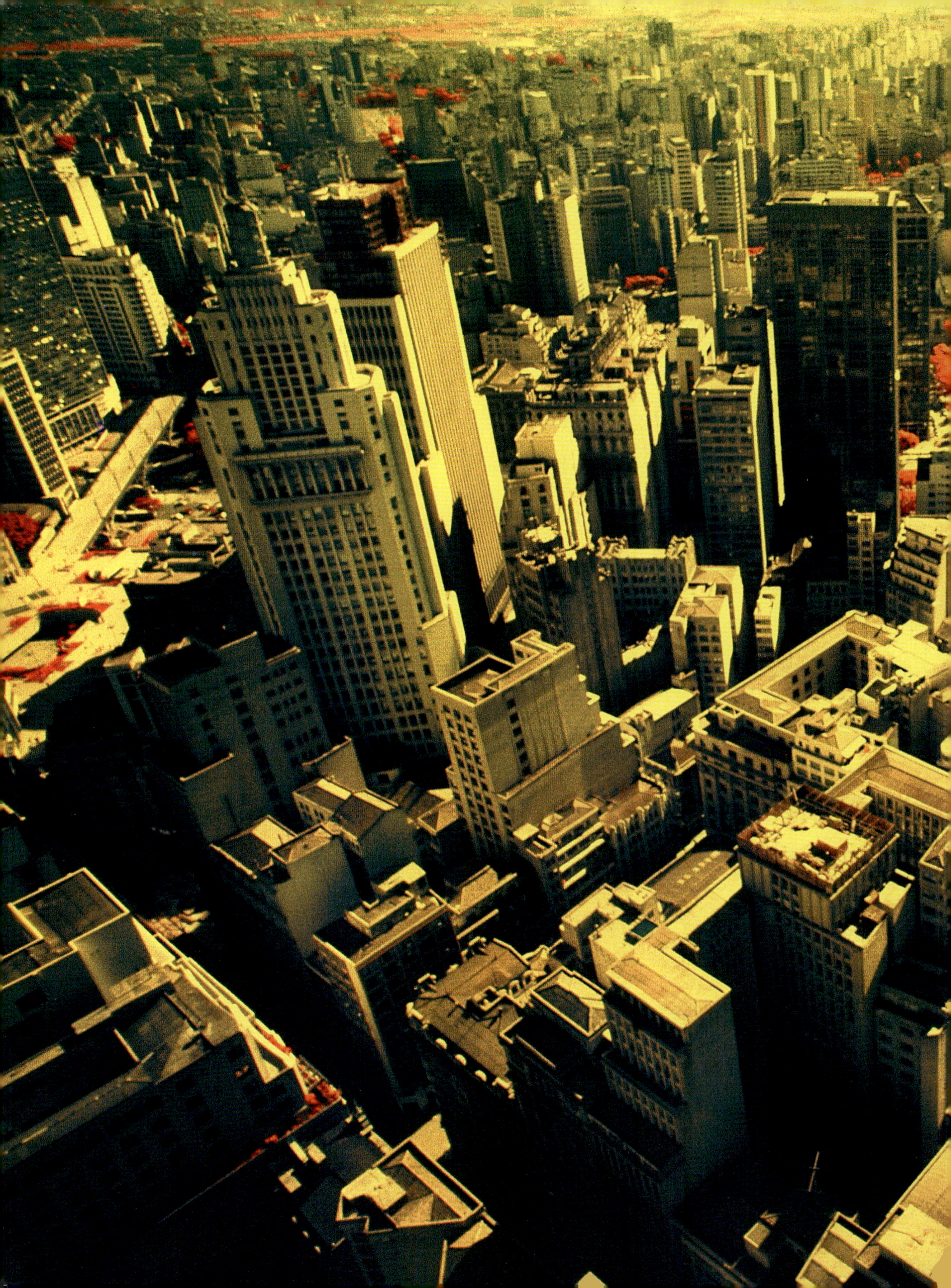

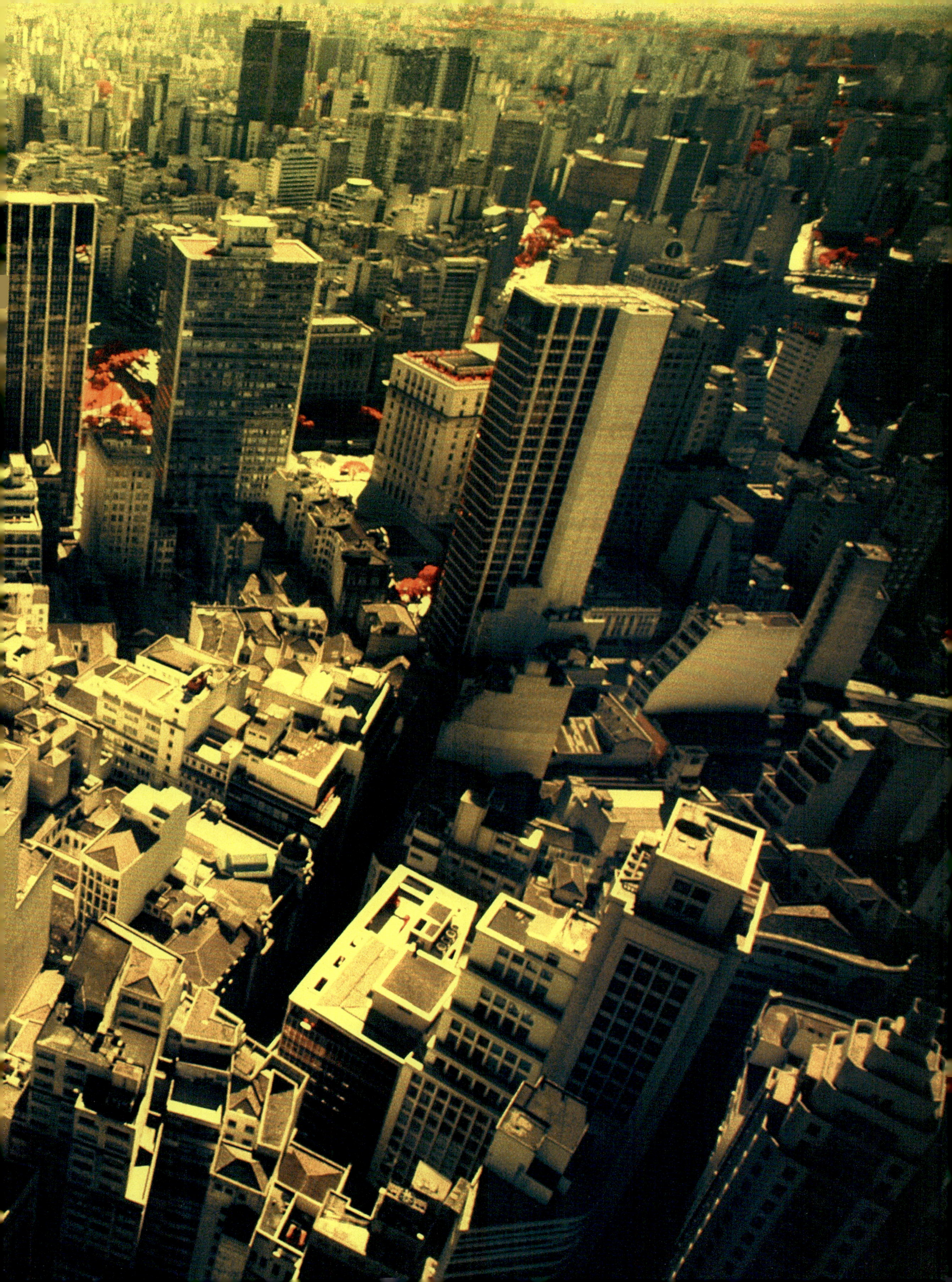

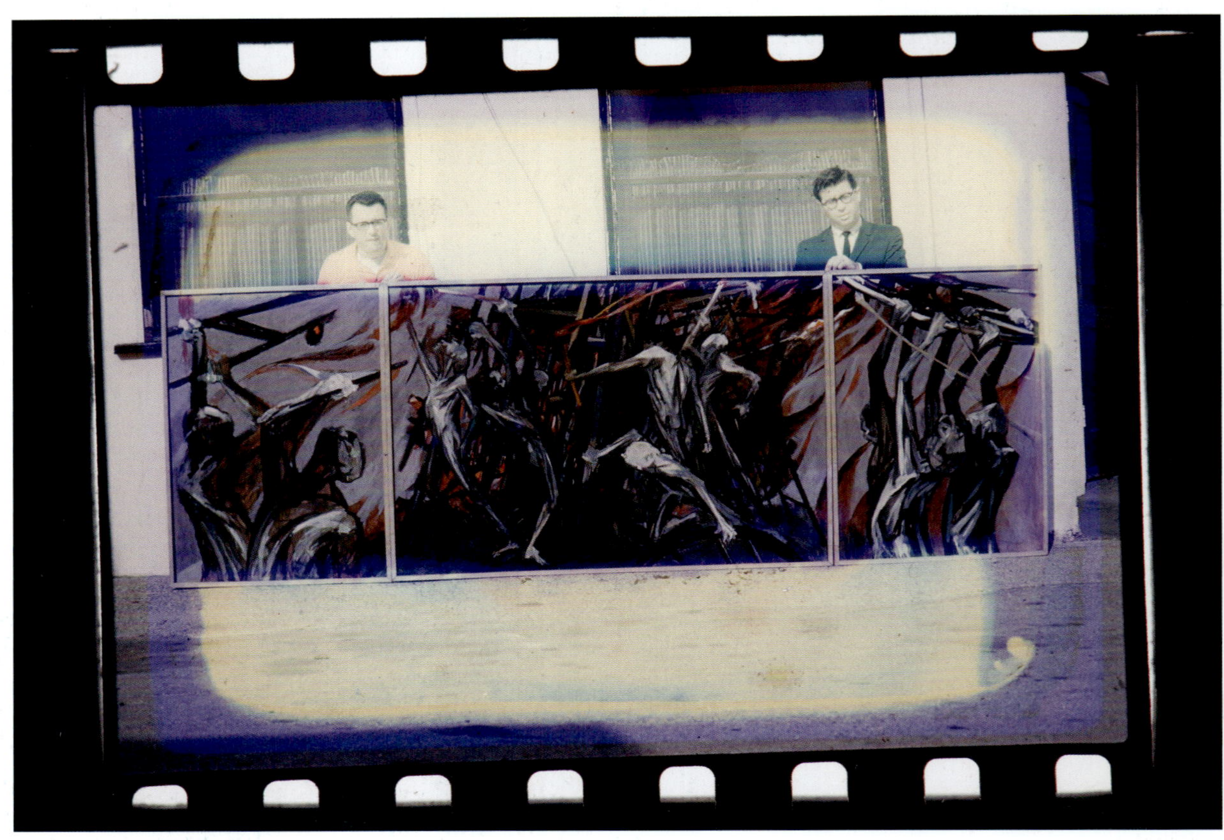

Founded in 1951, the São Paulo Biennial has cemented its place as a major global biannual art event; only the Venice Biennale, the model for São Paulo, has been around longer. The exhibition includes hundreds—some years even thousands—of objects, encompassing a wide range of mediums and filling the multiple sinuous levels of the Ciccillo Matarazzo Pavilion, an elegant Oscar Niemeyer building located in São Paulo's enormous Ibirapuera park, a verdant oasis that is home to a number of the city's major museums.

Over the past few years, the biennial's archivists have been at work preserving their 35-mm-slide documentation of hundreds of artworks exhibited—or considered for possible inclusion—during the sixty-two years of the show's existence. For conservation reasons, the slides' masks (an opaque border surrounding the documented artwork, often formed with ink, tape, cardboard, or other materials) were removed out of concern that they were damaging the slides. The unmasked slides offer not only a broader view of the documentation process but also clues about when and where they were photographed. In the slide pictured above, American artist Arnold Mesches and an unidentified curator hold up a painting by Mesches, *Celebration of the Survivors* (1958–59), to be photographed outside the artist's studio in Sun Valley, California. In other unmasked slides, paintings appear casually propped against playground equipment or a pillar in an unidentified interior. The brilliant sun and heat are palpable in many of these images, as they should be: No doubt the promise of plentiful light is what compelled artists and curators to bring these artworks outside to be photographed.

—The Editors